ULYSSES Fifty Years

Fifty Years

ULYSSES

Edited and with an Introduction by

Thomas F. Staley

INDIANA UNIVERSITY PRESS
Bloomington & London

Published in Canada by Fitzhenry & Whiteside Limited,
Don Mills, Ontario
Manufactured in the United States of America

Library of Congress Cataloging in Publication Data
Main entry under title:

Ulysses: fifty years.

"The essays in this volume were first presented at
a colloquium in the Graduate Institute of Modern
Letters at the University of Tulsa in July of 1972."
    1. Joyce, James, 1882-1941. Ulysses. I. Staley,
Thomas F., ed. II. Tulsa, Okla. University.
Graduate Institute of Modern Letters.
PR6019.09U75   823'.9'12   73-16538
ISBN 0-253-36160-5

CONTENTS

ABBREVIATIONS

Dubliners Joyce, James. *Dubliners*, ed. Robert Scholes in consultation with Richard Ellmann. New York: Viking Press, 1967.

Joyce, James. *"Dubliners": Text, Criticism, and Notes*, ed. Robert Scholes and A. Walton Litz. New York: Viking Press, 1969.

FW Joyce, James. *Finnegans Wake*. New York: Viking Press, 1939; London: Faber and Faber, 1939. (It should be noted that these two editions have identical pagination.)

JJ Ellmann, Richard. *James Joyce*. New York: Oxford Univ. Press, 1959.

Letters, I, II, III Joyce, James. *Letters of James Joyce*, I. ed. Stuart Gilbert, New York: Viking Press, 1957; reissued with corrections 1965. Vols. II and III, ed. Richard Ellmann. New York: Viking Press, 1966.

Portrait Joyce, James. *A Portrait of the Artist as a Young Man*. The definitive text corrected from the Dublin Holograph by Chester G. Anderson and edited by Richard Ellmann. New York: Viking Press, 1964.

Joyce, James. *"A Portrait of the Artist as a Young Man": Text, Criticism, and Notes*, ed. Chester G. Anderson. New York: Viking Press, 1968.

U Joyce, James. *Ulysses*. New York: Random House, 1934 ed., reset and corrected 1961. (This text is obviously imperfect, but it is the most accessible.)

INTRODUCTION

Fifteen years ago Richard Ellmann began his brilliant biography of Joyce with the statement that we are still learning to be James Joyce's contemporaries, to understand our interpreter. Today, perhaps a little more certain of their ground, critics and scholars are still involved in this learning process. The essays in this volume, written from a perspective of half a century after the book publication of *Ulysses*, represent a further attempt to establish ourselves as Joyce's contemporaries. By focusing on a variety of persistent critical and interpretative problems of the past fifty years in the study of *Ulysses*, the authors of this volume have also in a large way measured the influence of *Ulysses* on modern literature.

Even taking into account the interest and debate which *Ulysses* provoked when Joyce began publishing it serially in the *Little Review* between March 1918 and December 1920, *Ulysses* had anything but an auspicious beginning for a novel that was to become so important. Well aware of the impossibility of getting the book published in an English-speaking country, Joyce made arrangements with a young American bookseller in Paris, Sylvia Beach, to publish the book through her bookshop, Shakespeare & Co. It was not until 1934, twelve years after its original publication and following the famous Woolsey Decision, that the book was published in an English-speaking country. Of less importance is the fact that only within the last few years could a copy be purchased in Joyce's native Ireland. In spite of its delayed publication in England and the United States, the sales of the book, while not approaching Mickey Spillane's, are spectacular for a work such as *Ulysses*, as the following figures from *The New York Times* indicate:

> In the United States, Random House, which has published *Ulysses* since 1934, when a court ruled that it was not obscene, has sold 880,000 copies. Of these, 544,000 have been in the Modern Library Giant edition, 69,000 in the regular edition, and, since 1967, 275,000 in the Vintage paperback. This book is now selling 33,500 copies a year.
> The Bodley Head, publisher of *Ulysses* since 1936, when the censorship was lifted in Britain, has sold 350,000 hard-cover copies, including the original edition and a new edition in 1960. Paperback rights were sold to Penguin in 1967 for $180,000, the highest price Penguin had ever paid for such an arrangement. Starting with Penguin's limited edition in 1968 and continuing with a major printing the following year, soft-cover sales have totaled 300,000. [February 2, 1972, p. 35].

As impressive as these sales records are, it is, of course, the critical and intellectual response to the book that has established it as one of the foremost imaginative works of the century.

For fifty years critics have explored the innumerable facets of *Ulysses;* scholars have provided a word index, allusion lists, musical sources, character glosses, gazetteers of street and place names, and literally thousands of interpretations of various aspects of *Ulysses.* No novel written in this century has evoked more critical controversy or sparked such elaborate exegesis. The subjective consciousnesses of Bloom, Molly, and Stephen Dedalus have been examined in the most exhaustive ways imaginable, using every critical tool available to the modern scholar. The construction and design of the book, with its intricate scaffolding and thematic and metaphorical configurations, seem to turn *Ulysses* in on itself; the thousands of borrowings, echoes, and allusions having been noted and analyzed only lead back to the puzzling *quidditas* of the work itself. We learn more as we explore the mysteries of *Ulysses,* but we are perhaps more tentative in our conclusions.

In Joyce's work life and art seem to have turned mirrors on each other, and the triumph is not a system of order such as we see in Dante's *Commedia,* but rather the reflection of life on art and art on life, with the artist standing removed from his art, allowing other human beings of his century and future centuries to ponder the same questions which T. S. Eliot first asked in his seminal essay, "*Ulysses,* Order and Myth," a year after the book was published. "The question, then, about Mr. Joyce, is: how much living material does he deal with, and how does he deal with it: deal with, not as legislator or exhorter, but as an artist?" In *Ulysses* there is no grand overview of the human condition, no absolute image of man, but rather an exploration of the chaos, disorder, and disunity of man's existence mingled with his capacity to endure and even smile at his fate.

The art of *Ulysses* seems uniquely to embody the aspirations and artistic vision of our age, and fifty years is a very short time in which to assess its claim on our culture; nevertheless, its rich and original fabric, its implicit vision of the human dimensions of man, both progressive and regressive, have established it as a great work of art for our time. This very greatness which we have accorded it is an early testament to its universality, its meaning for subsequent generations.

The essays in this volume were first presented at a colloquium in the Graduate Institute of Modern Letters at The University of Tulsa in July of 1972 and later appeared in a special issue of the *James Joyce Quarterly* (Fall, 1972), commemorating both the fiftieth anniversary of *Ulysses* and the tenth anniversary of the *Quarterly*. Each paper concentrates on a particular critical problem in *Ulysses* and attempts to view that problem from the perspective of fifty years. It was within these broad guidelines that the essays were written, and they represent not only an assimilation of many of the major critical positions on *Ulysses,* but also extend the critical boundaries with new insights as we begin to live with Joyce's work for a second half-century.

THOMAS F. STALEY

October 25, 1973

ULYSSES Fifty Years

A. Walton Litz
POUND AND ELIOT ON ULYSSES:
THE CRITICAL TRADITION

It is part of the mythology of modernism that we habitually discuss *Ulysses* and *The Waste Land* as if they were simultaneous artistic performances, twin children of the Zeitgeist. In our desire to make those *anni mirabiles* of the early 1920's even more miraculous, we suppress the obvious fact that *The Waste Land* and its attendant masterpieces, such as Pound's *Hugh Selwyn Mauberley*, were written with Joyce's great novel clearly in view. During the years 1918-20, when the first half of *Ulysses* was appearing serially in the *Little Review* and the *Egoist*, Joyce's novel exercised a growing influence as its monumental dimensions became apparent. Few works can have received such intense publicity, or impressed themselves so deeply upon the literary consciousness, while still works-in-progress. *Ulysses* was a cultic object and cultural artifact long before its book publication by Shakespeare and Co. in 1922.

Recent studies in the literary history of this period have refined our sense of *Ulysses* as a work-in-progress, and have provided new evidence of its profound impact upon the literary development of Pound and Eliot in particular.[1] Robert Adams Day has demonstrated that from early 1917 onward "Eliot was as ardent and well informed a Joyce partisan as Pound or Harriet Weaver; and [that] he as well as Pound was seeing the episodes of *Ulysses* as soon as Joyce sent them to London" (p. 179). This means that both Pound and Eliot would have been familiar with the novel as far as "Proteus" by mid-1918, and as far as "Sirens" by mid-1919. The early episodes from "Nestor" to "Wandering Rocks" would have been specially impressed upon Eliot's mind, since he read them with the care of a proofreader while assistant editor of the *Egoist*. But beyond this early knowledge of the episodes published in serial form, Day makes a strong case (pp. 182-85) that by the fall and winter of 1921, when *The Waste Land* was written and revised, Eliot and Pound knew all of *Ulysses* except possibly "Ithaca" and "Penelope." In the light of this close involvement with *Ulysses* as a work-in-progress, many of the poetic accomplishments of Eliot and Pound in the period 1918-22 take on a "Joycean" cast. Eliot's use of myth and the mock-heroic in *Poems* 1920; Pound's imaginary conversation with Propertius in the *Homage*; the Odyssean frame for *Hugh Selwyn Mauberley*; the ritual background and much of the specific imagery in *The Waste Land*; the key role of Homer and "the epic"

5

in the recasting of the early *Cantos*—all these aspects of the poetic achievements of Pound and Eliot, and many more, can be related to the overwhelming example of Joyce's work-in-progress. Less attention, however, has been given to the impact of *Ulysses* on the development of Pound and Eliot as critics, although the years 1917-22 were crucial for both of them. It was in these years that Pound's critical ideas were brought to maturity, and shaped into the "pedagogical" schema which later appeared in *How to Read* and *ABC of Reading*; it was in these years that Eliot evolved the critical assumptions which underlie his most influential essays, and wrote all of the pieces in *The Sacred Wood* and *Homage to John Dryden*. It is no exaggeration to say that Pound and Eliot wrote their most important criticism under the shadow of *Ulysses*, and partly in response to Joyce's unsettling masterpiece as it gradually took shape before their eyes. Although the presence of *Ulysses* can be felt in almost all their criticism of 1917-22, this paper is focussed specifically on those essays and comments where Pound and Eliot are grappling directly with *Ulysses*. I hope such a focus will not only reveal some of the basic attitudes of the two most important poet-critics of their age, but will give a perspective on the long critical tradition that they initiated, and in large part defined: the critical tradition devoted to an understanding of *Ulysses*, which often seems nothing but an extended conversation between Pound and Eliot.

From Pound's first contact with Joyce in late 1913, when he chose "I hear an army" for the *Des Imagistes* anthology because of its "objective" qualities, the term "realism" dominated all of his formal comments on Joyce's work. In fact, Pound's ten-year effort to assimilate Joyce's achievement, from *Dubliners* through *Ulysses*, may be seen as a gradual definition of that "realism" which he hoped to capture from "the prose tradition" and make his own. Looking back on the decade from the perspective of 1933, when his immediate enthusiasm for Joyce's work had been somewhat cooled by *Finnegans Wake*, Pound still acknowledged Joyce as the first English writer to follow Henry James in extending "the art of the novel beyond the territory already occupied by the french." Building upon Ibsen and Flaubert, Joyce produced in *Dubliners* and *Portrait* a clean, hard surface where "English prose catches up with Flaubert," and then proceeded to break new ground in *Ulysses*. Speaking of his first enthusiastic response to *Dubliners*, Pound linked it as always with his own poetic aims:

As Madox Ford had been preaching the virtues of the French prose, of what he called impressionist prose, for some years, and as the Imagist FIRST manifesto had demanded 'Direct treatment of the THING whether subjective or objective, and the use of NO WORD that did not contribute to the presentation,' a few people recognized the significance of Joyce's first prose book at once.[2]

Pound encountered *Dubliners* at the time when he was developing one of the crucial discriminations in what was to become his abiding view of the usable "tradition": the notion that with Stendhal and Flaubert the major artistic impulse "went over" to prose, and that the job of the modern poet was to assimilate the discoveries of the prose tradition. Writing to Harriet Monroe in January 1915, with *Dubliners* and *Portrait* in the foreground of his mind, Pound identified the qualities which he most admired in "the prose tradition":

Poetry must be *as well written as prose*. Its language must be a fine language, departing in no way from speech save by a heightened intensity (i.e. simplicity). There must be no book words, no periphrases, no inversions. It must be as simple as De Maupassant's best prose, and as hard as Stendhal's . . . .
Language is made out of concrete things. General expressions in non-concrete terms are a laziness; they are talk, not art, not creation.[3]

First and last, it was the precision and "realism" of Joyce's language that Pound praised and hoped to imitate. He had already been groping toward a concept of poetic "realism" in his essays on the French poets Francis Jammes and Charles Vildrac, who along with D. H. Lawrence are evoked in his 1914 review of *Dubliners* as examples of poets who "have written short narratives in verse, trying, it would seem, to present situations as clearly as prose writers have done, yet more briefly."[4] Throughout the review of *Dubliners* Pound is trying to sort out his views of "realism," distinguishing the "exact presentation" of the Stendhal-Flaubert tradition from the softer effects of Impressionist prose, and the entire essay subtly tilts the axis of Joyce's achievement toward Pound's current artistic preoccupations. The symbolic dimensions of *Dubliners*, the covert thrust toward allegory, the effective uses of Symbolist prose—these are slighted in an effort to establish Joyce as a "realist" who writes "a clear hard prose." But even the focus on "realism" is not as precise as it appears to be on first reading: as in all of Pound's subsequent comments on Joyce, there is a not quite successful attempt to square Joyce's scrupulous attention to realistic detail with his ability to disengage the "universal element" through selection and concentration. "Mr. Joyce does not present 'types' but individuals . . . . He is classic in that he deals with normal things and with normal people." Here is the nub of Pound's critical problem: he wishes to found Joyce's universal appeal on his objectivity, his mastery of concrete detail, without denying his powers over general nature.

The various ambiguities inherent in the term "realism" inhabit all of Pound's criticism of Joyce between 1914 and 1922, and are never fully resolved. At times "realism" means simply defying the censor (whether political or Freudian), opening up new areas of human experience for serious art. In this sense the Joyce of *Ulysses* was the ideal modern Rabelais whom Pound had imagined in a limerick of ca. 1912:

> Sweet Christ from hell spew up some Rabelais,
> To belch and . . . and to define today
> In fitting fashion, and her monument
> Heap up to her in fadeless excrement.[5]

In *Ulysses*, Joyce lanced the boil of a sick culture, using gross realism as his scalpel. But by "realism" Pound also meant the Jamesian surface that he aimed at in *Mauberley*, a delicate record of contemporary manners made with objective irony: that "history of contemporary ethics-in-action" *(l'histoire morale contemporaine)* which the Goncourt brothers had called for, that record of "les moeurs de ses contemporains—leurs rêves, leurs vanités, leurs amours, et leurs folies" which Remy de Gourmont had found in Flaubert (Pound used this quotation to head his 1917 review of Eliot's *Prufrock and Other Observations*). And he meant by "realism" a third thing, something more subtle, the use of "luminous detail" which he was striving for in his poetry: an effort to locate the universal in the particular, to fulfill the Coleridgean aesthetic on a grand scale. At times Pound's "realism" takes on the aspect of Romantic symbolism, and echoes Goethe's famous distinction between the symbol and "mere" allegory:

> There is a great difference, whether the poet seeks the particular for the general or sees the general in the particular. From the first procedure arises allegory, where the particular serves only as an example of the general; the second procedure, however, is really the nature of poetry: it expresses something particular, without thinking of the general or pointing to it.[6]

Such an emphasis on the particular explains, in part, Pound's resistance to the late elaborations of *Ulysses*. All these gradations of "realism" are present in Pound's continuing response to Joyce, but none of them allows sufficient scope for Joyce's love of allegory, his Celtic delight in artifice and design, what Pound called his "mediaevalism." Therefore Pound's complex notion of modern "realism" ultimately led to a special—and somewhat limited—view of Joyce's *Ulysses*.

The challenge of Joyce and the "prose tradition" is clearly evident in the first draft of Canto I (1915-17), where Pound is uncertain whether the "semi-dramatic, semi-epic" techniques borrowed from Browning and his own earlier practice are up to a modern long poem: can they hold his vision, or will he have to "sulk and leave the word to novelists"?[7] As Forrest Read has pointed out, Pound "had not solved the problem of how to include novelistic realism and history in a modern literary work" when he began to write the *Cantos*, and this uncertainty is reflected in his 1916 notice of *Exiles*, "Mr. James Joyce and the Modern Stage."[8] This long and pessimistic survey of the modern stage, where *Exiles* cannot find an intelligent audience, ends with a question: "Must our most intelligent writers do this sort of work in the novel, *solely in the novel*, or is it going to be, in our time, possible for them to do it in drama?" If we read "poetry" for "drama," then Pound is asking a personal question which colors his entire response to *Ulysses*, and to Eliot's work as well. In reviewing *Prufrock* in 1917 Pound linked Eliot with Joyce, and singled out the novelistic qualities of the verse at the expense of qualities which seem more obvious to a later reader.

> James Joyce has written the best novel of my decade [*Portrait*], and perhaps the best criticism of it has come from a Belgian who said, 'All this is as true of my country as of Ireland.' Eliot has a like ubiquity of application. Art does not avoid universals, it strikes at them all the harder in that it strikes through particulars.[9]

This last sentence, when set against the background of Romantic symbolism and the foreground of Imagism, the "prose tradition," and Pound's comments on the Chinese Written Character, gives one a clear sense of the higher realism that he sought in *Ulysses*. The value which he attached to this realism and its accompanying precision of language is expressed with great passion in his 1917 review of *Portrait*, written at the nadir of war-time despair.

> Flaubert pointed out that if France had studied his work they might have been saved a good deal in 1870. If more people had read *The Portrait* and certain stories in Mr. Joyce's *Dubliners* there might have been less recent trouble in Ireland. A clear diagnosis is never without its value . . . .
> It is very important that there should be clear, unexaggerated, realistic literature. It is very important that there should be good prose. The hell of contemporary Europe is caused by the lack of representative government in Germany, *and* by the non-existence of decent prose in the German language. Clear thought and sanity depend on clear prose. They cannot live apart. The former produces the latter. The latter conserves and transmits the former.[10]

Pound's first brief notice of *Ulysses*, written in 1918-19 after the
opening chapters had passed across his desk, announces in staccato
form the direction of all his subsequent comments.[11] Joyce's place
in the Flaubertian tradition is particularized ("He has done what
Flaubert set out to do in *Bouvard and Pécuchet*, done it better, more
succinct"), anticipating the more elaborate analysis of the 1922 essay
on "James Joyce et Pécuchet"; and Pound, "tired of rewriting the
arguments for the realist novel," simply quotes in conclusion the
entire Preface by the Goncourt brothers to the first edition of
Germinie Lacerteux. A paragraph from this Preface, which had
become for Pound the master-document of prose realism, had been
used earlier in his meditations upon the difficulty of getting
Portrait printed in book form:

> 'Now that the novel is wider and deeper, now that it begins to be the serious,
> passionate, living great-form of literary study and of social research, now
> that it has become, by analysis and psychological inquiry, the history of
> contemporary ethics-in-action (how shall one render accurately the phrase
> "l'histoire morale contemporaine"?), now that the novel has imposed upon
> itself the studies and duties of science, one may again make a stand for its
> liberties and its privileges.'[12]

As *Ulysses* grew to its final dimensions in the years 1919-21, and
as Joyce's artistic aims departed more and more from those of the
Flaubertian "prose tradition," Pound's conception of the work
scarcely altered. In effect, his later essays of 1922-23 are simply
a working-out of the view of *Ulysses* already established in 1918-19.
There are several explanations for this, one of which has to do with
the history of the text: Pound's first and lasting impression of
Ulysses was based on the earlier and plainer versions of the first
nine episodes, before Joyce had revised them to harmonize with the
more complex second-half of the novel. Like Yvor Winters, who
seems to be talking of the first published version of Stevens' "Sunday
Morning" even when he has the final text before him, Pound was
conditioned by the Ur-*Ulysses* that he read in 1918-19. But these
circumstances of publication cannot offer a full explanation, since
Eliot read the first versions of the opening chapters in great detail
and still arrived at a quite different vision of the finished work. More
important are Pound's efforts at that time toward his own ideal of
poetic realism ("Langue d'Oc," "Moeurs Contemporaines," *Homage
to Sextus Propertius*, the early *Cantos*, *Hugh Selwyn Mauberley*),
works which fixed certain qualities of *Ulysses* indelibly in his mind.
As always, Pound was most interested in a literary work for what
it could contribute to a live tradition, in this case the tradition of his
own difficult poetic progress since 1912-13; and those aspects of the

developing *Ulysses* which did not jibe with his view of the modern literary tradition were pushed aside. Thus the "Sirens" episode, the first chapter to confront the reader with the inescapable implications of Joyce's *schema*, received a cool reception from Pound. "Pound writes disapproving of the *Sirens*," Joyce told Frank Budgen in June 1919, "then modifying his disapproval and protesting against the close and against 'obsession' and wanting to know whether Bloom (prolonged cheers from all parts of the house) could not be relegated to the background and Stephen Telemachus brought forward" (*Letters* I, 126). Joyce later remarked to Harriet Weaver that Pound's disapproval of *Sirens* "is based on grounds which are not legitimate and is due chiefly to the varied interests of his admirable and energetic artistic life" (*Letters* I, 128). Already Joyce must have realized that Pound's interest in *Ulysses* was inextricably bound up with his own critical theories and evolving artistic energies, and that the two men would inevitably diverge as Joyce's art ceased to match Pound's conception of what it should be.

In view of this resistance to Joyce's later methods in *Ulysses*, it is not surprising that Pound's encomium of 1922, which begins "All men should 'Unite to give praise to Ulysses,' " merely echoes his earlier opinions. The critical points of the earlier notices are repeated and sometimes amplified, and although Pound displays a detailed knowledge of the work's conclusion his remarks on the last episodes are curiously bland. The metamorphoses between past and present which resemble those of the *Cantos* are often acknowledged—Molly is both "Gea-Tellus the earth symbol" and "a coarse-grained bitch"—but the elaborate orders of the finished novel are of little interest to Pound, and even the Homeric frame is described as "simple reversal."

> In this super-novel our author has also poached on the epic, and has, for the first time since 1321, resurrected the infernal figures; his furies are not stage figures; he has, by simple reversal, caught back the furies, his flagellant Castle ladies. Telemachus, Circe, the rest of the Odyssean company, the noisy cave of Aeolus gradually place themselves in the mind of the reader, rapidly or less rapidly according as he is familiar or unfamiliar with Homer. These correspondences are part of Joyce's mediaevalism and are chiefly his own affair, a scaffold, a means of construction, justified by the result, and justifiable by it only. The result is a triumph in form, in balance, in main schema, with continuous inweaving and arabesque.[13]

In the delicate exchange between myth and reality which is one of the hallmarks of modernism, Pound—unlike Eliot—is firmly on the side of the present.

Like the 1922 *Dial* notice, Pound's essay on "James Joyce et Pécuchet" rehearses a familiar position.[14] Taking advantage of the Flaubert centenary, Pound made his most elaborate assessment of Joyce's inheritance from Flaubert and the Goncourts: *Ulysses* takes up where Flaubert left off in *Bouvard et Pécuchet*, laying bare through encyclopedic realism and satire the inanities of the modern world. "It is the realistic novel par excellence, each character speaks in his own way, and corresponds to an external reality." The symbolic and mythic frames are but "means of regulating the form," necessary but mechanical controls on the realistic narrative. "Joyce uses a scaffold taken from Homer, and the remains of a medieval allegorical culture; it matters little, it is a question of cooking, which does not restrict the action, nor inconvenience it, nor harm the realism, nor the contemporaneity of the action." Once again, the inherent antagonism between allegory and the "luminous detail" is apparent. Whereas Eliot saw *Ulysses* as a continuous parallel between contemporaneity and antiquity, Pound viewed the novel's *schema* as an ordering device not organically related to the narrative, a vestigial mediaevalism which has little to do with the work's essential realism. Since Pound chose to reprint "James Joyce et Pécuchet" in *Polite Essays* (1937), we may assume that he considered it his final statement on the unique place of *Ulysses* in the "prose tradition."

Forrest Read claims that in 1922, when Pound saw *Ulysses* "as a whole for the first time," he gained "a new awareness of the prose tradition as a development from the epic tradition."

> Pound wrote several 'Paris Letters' for *The Dial* on Flaubert and Joyce. Of Flaubert he wrote: 'More and more we come to consider Flaubert as the great tragic writer, not the vaunted and perfect stylist. I mean that he is the tragedian of democracy, of modernity.' Both Flaubert and Joyce were 'classic' in that they represent 'everyman' even while writing *l'histoire morale contemporaine*. Flaubert had adumbrated a new modern form in *Bouvard*; Joyce had perfected that form in *Ulysses* and at the same time conflated the novel and the epic.[15]

It is true that Pound gained a new appreciation of the "epic" dimensions of *Ulysses* in 1921-22, and that he acknowledged the "logic" given to the novel by its mythological correspondences; but he was still most interested in *Ulysses* as an extension of Flaubert's "encyclopedia in the form of farce." *Ulysses* is more unified than *Bouvard et Pécuchet*, although similar in intention: "Joyce combines the middle ages, the classical eras, even Jewish antiquity, in a current action; Flaubert strings out the epochs." After all the evidence cited by Forrest Read has been taken into account, the emotional balance in Pound's most comprehensive study of *Ulysses* remains firmly on the side of realism: Molly may be a reincarnation of Penelope, but Pound locates her reality in the language and behavior of contemporary life.

In January of 1923 Pound published a little-known essay, "On Criticism in General," which marks the dividing line between his early *engagé* criticism and his pedagogical essays of the 1920's and 1930's, where he is propagandizing a formed and static view of "the tradition."[16] Almost impenetrable when read in isolation, this essay provides a shorthand sketch of Pound's ten-year critical progress, and is alive with resonances for the reader familiar with his entire critical *oeuvre*. Addressed to a typical disciple, "On Criticism in General" is really a rough draft for the later *How to Read* and *ABC of Reading*. Here for the first time Pound summarizes all his scattered debts to his contemporaries, and outlines the figures from Homer to Joyce who have provided the essential "inventions." Central to the entire historical argument is his conviction that Stendhal, with "his remark about 'La poésie avec ses comparaisons obligées,' " marked the moment in time when "the best minds turned to prose." In a schematic genealogy stretching from Flaubert through the Goncourts, Dostoievsky, and Henry James to Joyce, Pound outlines the main channel of recent literary energy, as distinct from the "local history of the novel in England." In this "genealogy of the period" Joyce stands alone among Pound's contemporaries, followed by the bald statement "Fenollosa on the Chinese Ideograph." As Forrest Read has observed, Pound called "On Criticism in General" his *De Vulgari Eloquio* because it provided the theoretical basis for his new work on the *Cantos*, which would combine the organizational methods learned from Fenollosa's discoveries with his "decision to begin his own poem as a modern *Odyssey*, in the wake of the prose *Ulysses*."[17] But the essay also makes clear that Pound's use of Homer would be very different from that of Joyce, based on moments of metamorphosis rather than the great coordinating frames of *Ulysses*. Pound's special view of "realism" precluded his use or full appreciation of those qualities in *Ulysses* which Eliot was to identify as Joyce's major contributions to modern literature.

T. S. Eliot's relationship to Joyce's work-in-progress was more cautious, and at the same time more ambiguous, than that of Pound. *Ulysses* abrupted on the literary scene when Eliot's critical ideas were still malleable, and from the first he felt somewhat threatened by the overwhelming size of Joyce's achievement. Writing in the *Egoist* for June/July 1918, when he could hardly have read beyond the "Proteus" episode, Eliot spoke of *Ulysses* as "volatile and heady" but "terrifying," as any great new work of art must be;[18] and even in his finally measured assessment—"*Ulysses*, Order, and Myth" (1923)—he described Joyce's work as "a book to which we are all indebted, and from which none of us can *escape* . . . it has given me all the surprise, delight, and *terror* that I can require"[italics mine]. By mid-1918 Eliot had assimilated Pound's belief that *Ulysses* would finally upset the traditional view of prose as a "humbler vehicle" than poetry, although he seemed concerned that Joyce was operating within the medium of his own feelings and emotions, not "tempering and purifying" them as Stendhal did. He was disturbed by the "crudity and egotism" which Joyce shared with Yeats and other Irish writers, while admitting that in *Ulysses* it was "justified by exploitation to the point of greatness."[19]

Clearly Eliot was troubled from the start by the threat which Joyce's diverse and rambunctious prose might pose to the "classicist," and even in the London Letter to *The Dial* dated September 1921 (written shortly before his main work on *The Waste Land*) he linked *Ulysses* with the performance of Stravinsky's *Sacre du Printemps*, where he had sensed a lack of "interpenetration and metamorphosis" between the primitive and the modern.

> The effect was like *Ulysses* with illustrations by the best contemporary illustrator. . . . The spirit of the music was modern, and the spirit of the ballet was primitive ceremony. The Vegetation Rite upon which the ballet is founded remained, in spite of the music, a pageant of primitive culture. It was interesting to any one who had read *The Golden Bough* and similar works, but hardly more than interesting. In art there should be interpenetration and metamorphosis. . . . In everything in the *Sacre du Printemps*, except in the music, one missed the sense of the present. Whether Strawinsky's music be permanent or ephemeral I do not know; but it did seem to transform the rhythm of the steppes into the scream of the motor horn, the rattle of machinery, the grind of wheels, the beating of iron and steel, the roar of the underground railway, and the other barbaric cries of modern life; and to transform these despairing noises into music.[20]

Yet even when Eliot felt the unsettling "terror" and uncontrolled energy of *Ulysses* he also felt its surprise and delight, and much of his theoretical criticism in the years 1918-21 may be read as covert responses to Joyce's amassing novel. "Tradition and the Individual Talent" (1919) is founded on certain perceptions which Pound had adumbrated in *The Spirit of Romance* (1910), but it can also be viewed—along with the quatrain poems of *Poems 1920*—as an attempt to handle Joyce's bold challenge to the conventional relationships between past and present. Like a devoted but somewhat timid child, Eliot was trying to process Joyce's novel into a congenial world of "authority" and "tradition." The first breakthrough for him seems to have come during the writing of *The Waste Land* in 1921, when he must have discovered the full extent of his debt to Joyce. *Ulysses* had delivered to the modern artist a new and dynamic relationship between past and present, a usable attitude toward myth and history which—far more than Eliot's own *Poems* 1920—fulfilled the theoretical precepts of "Tradition and the Individual Talent."[21]

When *Ulysses* appeared in February 1922 Joyce clearly anticipated a public appreciation from Eliot, and on April 10th he wrote to Harriet Weaver in disappointment: "I expected that at least *The Dial* would have arrived today with Mr. Eliot's article but not even that has come" (*Letters* I, 183). Eliot may have delayed his expected encomium because of the enthusiastic notice which Pound wrote for the June *Dial*,[22] but it seems more likely that he held back because he had not yet come to terms with the novel, and was not yet prepared to make a definitive critical "statement." In the *Dial*'s September issue Eliot weakly echoed Pound when he referred to *Ulysses* as "at once the exposure and the burlesque of that of which it is the perfection . . . [it] is not a work which can be compared with any 'novel.' "[23] This comment prepares the way for "*Ulysses*, Order, and Myth," where Eliot claims that "the novel ended with ₁Flaubert and with James," and that Joyce—after trying one novel in *Portrait*—set himself a more expansive and problematic form in *Ulysses*.[24]

It seems obvious that the nature of Joyce's new form, and its particular manifestations, were still a cause of anxiety to Eliot in the period 1921-22. In his comments of those years he tried out a number of Pound's rationales for the greatness of *Ulysses* (as in the *Dial* London Letter of August 1921, where he praised Joyce's "constructive ability"), but it was only with the completion of the work and the publication of Valéry Larbaud's appreciation that Eliot found the key to his instinctive responses. Larbaud's essay, an expansion of his talk given at the Paris séance of 7 December 1921, was first published in the *Nouvelle Revue Française* for April 1922, and Eliot arranged to have an English translation printed in the first issue of *The Criterion* (October 1922) which also contained the text of *The Waste Land*. Written under Joyce's guidance, with the complete novel and Joyce's *schema* at hand, Larbaud's introductory essay emphasized the symbolic dimensions of *Ulysses* and the Odyssean backdrop, thus providing Eliot with the "classical" sanctions that he needed. In "*Ulysses*, Order, and Myth" (November 1923) Eliot makes no mention of Pound's 1922 essays, and refers to Larbaud as the only commentator who has appreciated the significance of Joyce's method: "the parallel to the *Odyssey*, and the use of appropriate styles and symbols to each division." The center of Eliot's essay is a mock quarrel with Richard Aldington, who had pretended to find *Ulysses* deficient in discipline and classical order; and the famous concluding paragraphs of the essay announce in triumphant tones Eliot's newly-discovered understanding of Joyce's "classical" method, an easy commerce between past and present, between tradition and the individual talent. Joyce's parallels with the *Odyssey* have "the importance of a scientific discovery" because they enable the artist to express both the pastness of the past and its eternal presentness. In Eliot's reading of *Ulysses*, Bloom is no more a Ulysses-figure than Ulysses is a Bloom-figure. The two levels of reality become one in a work which mediates between myth and contemporary manners, although from time to time the missionary-spirit of Eliot's essay tilts the balance toward myth and archetype.

> In using the myth, in manipulating a continuous parallel between con-temporaneity and antiquity, Mr Joyce is pursuing a method which others must pursue after him. They will not be imitators, any more than the scientist who uses the discoveries of an Einstein in pursuing his own, independent, further investigations. It is simply a way of controlling, of ordering, of giving a shape and a significance to the immense panorama of futility and anarchy which is contemporary history.... Instead of narrative method, we may now use the mythical method. It is, I seriously believe, a step toward making the modern world possible for art....

In the history of Joyce criticism, Pound's essay on "James Joyce et Pécuchet" and Eliot's essay on "*Ulysses*, Order, and Myth" have become touchstones to two important dimensions of the work. What Arnold Goldman has called "the fact/myth ambiguity" in Joyce's art is accurately reflected in the criticism of *Ulysses*.[25] It has been said that the history of literary criticism can be described as a running debate between Plato and Aristotle; the history of *Ulysses* criticism can be viewed with equal justice as an extended conversation—often amiable, occasionally irritable—between the spiritual descendants of Pound and Eliot. In our own time Hugh Kenner and Richard Ellmann have been the most prominent inheritors, but virtually every study of *Ulysses* can be located on a continuum that stretches between Pound and Eliot. What this means, quite simply, is that the· two most powerful literary sensibilities of the age responded in character-istic fashion to the two most powerful strains in Joyce's fiction. When asked to lecture on English literature at Trieste's Università

Popolare in 1912, Joyce chose as his subjects *verismo* and *idealismo*, Defoe and Blake, thus anticipating the poles between which *Ulysses* fluctuates. With the appearance of each new book on *Ulysses* the call goes out from the reviewers for some ideal "balanced" reading which will do justice to both extremes of Joyce's art, but that ideal criticism will never come. *Ulysses* itself is a meeting-place and battleground for all the diverse strains in the history of prose fiction, not a work of easy reconciliation, and only the enormous learning and energy which Joyce put into the work holds the warring elements together. None of our reactions can match this complexity and this energy: therefore our criticism must constantly fluctuate between partial visions, between fact and myth, between Pound and Eliot. For instance, the 1960's witnessed a general trend toward more "novelistic" readings of *Ulysses* and away from the headier symbolic readings of the 1950's, a trend set in motion by S. L. Goldberg's *The Classical Temper*; but in Richard Ellmann's *Ulysses on the Liffey*, published in this anniversary year, Joyce's *schema* reasserts all of its most outrageous claims. Since any critical study is bound to be a partial record of one reader's imperfect understanding we may expect future critics to re-enact over and over again, with various degrees of intelligence and originality, the debate which Pound and Eliot initiated while *Ulysses* was still a work-in-progress. It is our good fortune, and Joyce's, that the terms of this long critical conversation were established by the two greatest poet-critics of his time.

Princeton University

NOTES

1. The chief documents are Richard Ellmann's edition of the *Letters of James Joyce*, Vol. II; Forrest Read's edition of the *Pound/Joyce* documents (Norfolk, Conn.: New Directions, 1967); B. L. Reid's biography of John Quinn, *The Man from New York* (New York: Oxford University Press, 1968), which contains new letters from Eliot to Quinn; Forrest Read's article on "Pound, Joyce, and Flaubert: The Odysseans," in *New Approaches to Ezra Pound*, ed. Eva Hesse (Berkeley: University of California Press, 1969), pp. 125-44; and Robert Adams Day's study of the relationship between *Ulysses* and *The Waste Land*, "Joyce's Waste Land and Eliot's Unknown God," in *Literary Monographs*, Vol. 4, ed. Eric Rothstein (Madison: University of Wisconsin Press, 1971), pp. 139-210.

2. "Past History," *The English Journal* (Chicago), May 1933; *Pound/Joyce*, pp. 248-49.

3. *Letters of Ezra Pound*, ed. D. D. Paige (New York: Harcourt, Brace, 1950), pp. 48-9.

4. "*Dubliners* and Mr. James Joyce," *The Egoist*, 15 July 1914; rpt. in *Literary Essays of Ezra Pound*, ed. T. S. Eliot (Norfolk, Conn.: New Directions, 1954), pp. 399-402.

5. *Guide to Kulchur* (Norfolk, Conn.: New Directions, 1952), p. 96.

6. Quoted in Herbert N. Schneidau, *Ezra Pound: The Image and the Real* (Baton Rouge: Louisiana State University Press, 1969), pp. 79-80. Chapter III of Schneidau's study provides an elaborate and rather extravagant account of this aspect of Pound's literary theory.

7. *Poetry* (Chicago), 10 (June 1917), 117-18.

8. *Pound/Joyce*, pp. 48-49; Pound's review of *Exiles*, which first appeared in *The Drama* (Chicago), Feb. 1916, is rpt. in *Pound/Joyce*, pp. 49-56.

9. *Literary Essays*, p. 420.

10. *The Egoist*, Feb. 1917; *Pound/Joyce*, pp. 88-91.

11. *Literary Essays*, pp. 415-17.

12. *The Egoist*, 1 March 1916; *Pound/Joyce*, p. 71.

13. *The Dial*, June 1922, Paris Letter dated May 1922; *Literary Essays*, pp. 403-09.

14. *Mercure de France*, June 1922; trans. Fred Bornhauser, *Shenandoah*, 3 (Autumn 1952), 9-20.

15. "Pound, Joyce, and Flaubert: The Odysseans," p. 128.

16. *Criterion*, 1 (Jan. 1923), 143-56.

17. "Pound, Joyce, and Flaubert: The Odysseans," p. 129.

18. "Contemporanea," *The Egoist*, 5 (June/July 1918), 84.

19. "A Foreign Mind" (review of Yeats's *The Cutting of an Agate*), *Athenaeum* (4 July 1919), 553.

20. *The Dial*, 71 (Oct. 1921), 453.

21. For a detailed survey of Eliot's thematic and structural debts to *Ulysses* in *The Waste Land*, see Robert Adams Day, "Joyce's Waste Land and Eliot's Unknown God."

22. *Literary Essays*, pp. 403-09.

23. London Letter entitled "The Novel," *The Dial*, 73 (Sept. 1922), 329.

24. *The Dial*, Nov. 1923; rpt. in *James Joyce: Two Decades of Criticism*, ed. Seon Givens, (New York: Vanguard Press, 1948), pp. 198-202.

25. *The Joyce Paradox: Form and Freedom in his Fiction* (Evanston: Northwestern University Press, 1966), pp. 105ff.

Hugh Kenner
MOLLY'S MASTERSTROKE

I

Fifty years with *Ulysses*, surely by now the most written-about and lectured-about novel in any language, its margins black with cross-references: criticism after a seance of that duration has surely very little left to say? So much homework is done; so many, many facts have been checked out—Homeric facts, newspaper facts, city directory facts, in the post-Ellmann years biographical facts, more murkily present; and as for the naturalistic core, the old-fashioned novel's inventory of Things That Happen, surely Joyce (assisted by Gilbert, Budgen, Kain, Blamires, and so on to no last term) has left us in no doubt about any of that? It is understandable if we feel we have reached a point of negligible returns. We know the book, at last, too well to know any more. And suddenly it begins to look as though *Ulysses* has barely been read at all. That naturalistic core, precisely that, we have taken too much for granted.

For a fact has been all these years quietly awaiting attention, the fact that during the day covered by *Ulysses* a great many important things happen while the author is detaining us somewhere else. What occurred, for instance, at Westland Row Station? Whatever it was, it sufficed in Bloom's judgment to keep Stephen from being readmitted to the Martello Tower (*U* 619). Did he, pushed too far for once, take a swing at Mulligan, and is that why his hand commences paining him a couple of hours later (*U* 563, 589)? (We should be bringing our knowledge of life to such matters, the familiar knowledge for instance that trauma anaesthetizes and a violent blow doesn't hurt at first. Conversely, a blow that pains later was pretty severe. Now think of Mulligan's chin.)

And the most important happening of the day, so far as Bloom is concerned: Molly's tryst with Blazes Boylan—what really went on? It happens wholly offstage, and we seem not to think about it very much, unless to reflect how melancholy is Bloom's fate, to have a thing like that on his mind all day. Trysts, assignations, adulteries, these are banal. It seems part of Joyce's art to relegate that order of melodrama to the wings, and focus our attention instead on the perdurable texture of the ordinary. Bloom walking, Bloom musing, that is the kind of thing that occupies the foreground, the kind of thing that comes to mind when we think of *Ulysses*.

But Joyce was not priest of the Eternal Imagination for nothing, and as the priest's liturgies reflect and inflect the operations of the

19

Church Invisible, Joyce was always pleased to have the foreground action he dwelt on backed up by unseen happenings we can extrapolate. He never relaxes his concern for what we cannot see. In what seems to have been the first story he wrote for publication, "The Sisters," the real action took place long ago and elsewhere, in Father Flynn's mind as he sat alone in his confessional. In the second story he wrote, "Eveline," we are to locate the fulcrum of what happens in the intentions of a man we never see, the sailor who calls himself Frank. Eveline's story is worth a little attention. She appears to be a first sketch for Molly Bloom: a woman whose thoughts take up the foreground of our awareness of her, and whose fantasies of romantic escape structure the part of her life we are shown.

Everyone remembers the visible plot. We encounter the heroine posed like so many of Joyce's women, immobile in a setting carefully contrived to signify meditation. She is seated by a window, just as a 19th century illustrator would have posed her; we may remember Gretta Conroy posed on the stairs, and Gabriel Conroy thinking she looks like a picture one could call "Distant Music." Eveline is thinking of what is near at hand, her life with her father and her brothers and sisters, and reflecting that in some ways it is not a bad life. But it does not compare in glamor with the life Frank seems to be offering her; and Frank, she says to herself, "was very kind, manly, open-hearted." It is clear that "Frank" is the right name for a man like that; there would have been no story if he had told her his name was Boris. Frank has narrated his rise to affluence, a narrative not devoid of omissions; he specified "the terrible Patagonians," but seems not to have dwelt on how he "had fallen on his feet in Buenos Ayres." (And still a sailor?)

"He had fallen on his feet in Buenos Ayres [comma] he said [comma] and had come over to the old country just for a holiday." Great issues may be said to hang on those commas, which stipulate not only that Eveline is quoting Frank, but that Frank has been quoting also: quoting from the kind of fiction Eveline will believe, the fiction in which ready lads "fall on their feet." And he had come to Dublin, it seems, to obtain a bride, and take her back to Buenos Aires, where (to quote again) "he had a house waiting for her."

Caught up as we are in the pathos of her final refusal, we may not reflect on the extreme improbability of these postulates, that a Dublin sailor-boy has grown affluent in South America, and bought a house and sailed all the way back to Ireland to find him a bride to fill it. Nor are we normally struck by the fact that when Eveline halts paralyzed at the barrier Frank makes no apparent effort to return to her side, but instead boards the ship and sails off. That ship is not going to Buenos Aires, it is going to Liverpool, and Frank has not missed a lifetime in Buenos Aires with Eveline, he has missed a quick conquest which would have been consummated in an English seaport. The hidden story of "Eveline" is the story of Frank, a bounder with a glib line, who tried to pick himself up a piece of skirt. She will spend her life regretting the great refusal. But what she refused was just what her father would have said it was, the patter of an experienced seducer.

II

What nearly seduced her was the opportunity to step into a piece of newspaper fiction, in which a girl's dreams are fulfilled by a sailor from beyond the sea—think of Molly and Mulvey—a sailor who has risen to affluence moreover by the process newspaper fictionists abridge to the formula, falling on one's feet. Frank, if Frank is his name, has exploited that fiction skilfully, and come close to executing a masterstroke. Had he succeeded, then instead of making a story for the *Irish Homestead*, which paid James Joyce one pound, it might have made a story for *Titbits*, where payment is made at the rate of a guinea a column, and a story called "Matcham's Masterstroke" has earned "Mr Philip Beaufoy, Playgoer's Club, London" three pounds thirteen and six. Leopold Bloom read that story in the outhouse. Unlike "Eveline," it ends with the words *"hand in hand."* It begins, "*Matcham often thinks of the masterstroke by which he won the laughing witch who now*" (*U* 69). We may imagine the story of Frank's Masterstroke, though his name would have to be changed from Frank to something more masterful, and Eveline is hardly a laughing witch. Still, art alters these little details.

"*Matcham often thinks of the masterstroke . . .*": the assurance of such a sentence has great power. We have no difficulty imagining Matcham, merry with his bared teeth and curled moustaches, thinking back over his masterstroke (what a marital climate!), the laughing witch perhaps on his lap. Such fictions have a very primitive power. And one man at least in Bloomsday Dublin seems to have modeled his stance on the likes of Matcham: Hugh E. (Blazes) Boylan with his slanted straw hat and the carnation between his teeth, his skyblue tie and suit of indigo serge. We are present at the execution of a phase of Boylan's Masterstroke, the purchase (*U* 227) of a basket of "fat pears and blushing peaches," also a bottle and a small jar, sent by tram to arrive at Molly's just before he does.

We shall see Molly attempting a counterstroke of her own; or rather, we shan't see her attempt. We'll have to deduce it, though from ample evidence. When we're done deducing, we shall have reconstructed a hilarious melodrama.

III

The immediate present in which Joyce prefers to detain us is generally unexciting. Once in a while Joyce does permit something melodramatic to happen before our eyes, for instance the citizen throwing a biscuit-tin at Bloom, the enraged dog moreover in furious pursuit as the jarvey whips a frightened nag. This is by way of assuring us that, yes, melodrama seems to be the norm. We may remember the old priest going mad in his confession-box, or Mrs. Mooney the Injured Mother confronting Bob Doran (what a scene *that* would make!), or Michael Furey, dying of consumption in fulfilment of the chill sentiment of Gretta Conroy: "I think he died for me." Or Rudolf Bloom swallowing aconite; or a thwarted boy, son to the moneylender, being fished from the Liffey on the end of a boathook by the slack of his breeches, having tried to drown himself for the sake of "a girl in the case," or more likely to spite his father. Joyce prefers not to *write* such scenes, not the way he writes such a scene as Bloom frying pork kidney. We glimpse them as though in mirrors in the present we are shown.

There are details about the present that he doesn't tell us too, not till he's good and ready, and when he does tell us, something akin to deduction should take place, and earlier scenes be transformed. Thus we see Stephen gazing across a "threadbare cuffedge" at Dublin Bay, and remembering the basin of green bile beside his dying mother's bed (*U* 5). We may suppose him dreadfully insensitive to the charms of the morning landscape, until we learn very late in the book (*U* 560) that Stephen broke his glasses "yesterday" and thus has spent the whole of June 16 unable to focus further than, say, eight inches from his face. And then we understand why the fraying edge of his coatsleeve was so sharply defined, while the "ring of bay and skyline held a dull green mass of liquid."

A last principle, to serve us as premise when we confront Molly's Masterstroke: Joyce's most insidious techniques have to do with Point of View. "The ring of bay and skyline held a dull green mass of liquid," but only through Stephen's myopic eyes. Stephen

"lifts his ashplant high with both hands and smashes the chandelier" (*U* 583) but chiefly in his own intention; no one else sees time's livid final flame leap, and Bloom's inspection discloses no damage more catastrophic than a crushed shade and a broken chimney. And what really, given the state of his eyes, does Stephen see on the strand? For instance does he really discern, or just fantasize, that midwife's bag (*U* 37)?

Not even in "Ithaca," where the point of view seems that of cosmic intelligence, can we presume an absence of such distortions. "Compile the budget for 16 June 1904," the catechist commands, and one is compiled; but we do not find in the Debit column (*U* 711) either the half-sovereign Bloom laid on Bella Cohen's table (*U* 558), or the extra shilling (*U* 585) he gave for the broken chimney. This is not the budget *an sich*, but such a version as Bloom might let Molly inspect.

And most important for our present theme, what looks like a list of Molly's bedfellows compiled by the Recording Angel (*U* 731) proves to be chiefly a litany of Bloom's suspicions; she did not have intercourse with Mulvey (*U* 760), and Penrose was no more than a Peeping Tom (*U* 156, 754), and so on and on. Anyone whom this list misleads (as it did me for years) should consult David Hayman's summary (in *Approaches to "Ulysses": Ten Essays*, ed. Staley and Benstock [Pittsburgh: University of Pittsburgh Press, 1970], pp. 113-14) of the reasons why Boylan, once we come to think about it, must surely be participating in Molly's first affair. It was in the mind of an inexperienced adulterer that Molly's Masterstroke was conceived. Not that it worked.

IV

Eveline missed no home in Buenos Aires; Stephen saw no midwife's bag; Molly was no amoral Mother Earth: if inspection of Joyce's text keeps yielding conclusions like that, what order of evidence may we trust? We may learn from Sherlock Holmes and Flaubert: trust the furniture. "What great issues, Watson, may hang upon a bootlace!" Or upon a chair, or a piano, or a sideboard. Flaubert taught a generation of novel-readers to read furniture; amid his orchestrations of illusion, we are always to trust what we can deduce from the ornaments on mantels, or the posture of chairs. Everyone remembers the camera's-eye tour clear through the empty house, at the opening of *Un Coeur Simple*, from which we learn so much more about the people who live there than we ever do from their deeds or their exiguous words. His disciple Shem the

Penman, author of the "usylessly unreadable Blue Book of Eccles" (*FW* 179) may be glimpsed "writing the mystery of himsel in furniture" (*FW* 184). And Shem's *alter ego* the narrator of the "Ithaca" catechism places at our disposal any quantity of readable evidence moments after the right temporal lobe of Leopold Bloom's cranium comes into contact with a solid timber angle (*U* 705), much as Aristotle, reader of signatures, was "aware of them bodies before of them coloured" by "knocking his sconce against them" (*U* 37).

Bloom bangs his cranium in the doorway of his front room because at some time since he left the house that morning the furniture has been moved. This is one of the most massive of the book's many offstage events, and an inventory is supplied:

> A sofa upholstered in prune plush had been translocated from opposite the door to the ingleside near the compactly furled Union Jack (an alteration which he had frequently intended to execute): the blue and white checker inlaid majolicatopped table had been placed opposite the door in the place vacated by the prune plush sofa: the walnut sideboard (a projecting angle of which had momentarily arrested his ingress) had been moved from its position beside the door to a more advantageous but more perilous position in front of the door: two chairs had been moved from right and left of the ingleside to the position originally occupied by the blue and white checker inlaid majolicatopped table (*U* 705-06).

These chairs as described resemble Molly and Boylan, who have occupied them; we are encouraged to perceive not only "symbolism" but "circumstantial evidence"—we'll come back to those chairs. But the inventory has not ended; something else has been moved:

> What occupied the position originally occupied by the sideboard?
> A vertical piano (Cadby) with exposed keyboard, its closed coffin supporting a pair of long yellow ladies' gloves and an emerald ashtray containing four consumed matches, a partly consumed cigarette and two discoloured ends of cigarettes, its musicrest supporting the music in the key of G natural for voice and piano of *Love's Old Sweet Song* . . . open at the last page with the final indications *ad libitum, forte*, pedal, *animato*, sustained, pedal, *ritirando*, close (*U* 706).

Bloom contemplates the scene "with attention, focusing his gaze on a large dull passive and slender bright active": respectively "a squat stuffed easychair with stout arms extended and back slanted to the rere" and "a slender splayfoot chair of glossy cane curves." Here they are, his wife and her lover; here they sat. The Molly-chair, "repelled in recoil," has "upturned an irregular fringe of a rectangular rug." Bloom ("with solicitation"—envisaging such an impact?) turns the rug down. And the Molly-chair displays "on its amply upholstered seat"—one more particular in which it resembles its denizen—"a centralized diffusing and diminishing discolouration." Circumstantial evidence indeed, the mark of superincumbent Boylan, whose role, his eyes fixed on this stain, Bloom perceives "through various channels of internal sensibility." He then lights a cone of incense, rearranges a few disordered books, partially undresses, locks away Martha Clifford's letter and tiptoes barefoot next door to the bedroom. After a fashion, he has read the story in the furniture. But we have no indication that he has asked the question that cries out to be answered: who moved it?

Mrs. Fleming, who came in to clean late in the morning (*U* 93)? Not likely. Here's what else we are told about Mrs. Fleming: "that old Mrs Fleming you have to be walking around after her putting the things into her hands sneezing and farting into the pots well of course shes old she cant help it" (*U* 768). It's doubtful if Mrs. Fleming could have lifted even the lighter chair.

Molly? Nonsense. Pay attention. Bloom is 5 feet 9½ inches tall (*U* 727), and the walnut sideboard is high enough to fetch him a cranial blow. We may guess at the weight of that sideboard. It has been dragged far enough to clear a space into which a piano has been moved, from we are not told how far. Moving a piano, furthermore, is not an easy job for one strong man, let alone a fleshy woman. The two chairs, yes. The table, yes. The sofa, maybe. But not the sideboard, no, and not the piano. Not by Molly, nor Mrs. Fleming, together or singly.

So who moved the furniture?

Ah, that is the substance of the failed Masterstroke.

V

At 3:15 p.m. Mrs. Marion (Tweedy) Bloom, inexpert adulterer, student of the fiction of Paul de Kock ("Nice name he has") was whistling "There is a charming girl I love"; "and I hadnt even put on my clean shift or powdered myself or a thing" (*U* 747) though she expects her visitor at four. There is a knock; she peeps through the blind; it is not Boylan but a messengerboy bringing an oval basket containing peaches, pears, a bottle of Gilbey's invalid port wrapped in pink tissue, and a pot of Plumtree's potted meat (*U* 227, 675, 747). Her first thought is that Boylan himself will not appear ("I thought it was a putoff first"). Still, she waits, impatient, past four as she later reckons; "and I was just beginning to yawn with nerves thinking he was trying to make a fool of me when I knew his tattarrattat at the door" (*U* 747).

"One rapped on a door, one tapped with a knock, did he knock Paul de Kock, with a loud proud knocker, with a cock carracarra-

carra cock. Cockcock" (*U* 282). That is, more or less, the absent
husband's fantasy ("Knock at the door. Last tip to titivate" [*U* 284]).
It seems to have been rather like Molly's sense of things too: "I knew
his tattarrattat at the door": and there he stood. This is a moment she
has fantasized, but no longer fantasy. "That blue suit he had on and
stylish tie and socks with skyblue silk things on them" (*U* 749). He
wears the carnation he picked up in the store (*U* 228)—he tells Molly
he bought it but she guesses better (*U* 741)—and he smells of a
liquor she cannot identify: sloegin from the Ormond Bar (*U* 265,
741). This is real.

Here documentation lapses, leaving us, though, with that
irrefutable shifted furniture: that ponderous walnut sideboard, that
piano. Molly and Mrs. Fleming didn't move them. If anyone
else capable of moving them was in the house prior to 4 p.m. we
are not told, which seems impossible. Ergo Boylan moved them.

Boylan, "Boylan with impatience," huffing and puffing to shift
all the furniture in the front room? While the eager Molly boiled
with impatience too?

Ah, but did she? She is an inexperienced adulterer. Her bonds
with her husband have been long in the weaving. The moment to
betray him is at hand, the moment to step outside her role as
faithful Penelope. Yes, she has fantasized, Paul de Kock in hand,
but now years of fantasizing are replaced by confronted reality:
a vulgar fleshly reality, filling the room, notable for "his vigour
(a bounder), corporal proportion (a billsticker), commercial ability
(a bester), impressionability (a boaster)" (*U* 732). For Molly, it is
easy to assume, this was suddenly too much. Like Emma Bovary,
like Eveline, she has recourse to literary models. The literature
in which she is expert is pornography. Already she is in a pornographic novel, playing the conquered woman. She will modulate that
role with the help of one of pornography's simplest postulates,
that sexual and muscular vigor are manifestations of the same
energy. Drain him, therefore, with exercise. She will postpone,
perhaps evade, the physical moment: certainly reduce it. Across
her mind, as they stand in the front room, flits her husband's
frequent proposal to move that sofa to the ingleside (*U* 705).
Masterstroke! She will wear Boylan down moving furniture, heavy
furniture.

And so, it seems, we are to imagine Blazes Boylan, redfaced,
putting his shoulder to the sideboard, tugging at the piano, lifting
and carrying the sofa and the majolicatopped table, relocating the
heavy chair, the light chair. . . .

It is enough to redeem Molly in Bloom's mind forever, could he envisage it.

Of course it didn't work. Perhaps she slowly stopped wanting it to work. The music was spread out on the newly located piano. They sang. Was it *Love's Old Sweet Song* that melted her reluctance? She drew off her artiste's gloves. They smoked cigarettes (three butts, four matches; Molly, inexpertly dissolute, required two lights and abandoned her weed half-way). At some moment the easychair was "repelled in recoil" and disrupted the rug. Did he hurl himself on her? *That* would be a scene worthy of Paul de Kock.

If this sounds farcical, it is. Only by the most careful attention to their spoken and unspoken words could Joyce refrain from envisaging his characters' doings as farcical. (We remember Robert in *Exiles*, spraying the air with perfume from a hand-pump.) And Boylan, a cartoon-figure throughout the day, remains a pornographer's fantasy to the end, his capacity for orgasm seemingly inexhaustible.

Later "I made him sit on the easychair purposely when I took off only my blouse and skirt first in the other room" (*U* 769-70). She retains her illusions of delicacy: no strip-tease. Then she sat on his knee, and later hopes she was not too heavy. At some point the easychair acquired that stain. Still later in the bedroom Boylan assumed further initiative, "pulling off his shoes and trousers there on the chair before me so barefaced without even asking permission and standing out that vulgar way in the half of a shirt they wear to be admired" (*U* 776). "I took off all my things with the blinds down after my hours dressing and perfuming and combing" (*U* 742). He is then so vigorous she deduces from de Kockian premises that he must have eaten oysters ("I think a few dozen"). Or—she augments this impression—"a whole sheep" (*U* 742). "I suppose they could hear us away over the other side of the park till I suggested to put the quilt on the floor with a pillow under my bottom" (*U* 769). It is Homeric. Later they have the port and the potted meat in bed, and when Boylan leaves he slaps her behind for not calling him by his first name (*U* 776). "No manners nor no refinement."

Afterward she slept, "lovely and tired," till the thunder burst about 10: "God be merciful to us I thought the heavens were coming down about us to punish" (*U* 741). Earlier a thunderbolt of sorts had struck Boylan: news from the stop press he rushed outside to buy that his flutter at the track had not paid off. He came back inside and tore up the race tickets in a fury (*U* 749-50). That was in the kitchen, where Molly would have been disposing of some of the evidence: putting the empty Plumtree's jar and the port-bottle on the middle shelf of the kitchen dresser, and the basket too in which one pear is uneaten. The torn tickets are on the apron of the dresser (*U* 675) where they catch Bloom's attention, but there is no indication that he notices basket or jar or bottle.

Molly is content, and her night-thoughts afterward touch on the front room furniture only once: "the room looks all right since I changed it" (*U* 779). "I," indeed. As for Bloom, he is in a state of which one component is "equanimity" (*U* 733). He does not reflect on how the furniture got moved, though like Aristotle he had been jarred by physical evidence into what might have been "Sherlockholmsing" thought: "How? By knocking his sconce against [it], sure" (*U* 37). That sofa had moved from opposite the door to the ingleside, where he had often intended to move it himself: one tiny score for Poldy. It would have given him satisfaction and amusement to envision Boylan moving it, and moving all those other things too, notably two heavy things nearly immovable, the adulterer Demiurge to the husband's intentions, or lending a hand at the weaving of Penelope's web.

University of California
at Santa Barbara

Fritz Senn

BOOK OF MANY TURNS

Joyce's works can be seen, with equal validity, either as one great whole or as a series of self-contained units. Seemingly contradictory statements can make good sense: Joyce kept reshaping the same material in more complex ways—he never repeated himself. The reiteration, even permutation, of some fundamentals is striking. We can trace the terminal actuality of *Finnegans Wake* from the germinal potentiality of *Dubliners*; but conversely we are also tempted to emphasize the unique whatness of every single work. Joyce kept repeating himself in metempsychotic succession—but if we highlight the individual incarnations, each of his major works is essentially and unpredictably different from its predecessors.

In coming to terms with Joyce's particular other world of words, we can choose between two different sets of terminology. Taking up Joyce's own, or Stephen Dedalus's, insistent metaphors, we can see literature as a process of conception and parturition. A quasi-biological vocabulary suggests itself which serves to describe an evolution of powerful, vital drives in a teeming world of luxuriant growth. In fact, such a monstrosity as the "Oxen of the Sun" chapter in *Ulysses* can be read as a hymn to fertility in its theme and by its very nature—a misbirth maybe, but the offshoot of some generative (perhaps too generative) force. If we were not trying to be so erudite about this chapter, we might be impressed by its sheer animal exuberance. It seems that all of Joyce's creations came into being through some analogous biological force and were subject to many changes during their prolonged periods of gestation. The works are not only separate, though related, but they all got out of hand in the workshop; they could not be contained within whatever original ground plan there was. They proliferated into something never imagined at the instant of conception.

Even the smallest elements in a literary universe, the letters of the alphabet, can be fertile. Long before Joyce thought of *Finnegans Wake*, he made one of the characters in his first short story reveal her ignorance with an illiterate "rheumatic wheels" (*Dubliners* 17). The life force, like everything else in the story, has gone wrong; it has been turned into decay. So, through a tiny change of two letters or one sound, an appropriate word "rheum" (suggesting a disease: natural development gone wrong) replaces another word.[1] In *Ulysses*, a typographical misbirth, which disfigures the funeral report in the newspaper, is called, with good reason, "a line of bitched type"

29

(*U* 648), bitches being proverbially and indiscriminately fertile. The simple letter "l," whether superfluous as in "that other world" (*U* 77), or missing as in "L. Boom" (*U* 648), has a pullulating force and invites speculation.

But then it is exactly such exuberant, freakish offshoots as the "Oxen of the Sun" chapter that can be demonstrated to be the disciplined, programmed, calculated, systematic completion of an elaborate plan by a meticulous artificer—perhaps an`obsessed one. Chaos resolves itself into the painstakingly structured order of layered symmetry, of catalogues and charts, schemas, correspondences, and parallels. The jungle is also a garden. Much of our labor actually consists of exposing the manifold coordinates in the system. To some of us the existence of such a system amounts to the major justification of a work of literature. To others, Joyce has become too exclusively a cerebral constructor and callous arranger.

In *A Portrait*, the two aspects are clearly interfused. We have now been trained to see its rigid structure as a verbal and symbolic system. But to early readers sheer disorder seemed to prevail. Richard Ellmann, drawing on internal as well as biographical evidence, uses biological terms to characterize the novel as embryonic (*JJ* 306-09).

I take my starting point from a different but related ambiguity. It is contained in the title of the novel, that oddly trailing, spiraling, threefold phrase: "A Portrait—of the Artist—as a Young Man." It looks like an attempt, pedantic and verbose, to fix the subject as accurately as possible. The incongruous effect is that the subject becomes all the more elusive. A less clumsily delimitative title might not have made us aware of the aim of portraiture to pinpoint quiddity in the way that those portraits adorning the walls of Clongowes Wood (*Portrait* 55) preserve something unchangeable for all eternity.

The title implies, however, that there is no portrait as such, that a choice must be made. Out of a wide variety, only *one* phase or pose can be selected. So the implication is that there must be other poses or phases perhaps equally pertinent in the room of infinite possibilities. In the novel Joyce of course gives us a series of such poses and aspects, a chronological succession in which each phase extends and modifies the previous ones. Perhaps only in perpetual qualification can that quintessential quality be circumscribed which, in itself—as the title indicates—remains beyond our grasp. The specification "as a young man" is necessary to the nature of portraiture, but it also contradicts its concept.

In the title it is the unstressed but potent conjunctive particle "as" which seems to infuse the novel. This particle denotes, as the dictionary will tell us, something or someone "in the character, in the capacity" or "in the role" of something else. The *Portrait* is a sequence of such parts of character. Stephen, knowingly or un-knowingly, assumes an amazing number of character roles as he grows up. Before he appears in the flesh, Stephen has already been transformed into a fairy tale character which is specifically glossed ("He was baby tuckoo" [*Portrait* 7]). He soon learns to play some parts, often protective ones, with varying degrees of skill and success. Stephen learns to imitate and to pretend: on the second page he is already "feigning" to run. A number of roles are prescribed to him by the communities of family, school, church, and nation, and it takes some growing up to make him realize the reticular hazards involved. His reading provides a further set of models to be imitated. In the second chapter Stephen actually prepares for a stage per-formance in a school play, a take-off on one of his masters. He deliberately and, at times, histrionically rejects some roles, whereas he remains quite unaware of certain others. It is easier for us than it was for some earlier readers to recognize the stagey nature of some turning points in Stephen's career. Finally Stephen chooses to become an artist, that is, a creator of fictional roles. And in *Ulysses*, the same Stephen singles out, for a dazzling display of theorizing, the writer who probably created more roles than anyone else, Shake-speare (and Stephen is aware that Shakespeare also played real theatrical parts on the London stage). Stephen's artist is compared to "the God of the creation" (*Portrait* 215), and this God is immediately epiphanized in one particular pose—"paring his fingernails."

Somehow Stephen, who enumerates with such gusto the chosen roles of his father: " . . . a tenor, an amateur actor, a shouting politician . . . a taxgatherer, a bankrupt and at present a praiser of his own past" (*Portrait* 241), is a chip off the old block, with a self-written scenario that is just a bit more *recherché*. A predominant role is preordained in the family name, Dedalus, which was taken, along with the motto of the novel, from an ancient book of roles and trans-formation scenes entitled *Metamorphoses*.

All of this is carried over into *Ulysses* and magnified there. The conjunctive potential of that word "as" permeates all of *Ulysses*. But Joyce need no longer plant it into his title. The title *Ulysses* proclaims a role, one Leopold Bloom *as* Odysseus, or Odysseus *as* modern man. And once we catch on to this new game of aliases or analogies, there is no holding back. *Ulysses* is Joyce's *Metamorphoses*, a book of roles and guises, a game of identities, of transubstantiations. It is panto-mimic in the sense of imitating everything. Molly Bloom tells us that her husband is "always imitating everybody" (*U* 771). But even without Molly's corroboration it would be superfluous, after fifty years, to reiterate all the parts that all the characters play in the book.

It is sufficient, by way of recall, to mention the first appearance of a character in the novel. Joyce portrays a real Dubliner, Oliver St. John Gogarty, who was well known in Dublin and remains in Dublin memory just because he was able to carry off so many roles with impressive alacrity. In the book he immediately assumes one particular role, that of a priest, pretending to be a vicar of Christ and a follower of St. Peter. And one of Buck Mulligan's first mocking actions concerns the miraculous eucharistic metamorphosis of mundane into divine substance. He does it, profanely but tellingly, to the pretended accompaniment of slow music, as an *artiste* in the music hall sense, a conjurer. And by means of electric current, as magic trickery, cunning deceit. His subject, however, *is* transformation, and he keeps transforming himself according to whim or opportunity. A true panto-mime, he becomes, in skillful mimetic turn, a priest, a military commander, patron of an artist, friendly adviser, medical rationalist, and so on. His repertoire transcends the boundaries of sex or humanity: he can imitate Mother Grogan or become a bird or an ascending Christ. His observer, Stephen, projects yet other roles onto him, while behind or beyond or above his handiwork an increasingly conspicuous author dangles another assortment of analogies. All of this takes place within some twenty pages comprising the first chapter.

It is no wonder that Gogarty, who could successfully bring off so many roles as doctor, athlete, poet, and later on as nationalistic senator, aviator, and carouser with the British nobility (quite apart from his histrionic talent *ad hoc*), resented the perpetuation of some post-adolescent roles in fictional permanence. Joyce had obviously and maliciously encroached upon his own chosen territory, and Gogarty was only paying back in kind when he revealed (to an audience of would-be Joyce idolators) the real, as he maintained, meaning of the term "artist" in Dublin parlance, reducing, in intention, Joyce's and Stephen's role to the limited one of a poseur.[2]

The simplest way of playing imitative roles is by repeating someone else's words: thus *Ulysses* opens with an explicit quotation. The first words spoken aloud, "*Introibo ad altare Dei*" (*U* 3), are not of that everyday common speech that Joyce could evoke so well; they are neither everyday English, nor even English, nor even speech. They are "intoned," in Latin, that dead tongue with which the Church until recently chose to transmit its messages. The stability of the ritual from which these words are taken contrasts of course with Mulligan's volatile flexibility and lack of principle. The words, in any case, are imitation, resounding for the millionth time, as prologue to the book whose characters play parts, whose actions often consist in acting, and many of whose words are quotation to an extent that the author never even attempted to single out individual quotes by customary typographical marks. A quotation also links the present occasion with a former one; it is a strandentwining chord back in time. So the first words uttered aloud in *Ulysses* take us even beyond the Roman Catholic Mass to the Hebrew Psalms of the Old Testament. They span several millennia.

One capsular reflection of the whole is this: that the novel, whose Latin title suggests a Greek hero based (as Joyce believed) on Semitic tales, begins like a play, with stage directions in the first paragraph and an opening speech by an Irish character whose language is English and who, with a flair for imitation, intones a sentence from the Latin Mass, which is in itself a translation of a Hebrew Psalm. The ethnological and literary multiplicity is already present, while on the surface of it we never for a moment leave a simple, realistic story.

Joyce, who reveals the identity of Buck Mulligan at the outset, keeps the question of who and what he really is suspended throughout. We first witness mimicry, mummery, and mockery; the first voice we hear is put on, and it continues to change. It would be hard to determine exactly where Buck Mulligan drops all of his guises and pretenses and speaks in his own voice, if ever he does. I think that for all his imitative zeal we can feel the man's character behind the sequence of adornments. But it is interesting to note how much at variance all our feelings are once we try to bring them into the open. And so, it is no wonder that critics disagree in their assessment of Buck Mulligan; this is in keeping with mercurial Malachi cheerfully contradicting himself while manipulating his various *personae*.

Hence *Ulysses* appears, from the start, as a reapplication of a principle evolved in *A Portrait*. The artist is re-portrayed as a slightly more disillusioned young man with some newly acquired roles. But the foreground is dominated by his mercurial counterpart, who condenses a whole portrait gallery of a vaudeville *artiste as* (to pick some more items from the script) a mocker, *as* St. Peter, *as* a sycophant, *as* Cranly, *as* a Homeric suitor, or, in the overall view, *as* a Shakespearean clown who sets the stage.

This stage will before long be occupied by Leopold Bloom, whose verbal and mimetic repertoire is much more limited. Mulligan's brilliance is set off against Bloom's lackluster commonness and common sense. Bloom's opening words could not possibly elicit the same sort of extended commentary that Mulligan's require. But with his trite "O, there you are" (*U* 55), Bloom at least reaches his speechless partner, the cat, and attains whatever contact is called for. His concern for that partner is unfeigned. And the cat immediately responds with "Mkgnao," and two variations of the same theme: "Mrkgnao!" and "Mrkrgnao!"

The first book begins on top of a tower with imitative words and divine reverberations. The second book begins below ground in Bloom's kitchen, with simple words and onomatopoetic animal noises. It is intriguing to follow one reader, the Italian translator of *Ulysses*, who claims that the consonantic structure of the cat's "Mrkrgnao" utterance is a covert evocation of Mercury.[3] This would introduce either the Homeric messenger Hermes appropriate to the chapter, or else constitute an animal echo of Mulligan's mercurial role in the parallel chapter. As the novel moves on, Mulligan's brilliance can hardly be increased, while Bloom's earthy wit with and less ostentatious resourcefulness have a way of growing on most readers.

But then of course Bloom is accorded a great deal of scope. Although he is remarkably awkward in acting out such roles as he might enjoy playing in real life, like Philip Beaufoy or Don Juan, he is unconsciously carrying a much greater load than all the other characters. Most roles (Mr. Bloom *as* Odysseus, Christ, Moses, Wandering Jew, etc.) have been well studied. I would like to single out a far less personal role. Within the totality of the novel, Bloom is also a part of speech. In purely grammatical terms, Bloom is also an all round man. His name is taken through all the cases of the singular: "Bloom. Of Bloom. To Bloom. Bloom" (*U* 453), and he seems to have become a grammatical case history. On occasion he resembles a noun with a relative pronoun in various inflections like "Bloowho" (*U* 258), "Bloowhoose" (*U* 259), "Bloohimwhom" (*U* 264), in passages that seem to bring out Bloom's relativity. An inflated version is "puffing Poldy, blowing Bloohoom" (*U* 434). At times perhaps Bloom appears more like a verb than a noun, the *verbum* of Latin grammar or else of the Gospel of St. John. In the course of the novel he seems conjugated in all tenses, past, present, and future; in the active and the passive voice; in all the possible moods—indicative, imperative, subjunctive, optative—not to forget participial forms like "blooming." He becomes a universal paradigm of the school book; if we can parse him, we can parse humanity. Beyond grammar, he is anagrammatically transformed into "Old Ollebo, M. P." (*U* 678). And "POLDY" is the basis for an acrostic (*U* 678).

Bloom's nominal existence is diverse too. He has been translated from Hungarian *Virag*, and he is translating himself into such fictitious roles as Henry Flower, to which Molly adds "Don Poldo de la Flora" (*U* 778), and the author such variants as "Professor Luitpold Blumenduft" (*U* 304) or "Senhor Enrique Flor" (*U* 327). Other transformations are geometrical, a concave distortion like "Booloohoom," or a convex "Jollypoldy the rixdix doldy" (*U* 434). Typography adds an insult, "L. Boom" (*U* 647), to the catalogue. Etymology extends the range further: Skeat's *Etymological Dictionary* relates "bloom" to "blood." Leopold Bloom does not read Skeat's by the hour, but he substitutes his own name for "Blood" in a throwaway (*U* 151), unaware of a momentary eucharistic function. No wonder there are Bloomites in the book, and that the hero is sartorially celebrated in "bloomers" and even citified into "Bloomusalem." Thus, on the merely nomenclatural level of this ominously cluttered novel, Bloom is awarded unprecedented scope as a paradigm.

We know that Joyce found in Homer's Odysseus the universal paradigm from myth that he needed. Hence, I would like to rephrase some of my remarks in the light of Homeric analogies. I have to admit first that I always thought these analogies meaningful, fruitful, and even helpful, even if some of our heavy-footed glosses may not be so. The Homeric ground plan provides another link with the past; it takes us back, as Joyce always tries to do, to first beginnings. Homer's epics are, for all practical purposes, the origins of Western literature. *Ulysses* comprises all literature from its Greek roots (as well as its Hebrew roots in the Old Testament) to its latest ramifications in Yeats and a just emerging Synge. In between, English literary history is amply documented, notably in "Scylla and Charybdis" and "Oxen of the Sun," and there are vestigial traits of Italian, French, and German literature throughout. Homer's highly finished art is a beginning for us, but it was in turn already the culmination of a long development now lost in obscurity. It is an end turned into a new beginning, which makes it all the more fitting for Joyce's purposes.

That the Homeric poems were not, originally, written down and read but passed on orally and recited with musical accompaniment moreover conveniently ties them to an oral tradition very much alive in Ireland. The art of storytelling was still practiced in Joyce's Dublin in those communities that had to be culturally self-sustaining.

Joyce preferred the *Odyssey* to the much more martial *Iliad*, not merely because of his pacifist inclinations nor because he needed more social relationships than a war report can provide, but also because the action of the *Iliad* is subsumed in its sequel. The *Odyssey* is wider in scope: temporal, topical, and simply human.

Even though the so-called Homeric parallels, the transposition of characters and situations, have definite purposes, it is sometimes useful not to insist on the strictly parallel nature of the correspondences: the pattern is often a crisscross one, and similarities often go by contrast. Perhaps the most pervasive Homeric features in *Ulysses* are not the one to one relationships that Stuart Gilbert began to chart for us, but principles or motive forces—such as the Protean force of transformation in the third chapter. Homer and Joyce both had the ability to condense certain overall principles into concise verbal form. Joyce was fond of condensing themes and techniques of his whole works into his opening words (as on the first page of *Ulysses*, which I have dwelt upon in the preceding pages). I believe that Joyce realized that the opening of the *Odyssey* is similarly fashioned, and that he was aware that Homer, much more pointedly and literally than Vergil, Milton, or Pope, put the subject of his poem right in front of us. The subject is Man. The *Odyssey* begins with that word—"*Andra*"—in the objective case, the central object, and Homer keeps it suspended over the first line. It is fortunate that Joyce, who knew little classical Greek (though a Zürich friend, Paul Ruggiero, taught him some modern Greek), recorded the first line of the *Odyssey* in the original, or very close to it. Ellmann implies that it was quoted from memory (*JJ* 585). It is misquoted, of course, and we can explain Joyce's faulty accents as the result of understandable ignorance or, maybe, as a shift in emphasis. At any rate, Joyce knew by heart, and was ready to scribble beside the only authentic portrait of Mr. Bloom we have, the well-known line:

Andra moi énnepe, Mōusa, polýtropon, hòs mála pollà᾽

It happens, fortuitously, that in Greek the accusative noun can be placed before us without a definite article and with its defining adjective being cleverly withheld for a few beats. Thus "Man" is placed before us in his most universalized form before the focus narrows to one particular individual. This obviously suits Joyce's purpose.

In the Homeric text the second noun is "Troy, the holy city" (*Odyssey* I, line 2). So even here Joyce's favorite coupling of the individual and the community of the city seems anticipated. But the word that is especially emphasized in Homer's first line and which is skillfully introduced after a weighty pause, is the epitheton that accompanies "man"—"*polytropos*." It has occupied commentators a good deal, and W. B. Stanford in his excellent study, *The Ulysses Theme*, devotes some pages to it.[5] Joyce could have found most of the glosses in reference books or in the standard Greek dictionaries that he was quite able to consult. Any Greek dictionary would have given him more or less the same information that Liddell and Scott provide: Literally, *polytropos* means "much turned," "of many turns." It is taken to mean that Odysseus is a man much traveled, "much wandering." But the meaning was soon extended to suggest characteristic resourcefulness—"a man capable of turning many ways," a versatile character. It acquired a pejorative use too: it came to mean "shifty" or "wily" (in this sense the adjective is applied to Hermes, i.e. Mercury). It can mean "fickle" or just "changeable," or become a vague term for "various" and "manifold."

I submit that all of these potential meanings of the one word[6] are, literally or figuratively, transferred into *Ulysses*. When Joyce described an early plan of his novel to Stanislaus in 1915, he referred to the central section as "Ulysses Wandlungen."[7] Since Stanislaus at the time was interned by Austrian authorities, the postcard had to be written in German. What Joyce probably wanted to say was "Wanderungen"—wanderings—but he was either confused by the intricacies of the German vocabulary (where the verb *wandeln* can mean both "to wander" and "to change") and hit on *Wandlungen* (which means "changes" but not "wanderings"), or he was trying to entertain his brother by a double entendre. The result, in any case, is that "Ulysses Wanderungen" happens to be an excellent summing up of the novel and also of the two main meanings of Homer's adjective, stressing the hero's travels as well as his versatility.

But to return to the Greek dictionary. Its philological lore seems to appear, in part verbatim, throughout the book. "Wily," for example, is an epithet reserved for the voluble sailor in "Eumaeus," whose pseudo-Odyssean role we have known all along ("such a wily old customer" [*U* 630]). He pretends to be much traveled, and he is in fact a resourceful inventor of tales. Another adjective, "shifty," is applied by Bloom to such "crawthumpers" as one of the Carey brothers who plotted murder and then turned on his accomplices (the negative side of Odyssean changeability): "there's something shiftylooking about them" (*U* 81). The other adjective of the dictionary, "fickle," occurs in "Nausikaa." The boy whom Gerty MacDowell admires in vain seems to her a "Lighthearted deceiver and fickle like all his sex" (*U* 362). Actually Homer's hero had appeared in just such unfavorable

light to some of the early unsympathetic commentators.[8] Now I am
not sure how far Gerty's boy friend qualifies for an Odyssean role of
tertiary importance, but he is apparently capable of doing clever
turns on his bicycle, and it is a nice touch that his name is Reggie
Wylie. Since Joyce invites us to compare Odysseus with Leopold
Bloom and since Gerty compares Bloom with Reggie Wylie, this may
be a peripheral instance of Joyce's reserving some Odyssean versatility for minor characters as well.

Most editions of the *Odyssey* list, in their variant readings of
polytropos, a different adjective "polykrotos." This is in fact usually
the first textual note in the book. The meaning is generally given as
"wily, sly, cunning" (which corresponds to "polytropos"), but
originally it meant "ringing loud, resounding." Somehow this might
contribute towards making L. Boom a noise in the street. Stanford's
interpretation of the adjective as "knocked about"[9] would also apply
to Mr. Bloom. But even if this philological spectrum were outside of
Joyce's ken, it is worth noting that Homer's first emphasized
adjective was soon changed, distorted, or parodied—the earliest anticipation perhaps of Joyce's technique of meaningfully distorted
readings.

The translation of the *Odyssey* by Butcher and Lang, which Frank
Budgen assured me Joyce had used and for which Phillip Herring
found notebook evidence, renders the first epithet as "the man, so
ready at need." I cannot help being amused, perhaps coincidentally,
by Bloom's being described as "a man and ready," and rising to make
for the "yard," contemplating on his way Greek goddesses yielding to
Greek youths (*U* 176-77). Immediately afterwards his elusiveness is
commented upon. But this connection may merely be an instance of
one reader's mind being polytropically affected.

Homer's Odysseus appealed to Joyce because of his universality
and his encyclopaedic turns. In him the two opposites, the individual
and the universe (poles that appear throughout in Joyce's works,
from Stephen's geography book in *A Portrait* to Shem's riddle of the
universe), are combined. I cannot help but think that Joyce was
conscious of a translation of *polytropos* into Latin, which would yield
multi-versus, the exact anthetical correspondence to *uni-versus*.

Naturally it does not matter too much whether some general
principle in either the *Odyssey* or *Ulysses* finds one particular verbal
incarnation. But Joyce had a way of expressing in representative
detail what is also present in the organic whole. The preceding
philological digressions are justified, perhaps, simply because Joyce
was a philologist, in the etymological sense of being a lover of words

and also in the sense of being a commentator of Homer. He attributed the art Philology to the chapter devoted to change and Odyssean flexibility.

Diverging from Homer, Joyce does not start with an invocation stating his theme, but he puts the principle into action by putting he most conspicuously *polytropos* man in the novel right in front of us, Buck Mulligan, whose shifting roles can now be reinterpreted as Odyssean. Buck Mulligan does not know how much he is in fact hellenizing Ireland (*U* 7). Fairly early he uses the Homeric type of adjective himself, both in the hackneyed original "*epi oinopa ponton*" and in parodistic variation "the scrotumtightening sea" (*U* 5). His early Greek samples, incidentally, refer to the eminently changeable elements of water ("ponton," "thalatta") or wine.

Mulligan is resourceful and skillful in dealing with any situation at hand. But he also incorporates these qualities of trickery and deceit that the detractors of Odysseus had pointed out in antiquity. Again there is the tenuous possibility that Joyce had heard of one such detractor who claimed that Homer's account was a tissue of lies. Stanford goes on to say that this critic, whose "oration is bland, persuasive and superbly argued," is hardly trying "to do more than dazzle and astonish his audience," his aim being "to gain admiration for skill in rhetorical technique."[10] There is something very Mulliganesque in all this, but what makes the connection particularly intriguing is that the name of the critic was—Dio *Chrysostomos*.

We are on safer ground by taking Bloom's word for it that Buck Mulligan is an untrustworthy but "versatile allround man, by no means confined to medicine only" (*U* 620). "Versatile" is, of course, the standard definition of *polytropos*; "allroundman" echoes Lenehan's grudging concession of Bloom as "a cultured allround-man" (*U* 235). It echoes, moreover, Joyce's conversation with Frank Budgen in Zürich about Odysseus as a complete all-round character.[11] Lenehan, as it happens, is a little Odysseus in his own small cadging way, wandering and wily and versatile (in "Two Gallants" he is described as a "leech" and is performing an Odyssey in a minor key). It is remarkable how frequently the Odyssean characters in *Ulysses* comment on each other, and often in Odyssean terms too: Lenehan comments on Bloom; Bloom on Buck Mulligan, Lenehan, Simon Dedalus, and on the Sailor; Simon Dedalus on Buck Mulligan ("a doubledyed ruffian," [*U* 88]); the Sailor on Simon Dedalus (his yarn presents Dedalus as polytropos, much-traveled: "He toured the wide world" [*U* 624]); Buck Mulligan on Bloom, etc.

Our first glimpse of Buck Mulligan shows him literally and

physically as a man of many turns. Within the first few pages he is
choreographically living up to his polytropic nature: he faces about,
bends toward Stephen, peers sideways, shows a shaven cheek over
his right shoulder, hops down from his perch, mounts the parapet,
and actually "turn[s] abruptly" (*U* 3-5).[12]

Polytropia in *Ulysses* then is not limited to any one feature, or
level, or any one person—not even to persons. It is polytropically
distributed and incarnated throughout. Animals too, like Stephen's
protean dog on the beach or the dog following Bloom into the by-
ways of "Circe,"   perform feats of amazing versatility. Even
inanimate objects, such as Bloom's newspaper, his wandering soap,
or Stephen's ashplant, are capable of transformation. One whole
chapter hinges on the volatile mutability of all things, the "Circe"
episode. It is made up of all the previous roles in the novel and a
number of new ones, a gigantic transformation scene in panto-
mime, where old roles are continually permuted. Among its
polymorphic turns are the deviate turns of the psyche, with such
authorities as Krafft-Ebbing being responsible for parts of the script.

It is appropriate that Stephen comes to grief in this sequence,
also because, for all the flexibility of his mind, he fails, or refuses,
to be flexible enough to deal with a real situation and to evade a blunt
danger. He is not trying to select a more opportune role, but rather
continues a monologue that is unintelligible and must appear
provoking to the soldiers, who of course are equally inflexible.
The physical altercation in '"Circe" is between characters who
are rigid and might be called "monotropic." Stephen, in crucial
moments, is scornful of such advice as Buck Mulligan has given him
in the morning: "Humour her [his mother] till it's over" (*U* 8).
Mulligan does a lot of opportunistic humoring, and Bloom is good-
humoredly trying his best.

The culminations of "Circe" can be regarded as outgrowths of
such mimetic features as are already present in the first chapter.
"Circe" is made up almost entirely of Mulliganesque poses and
projections. In the morning Buck Mulligan begins by quoting Latin
from the Mass. Near midnight Stephen enters the scene by actually
responding to Mulligan's opening words: "*ad deam qui laetificat
juventutem   meam*" (*U* 433). His version contains one small
change (*deam* for *Deum*), but it is an entire perversion, a wholly
new and utterly Circean turn. The first sounds heard in "Circe"
are the call and answers of the whistles (*U* 429) which are an echo of
the first page. The first words spoken aloud, "Wait, my love," are
a variant of Mulligan's "Yes, my. love" (*U* 429, 4). With his

conjuring imitation of the transubstantiation, Mulligan has also prepared us for magic, the technique of the Circean transformations.

An interesting scene in the first chapter foreshadows many phenomena of "Circe." Mulligan, who has just challenged Stephen "Why don't you play them as I do?" puts on some clothes with the remark that "we'll simply have to dress the character"—a dress rehearsal for the rapid costume changes in "Circe." Mulligan justifies the contradictions in his words and actions with a quotation from Whitman. In "Circe" all contradictions are staged. The paragraph in which Buck Mulligan is dressing (*U* 16-7) is, incidentally, the first in the book in which we cannot be certain which words are actually spoken by Mulligan and which are part of Stephen's thoughts. The distinction between speech and thought will make little sense in the hallucinations of "Circe." Thus we do not know whether "Mercurial Malachi" (*U* 17) is actually spoken by mercurial Mulligan or not, but Mercury, Hermes, the wily, roguish god, is also presiding over the "Circe" chapter just as he was instrumental in helping Odysseus.[13] Mercurial Malachi paves the way for the technique of "Circe."

In this view, then, an extravagant convolution like "Circe" is a polytropical reconjugation of familiar elements met before. Joyce manipulates his material in the most suitable manner. This technique—of adapting one's approach to the situation—is in itself an Odyssean one. Like Odysseus, Joyce chooses his speech, his role, and his narrative stance carefully and ruthlessly. Every style is a role adapted for some purpose. Part of our difficulty as readers is that we are too rigidly fixed to follow the abrupt turns, the changes of the stage, so that the verbal, situational, and narrative texture is too polytropic for our customary inertia.

Odysseus, as well as his presidential adviser, Athene, was not particularly scrupulous in the means he employed to attain a given end, and literal truth is not his overriding concern. Nor, in a way, is it Joyce's. He is not exclusively concerned with realistic verisimilitude and can depart from it entirely. The roles, the styles, the perspectives are chosen for optimal effect *ad hoc*.

Ulysses is Homerically polytropical. Voices change, characters are not fixed, language is versatile and polymorphous. The reader is puzzled by new turns. Where passages, or even chapters, are monotropic, their effect is parodistic, and they strike us by their inadequacy and incongruity; in their totality they add up to the most encyclopaedic mosaic in literature.

In the "Wandering Rocks" chapter the many turns are those of a labyrinth, solidified into the bricks and stones of the city. "Aeolus," the first of those extravagant chapters in *Ulysses* which draw attention to their form, is made up of all the traditional rhetorical figures. It is literally composed of many turns, of *tropes*—all the preformed roles available in human speech. Language is intrinsically metaphorical. Part of the dynamism of Joyce's prose arises from the contrast of figurative to literal meaning, or the ironic unfittingness of a metaphor or a cliché fixed in some no longer congruous roles. Language, the most polytropic invention of the human mind, fascinated Joyce. Skeat's *Etymological Dictionary*, a catalogue of the historical roles of words, makes us aware of morphological and semantic transformations. Joyce makes us aware, moreover, of the various roles that even the most ordinary and familiar words always play. Such a simple and seemingly unambiguous unit as "key," for example, is capable of amazing variety and change of identity. That it can refer to those domestic objects that Bloom and Stephen find themselves without, or to symbols of power (as with St. Peter), to musical notation in "Sirens," to a political institution (the House of Keys), to a name (Alexander Keyes), to connotations like a keyhole in "Circe," or else to a woman "properly keyed up," etc., is all very commonplace and generally unnoticed, but belongs to the polytropic potential that Joyce found in everyday language.

Fortunately for him, the English language is particlarly flexible. Its powers of assimilation, its wide and varied vocabulary, but above all its lack of determining inflection, allow Joyce the scope he needed. In English the miraculous fact that "A belt was also to give a fellow a belt" (*Portrait* 9), which puzzles a young Stephen Dedalus, is easily possible—but perhaps only in English. Native English speakers may not realize, for example, what duplicity the simple title "The Dead" contains. A foreigner, especially if he wants to render it into his own language, may well wonder whether "Dead" is singular or plural. In the course of reading the story we could easily fluctuate in our view, at times taking the word in its more general sense until at one point it seems limited to Michael Furey before it is universalized again in the last paragraph. In other words, it seems to be a title that changes with our experience. Its flexibility is possible in English—in all other languages the meaning would probably remain fixed.

Bloom can beautifully make a trite phrase—"Another gone" (*U* 74)—do double duty, neatly referring, superficially, to Dignam's demise and internally to voyeuristic frustration. Once you try to do this in another language you will find that gender and inflection present some serious obstacles. Similarly, a "goal" scored in hockey cannot play the role of the great "goal" toward which all history moves (*U* 34) outside of the English language. English must be one of the most Odyssean languages; resourceful, pliant, homophonous, versatile, it allows Joyce to assume the voice appropriate for the occasion, multiple guises, mercurial transformations. Now the virtuoso performances of cunning and punning have appeared to some critics as questionable manipulations, forms of trickery. Interestingly enough, the two contradictory evaluations of Joyce's ways happen to reflect the two views held of the character of Odysseus—the superbly agile and ingenious hero, or else the artful, deceitful trickster. Not very surprisingly, the first one to take this negative view was the Homeric Cyclops, an early victim. It may be significant that his vision was troubled from the outset and worsened in the process. In his naiveté his one-track mind trusted words and names. For Polyphemus, at any rate, the pun on the name of Odysseus was a mean trick of some consequence, and it taught him the treacherous and potent nature of words. It taught him, one presumes, to trust no man and no man's words.

Language in the *Odyssey* and in *Ulysses* can be deceptive, elusive, often unreliable. "Sounds are impostures," says Stephen (*U* 622), and he says so in a chapter particularly suited to presenting the untrustworthy nature of all communication. The neatest instance is the funeral report in the newspaper. It contains untruths of two kinds. First the conventional hyperbolic formulae that have little relation to a real emotional involvement which they pretend to express: *"The deceased gentleman was a most popular and genial personality in city life and his demise . . . came as a great shock to citizens of all classes by whom he is deeply regretted"* (*U* 647). This form of falsification is less conspicuous but more ubiquitous than such strident deviations from factual truth as the listing of mourners present like Stephen Dedalus, J.P. McCoy, L. Boom, and M'Intosh. The reader of the novel is contextually privileged; but readers of the *Evening Telegraph* would have been seriously misled. And the characters of *Ulysses* are being similarly taken in. Even the author himself at times assumes the pose of trusting speech and language naively, by pedantically transforming, in one case, a glib and bibulous and next to meaningless "God bless all here" into a prolonged scene depicting a ceremonial benediction (*U* 338-40), one example of the rigid belief in the literal meaning of powerful words. This happens in the "Cyclops" chapter, which shows the clash of the unifocality of view with the multivocality of language.

The reader, as against the more shortsighted of the characters involved, has enough information at hand to adjust his views. But even today it does take a reader with at least a minimum of Odyssean agility. After half a century of *Ulysses* we have learned to regard any information provided within the novel with skeptical, in fact Bloomian, reserve. On the other hand, we invest the words of the text with unusual trust. We know that "L. Boom" is, on the realistic surface of it, simply a piece of misinformation. But we tend to rely on the assumption that the distortion means something, and usually more than just one thing. A principle of obverse truth seems to pervade the novel: somehow, "Boom" is literally true and relevant; its incongruity serves intricate purposes.

And perhaps the Latin phrase from the Mass that is irreverently quoted at the beginning of "Telemachus" also indicates that the book is also perversely like the Mass. Not only because it deals with transubstantiations, significant changes, but also because in it, as in the liturgy, every detail—gesture, word, vestment, etc.—is meaningful, a product of a process of condensation and accretion, and generally overdetermined.

So language as a means of communication in *Ulysses* cannot be trusted and at the same time justifies unusual trust, within a hierarchy of potential contexts. An ignorant rendering of "metempsychosis" as "met him pike hoses" is plainly erroneous in one context, but it is appropriate, word for word, to the character who enunciates it and to some major themes of the novel. Bloom's innocent statement, "I was going to throw it away" (*U* 86) is met with distrust, and its unambiguous everyday meaning is disregarded. Bantam Lyons, a particularly biased person, considers it *purely* allusive and is even willing to back his trust in it as an allusion with hard cash. Reality then turns the initial error into unexpected truth, and the reader can rely on some further nonrealistic relevance. Sounds are tricky, but even their trickiness has a communicative value.

In the episode in which a false Odysseus tells obvious falsehoods, in which the novel's real Odysseus warns Stephen against trusting the novel's preparatory Odysseus, and in which Stephen declares sounds to be impostures, the language of even the tritest of clichés has an odd way of sidelighting some truths. I have had occasion to stress some similarities between Leopold Bloom and Buck Mulligan (they concerned me for the present purposes more than their patent dissimilarities). The two form an uneven pair each with Stephen in the respective chapters of Book I and Book III.

Now, besides some parallels already mentioned and others easy to work out, I think a few different ones are potentially contained as homonymous asides in the first sentence of the "Eumaeus" chapter:

> Preparatory to anything else Mr Bloom *brushed* off the greater bulk of the *shavings* and handed Stephen the hat and ashplant and *bucked* him up generally . . . (*U* 612-13).

I have italicized "brushed," "shaving," and "bucked" because to me they echo, unassumingly, a-semantically, and in-significantly, the first scene in which Buck wields his brush to shave himself. A few sentences later a connection is further made with Stephen's handkerchief "having done yeoman service in the shaving line." These frail links do not contribute much to the passage, but they do bring out, once more and in a different guise, the principle of the same elements being reshuffled within the novel, and here the elements are partly phonetic. The tiny point is that those signs singled out here are not *only* impostures. They contain a measure of oblique truth. (Incidentally, the vowel sounds of "shavings," "brushed," and "bucked" are the same as of "Stately, plump Buck.")

Or perhaps, to improve on my phrasing, these words and sounds are, literally and etymologically,[14] impostures, being imposed upon the text as an additional layer of gratuitous correspondence, ironic contrast, deviate reliability, or polytropical pertinence.

The novel's versatile and occasionally tricky resilience then can be accounted for as a quality that Homer ascribed to his hero. Joyce went on the write an even more *polytropos* novel with an entirely pantropical hero; also, among countless other things, an Irish Ulysses: "Hibernska Ulitzas" (*FW* 551.32). Because of its polytropic nature, *Ulysses* is capable of meeting us all on our own terms, or on any other terms we may think of. Strangely enough, we still tend to forget the lesson we might have learned and to fall back on monotropical statements of the form "*Ulysses* is basically this or that," and we can only do so by emphasizing one of the potentially multiple turns in our own Cyclopean fashion.

If there is any quintessential formula for *Ulysses*, I do not think it will be contained in a resounding, world-embracing YES, nor in an equally reductive nihilistic NO and rejection of our time, but in a modest, persistent, skeptical, Bloomian "Yes but."

Zürich, Switzerland

NOTES

1. Fritz Senn, " 'He Was Too Scrupulous Always': Joyce's 'The Sisters,' " *JJQ*, 2 (Winter 1965), 70-1.

2. "In Dublin an 'artist' is a merry droll, a player of hoaxes," Oliver St. John Gogarty, "They Think They Know Joyce," *Saturday Review of Literature*, 33 (Mar. 18, 1950), 70.

3. "Notice that the first time [the cat's meow] is spelled with Mk, the second time with Mrk, the third with Mrkr. . . . That's the Greek spelling of Mercury. The cat is Mercury," Sidney Alexander quoting Giulio de Angelis in "Bloomsday in Italy, *The Reporter*, 24 (Apr. 13, 1961) 42.

4. Joyce's version, as reproduced by Ellmann, *JJ* facing p. 433, is faulty and has here been substituted by the transcription of the standard Greek text.

5. *The Ulysses Theme: A Study in the Adaptability of a Traditional Hero* (1954; Ann Arbor: University of Michigan Press, 1968).

6. A selection of phrases with which translators of Homer tried to come to terms with *polytropos* is revealing: the hero fated to roam; who roamed the world over; who drew his changeful course through wanderings; that Great Traveller who wandered far and wide; an adventurous man who wandered far; of craft-renown that hero wandering; man of many changes; that sagacious man; resourceful; so wary and wise; various-minded; skilled in all ways of contending; steadfast, skilful and strong; for wisdom's various arts renown'd; who was never at a loss; ready at need; ingenious hero; the shifty; famous for cleverness of schemes he devised.

7. Reproduced in "Album Joyciano," p. 39 in Stelio Crise, *Epiphanies & Phadographs: Joyce & Trieste* (Milano: All' Insegna del Pesce D'Oro, 1967); it is also in the Frankfurt edition of Joyce: *Werke* 5, Briefe I 1900-1916 (Frankfurt: Suhrkamp Verlag, 1969), p. 574. The postcard is dated June 16, 1915.

8. "The Grandson of Autolycus," in Stanford, pp. 8-25, et passim.

9. Ibid., pp. 260-61.

10. Ibid., p. 148.

11. Frank Budgen, *James Joyce and the Making of "Ulysses"* (1934; London: Oxford University Press, 1972), p. 15ff.

12. After this paper was read in Tulsa a member of the audience suggested that "plump," second word in the book, also somehow means "all-round."

13. "Moly is the gift of Hermes, god of public ways . . . . Hermes is the god of signposts: i.e. he is, specially for a traveller like Ulysses, the point at which roads parallel merge and roads contrary also. He is an accident of providence" (*Letters* I, 147-48).

14. Relying on etymological potential is a form of circuitous trust.

Robert Boyle, S.J.

MIRACLE IN BLACK INK:
A GLANCE AT JOYCE'S USE OF HIS EUCHARISTIC IMAGE

In his recent *Ulysses on the Liffey*, Richard Ellmann, through a consideration of Joyce's image of art as Eucharist, arrives at one of the most penetrating and powerful critical insights the last fifty years of *Ulysses* criticism have seen.This is his perception of Molly's (and the other Dublin women's) menstruation as intimately allied to the various consecrations throughout Dublin of Christ's blood and body. This paper aims at bolstering, specifying, and, hopefully, enlarging Ellmann's presentation.

Joyce's use of the eucharistic image can be readily traced from *Portrait* through *Finnegans Wake*, and the earlier and later uses help, it seems to me, to throw light on what Joyce does with the image in *Ulysses*. I will attempt to demonstrate, through the analysis of Joyce's own manipulation of a number of theological terms, how Joyce, bringing many centuries of Catholic tradition to bear on his vision of literary art, comes face to face with the ultimate mystery of human existence, and how he responds when that epiphanic *quidditas* demands expression. The terms are: transmutation, transubstantiation, consubstantiation, subsubstantiation, and transaccidentation.

I have written elsewhere of the theological oddity of "transmuting" in Stephen's careful statement in *Portrait* that "to him, a priest of eternal imagination, transmuting the daily bread of experience into the radiant body of everliving life" (*Portrait* 221). Stephen introduces a term from alchemical tradition into a context where the change from bread to Christ's everliving body would be most properly expressed, in Catholic terms, by "transubstantiating." That Stephen is aware of the distinction and implications involved becomes clearer as we trace the image through the transubstantiations of *Ulysses* into the transaccidentation of the "first till last alshemist" in·*Finnegans Wake*.

In *Ulysses*, Joyce (or Stephen) with sophisticated skill shifts the terms, which operate in different ways when applied to different dogmas, from one theological context to another. The three principal mysteries involved, the Trinity, the Incarnation, and the Eucharist, are characteristically linked in this passage from the *Catholic Encyclopedia*'s article on "Eucharist" (the turn-of-the-century-theology of these volumes usually accords closely with the doctrines and theological speculations Joyce learned)—the movement is from the Trinity through the Incarnation to the Eucharist:

According to a well-known principle of Christology, the same worship of
latria (*cultus latriae*) as is due to the Triune God is due also to the Divine
Word, the God-man Christ, and in fact, by reason of the hypostatic union,
to the Humanity of Christ and its individual component parts, as, e.g. His
Sacred Heart. Now, identically the same Lord Christ is truly present in the
Eucharist as is present in heaven; consequently He is to be adored in the
Blessed Sacrament, and just so long as He remains present under the
appearances of bread and wine, namely, from the moment of Transubstantia-
tion to the moment in which the species are decomposed (cf. Council of
Trent, Sess. xiii, can. vi).

The term "consubstantial" changes its meaning in *Ulysses*
according to the theological context. When it involves the Son's
relation to the Father, the context is Trinitarian, and the term refers
to the *one* divine substance shared by the two persons. When
"consubstantial" shifts from a Trinitarian to a Eucharistic context,
however, it then refers to *two* substances, the substance of Christ
and the substance of the bread (or of the wine). When, in opposition
to the Catholic view, both Christ and the bread are considered to be
substantially present in the Eucharist, they are, in this view,
"consubstantial." I take it that Stephen is using this notion in
"Oxen of the Sun" (*U* 391) when he puts consubstantiality in
relation to transubstantiality and subsubstantiality. "Transubstantiality" determines the Eucharistic context, since it has no
meaning or use in other contexts. Then "consubstantiality" in its
meaning of two contiguous substances could imply Mary's congress
with a human male, and "subsubstantiality" a subhuman congress
with a beast—panther perhaps, *sacré pigeon*, or, like Leda, a swan.

"Transubstantiation" is used theologically only for the Eucharist,
where it refers to the mysterious (not available to observation, or to
human reason unaided) replacement of the substance of the bread by
the substance (and accidents) of Christ's body. Through the divine
power, Christ, as it were, comes across ("trans") the void to replace
the substance of the bread, though the accidents (or appearances) of
bread remain, inhering in no substance at all, but somehow sustained
in existence by divine power in some relation to Christ's body. Thus
when I move the appearances of bread I really move Christ's
sacramental body. Thus I can eat the living Christ as divine
nourishment and a source of ever-living life for me. A new
conscience—a *knowing-with* Christ, like what I take to be Stephen's
basic meaning in forming a new conscience for his race, a *knowing-
with* the artist—is thus nourished.

The term "transubstantial," then, involves divine action, direct
intervention. On this base Joyce uses the term in contexts other
than Eucharistic ones. He speaks (*U* 682) of Bloom as Virag's

"transubstantial son," and of Stephen as Simon's "consubstantial son." This may imply that, since transubstantiation requires deliberate action of the priest and consubstantiation requires merely the acceptance of the natural situation, the doing of "the coupler's will" (*U* 38), Bloom's father wanted his son more intensely than Simon wanted his. But the theological auras of the words, I judge, suggest much more. In the first case, since the context involves Bloom's Jewishness as contrasted with Stephen's Christianity, the interest of the Jewish father in the divine activity in regard to his son seems to be involved: "and every male that's born they think it may be their Messiah" (*U* 338). In the second case, all Catholics accept the fact that Stephen and Simon share the same generic nature, and receive divine grace, if they do, not directly from God but from Christ operating through the sacraments, in the normal course of events. Stephen and Simon are therefore referred to here as consubstantial, because of their natural sharing of the human principle of operation. Also on page 38 the term is applied to them on the basis of their sharing of human nature, though in that instance their distressing duality as opposed persons is involved as well.

"Subsubstantiation" must be formed on analogy with "subhuman." Stephen uses it in his discussion of the "knowing" which resulted in Mary's pregnancy (a passage I discuss in "The Priesthoods of Stephen and Buck," in *Approaches to "Ulysses": Ten Essays*, ed. Staley and Benstock [Pittsburgh: University of Pittsburgh Press, 1970], pp. 47-52). Ellmann considers it as a discussion of the nature of Mary's own substance: "In other words, Mary was either of divine or of human substance, but in no case was she less than substance or had she less than sexual intercourse."[1] I read the passage differently, since the context, as I now see it, does not deal with the question of the kind of substance Mary had. Her human substance is not here questioned, as it is not, as far as I know, anyplace in the book. Ellmann had earlier introduced the question of divine substance in regard to Mary: "Mariolatry and coyness resemble each other in that the one seeks to qualify the austere three-personed maleness of the Trinity by introducing a female presence into it . . ." (*UL* 128). That point may have some relevance elsewhere. Stephen speaks of "the madonna which the cunning Italian intellect flung to the mob of Europe," (*U* 207) as if this were a Vatican divine lure to enchant the world to weary ways. And maybe the idiocies of Mariolatry, which Stephen in *Portrait* amply illustrates, and the resentment of God as a stern Justius, a cosmic policeman, a Jesuit pandybatter, might give some basis to Ellmann's introducing the possibility of any question of Mary's divinity—but not much, if indeed any. At any rate, in this passage (*U* 391), as I can now read it, the whole question is whether the human Mary has been impregnated by divine power, by human power, or, as Taxil's crude blasphemy, allied to Buck's, suggests, by subhuman power, "*le sacré pigeon.*" As I see the matter now, then, it appears preferable to consider that "subsubstantial" refers here to "bestiality," and is allied to Buck's rationalistic attempt to reduce the death of Stephen's mother—and thus, by implication offensive to Stephen, Stephen himself—to a beastly event: "*O, it's only Dedalus whose mother is beastly dead*" (*U* 8). While Stephen is willing, in this discussion of Mary's conceiving the Word, to accept the notion of intercourse with God or with a human man, he pretends indignantly to reject the Leda-and-the-swan situation which Buck had vulgarized in his "Ballad of Joking Jesus."

Stephen orgulously goes on to mock, in terms more intellectual than Buck's, the problems Mariology had fussed over for centuries—e.g., "a body without blemish" thus would refer to the hymen of the inviolate Virgin, which many Mariologists asserted must have remained unbroken in the birth of Jesus, so that he passed through it as he passed through the locked door of the Upper Room some years later. Such matters, Stephen asserts, the faithful may assent to, echoing Mary's version of the Christian "Thy will be done," but the artist-priest and his ephemeral disciples will *with-stand*—perhaps in the old sense, stand *against* the dogma, and in the newer, stand *alongside* the artist-priest. He preaches, in any case, the human resolution of the situation: Mary had intercourse with Joseph (or perhaps with Panther). The lewd—that is the lay-folk, *unlearned* in the Latin root of "lewd"; *vicious* in the Anglo-Saxon root mingled with the Latin—may accept anti-natural dogmatizing, but we artists, truly consubstantial with each other in this human Eucharist of alcohol, can withstand and, as speakers of the Word (Burke's it turns out), can with-say (*against* the Holy Spirit and speak *alongside* licensed spirits). Thus our will, not Nobodaddy's, will be done, and we show ourselves superior to the Blessed Virgin and her credulous admirers. This reading of the passage, while not totally satisfactory to me, nevertheless seems at the moment preferable to Ellmann's. But I certainly agree altogether with his main point, that "consubstantial" here refers to human substances as opposed to divine substance or to anything less than human substance (Ellmann seems to want to use "substance" as a synonym for human substance).

In his preparation for the statement of his great insight into Molly's role in the Eucharistic image, Ellmann states: "This synthesis was prepared for long before in the book; in the *Proteus* episode Stephen brooded on the oddity of God's transubstantiation into flesh occurring in so many communions in so many times and places . . ." (*UL* 170). That is not happily stated, since Ellmann introduces a confusion which I judge that the Catholic Stephen (and Joyce) would not allow in this context. In the Eucharist, God does not assume flesh (the term "transubstantiation" does not at all fit into the context of the Word being made flesh); that is done in the Incarnation. In the Eucharist, Christ (not simply God, but God-made-man, anointed with chrism) assumes, as it were, without change of any kind in him, the accidents of bread and wine.

Stephen had considered this matter in "Proteus," when he thought of "the imp hypostasis" tickling Occam's brain (*U* 40). This consideration is most important in the eucharistic image Joyce develops, as Ellmann perceives in linking these varied consecrations of the hosts to the menstruations throughout Dublin (and the whole human world, for that matter). I judge that Weldon Thornton is mistaken in stating, in his annotation on this passage that "Stephen's use of *hypostasis* here is misleading since hypostasis refers to the union of God and man in Christ, not to Christ's real presence in the Eucharist . . . ."[2] Stephen is considering, as Occam did, that the hypostatic union effected in the Incarnation is the basis for the multilocation effected in the Eucharist. "Hypostasis" literally means exactly what "substance" means, and theologically it refers to the union of two natures, divine and human, in one divine person. Because that one person has both divine power and material extension, he can effect the transubstantiation of many diverse pieces of bread in different times and places and, without change in himself, become mysteriously present under their accidents (their extension, whiteness, and other sensible manifestations). It perhaps should be stressed that theologians do not operate on the basis of imagination, as artists do, so that Stephen's broodings on Occam's speculations might be quite novel to Occam. Stephen, like Joyce, is concerned merely to use the theological materials for his artistic and imaginative purpose. Here, his ultimate aim, as I conceive it, is to prepare for the image of the multilocation of the life-giving artist under the accidents of ink.

Now, if Stephen's thought is carefully considered, it will be seen that "transubstantiation" fits the bread very well, since the imagination tends to picture the substance of the bread (in the theological explanation Joyce most likely learned) passing, "transiting," into the potency of matter and disappearing altogether, while the accidents of the bread, those things which make it manifest to our senses, its extension, color, texture, etc., somehow mysteriously remain. How this can be merits some attention if we are to grasp the force of Joyce's later and most revealing Eucharistic coinage, "transaccidentation."

Human reason would surely judge, by available natural evidence, that where accidents appear there must be a substance in which they inhere. A baseless or rootless accident simply cannot be conceived or imagined, like a line with only one end. Or perhaps a faint analogy might be that engineless automobile which "Candid Camera" arranged to have apparently driven into a garage, to the stupefied consternation of the observing mechanic. Yet some such situation does confront the Catholic theologian. The *Catholic Encyclopedia*, under "Eucharist," presents this solution:

> If it be further asked, whether these appearances have any subject at all in which they inhere, we must answer with St. Thomas Aquinas (III, Q.lxxvii, a.1), that the idea is to be rejected as unbecoming, as though the Body of Christ, in addition to its own accidents, should also assume those of bread and wine. The most that may be said is, that from the Eucharistic Body proceeds a miraculous sustaining power, which supports the appearances bereft of their natural substances and preserves them from collapse.

Now it is clear that the point of view of Christ and that of the bread, in this situation, will differ radically, as theologians have realized: "Accordingly, the continuance of the appearances without the substance of bread and wine as their connatural substratum is just the reverse of Transubstantiation" (*Catholic Encyclopedia*, "Eucharist"). I take it that this means that the losing of substance by the bread is the reverse of the gaining of a substance by the Eucharist. In any case, as I understand the play of Joyce's imagination with this notion, the situation of the bread which has lost its substance but, in some sense, gained Christ as a base is the reverse of Christ's situation, who has lost nothing but, in some perhaps applied sense, adopted the orphaned accidents of the bread. Thus Joyce the artist prepares to move, complete and living, under the accidents of his ink, more durable than flesh.

In the Eucharist, Christ has not changed at all, but the bread has changed more than the human mind, without faith, can grasp. Thus if we asked the bread, "What has happened to you," the bread (or the remaining accidents) deprived of its substance, could answer with fervor, "I have been transubstantiated." But if we ask Christ, who has not changed, not moved, and is yet really present, he can at most say, "I have been transaccidentated." He somehow supports accidents not proper to him, as if he had moved under them, and thus he becomes available to all throughout time and space.

This is Joyce's development of the Eucharistic image of the artist in *Finnegans Wake*, where Shem, having prepared a caustic ink out of his own body wastes, is described, after he has written human history on his own skin, as "transaccidentated through the slow fires of consciousness into a dividual chaos . . ." (*FW* 186). Thus the image which formally began in the smithy of Stephen's soul in *Portrait*, where he planned to forge with the fires of slow perseverance through millions of real experiences a conscience for his race, which could now *know-with* or *experience-with* him, comes to full flower in its reversed condition, where not the experience is changed but the experiencer. Now instead of the daily bread of experience becoming a record or reflection of the maker's own human experiences through transmutation as in alchemy, as we surely understood it in *Portrait*, it becomes the Artist himself, as the bread in the Eucharist becomes Christ. Thus, under the accidents of this human ink, composed of faeces and urine as the Eucharist is composed of bread and wine, the artist makes himself available to his race, to give them conscience—to make them share, as the *FW* passage makes clear, in all human history by plunging with the individual artist into the dividual human chaos, substantiated in the verbal chaosmos of *Finnegans Wake*. So Joyce as a human being, like Dublin as a city containing all cities, contains in himself all humanity, as the particular contains the universal.

One danger in stressing the ultimate implications of the Eucharist image, I might digress to observe, Ellmann has not, as it now seems to me, altogether avoided. About the Eucharist it is possible to say that the word "love" expresses best of all what it means and what it is. Ellmann says exactly that about *Ulysses*, too, so that, as with great insight he observes, all levels of the book "have their summit in love, of which the highest form is sexual love" (*UL* 175). My mind gives enthusiastic assent to Ellmann's stance, but on some subliminal level I feel a stubborn squirm of resistance. And I further feel that this doctrine of "Amor super omnia" is the source of Ellmann's finding in Joyce, writing the final stages of *Ulysses*, "a certain embarrassment and reticence. He speaks of love without naming it . . ." (*UL* 175). Indeed! Joyce's aim, I suspect, is different from Ellmann's, who seems to long for and find, so he thinks, though

with infinitely greater depth and subtlety than Tindall, triumphant
Beethovenian chords assenting to *Liebe über alles*!

I judge, with some reluctance, from what I can see and feel, that
Joyce never totally abandoned the youthful cynicism evident in
Number XXVII of *Chamber Music*:

> For elegant and antique phrase,
>   Dearest, my lips wax all too wise;
> Nor have I known a love whose praise
>   Our piping poets solemnize,
> Neither a love where may not be
>   Ever so little falsity.

Ellmann, in his finding "a certain embarrassment and reticence" in
this usually bold but now suddenly coy Irishman, seems to picture
Joyce hanging back from the happy cosmic triumph, and suspects,
as he goes on to say that Joyce fears didacticism and is therefore
embarrassed and reticent. I cannot at this moment see how Ellmann's
attitude here totally avoids a tinge of Disney-like optimism. I myself
suspect that Joyce did not name love as the word known to all men
because he didn't see it or feel it that way. Love, in a human
universe, does exclude a great deal—all negative, perhaps, but profoundly operative nevertheless. At Buck's Black Mass in "Circe," the
server, Mr. Haines Love, hypostatically combines, like Butt and
Taff in *Finnegans Wake*, the human moral opposites in one person.
Joyce, as I see it now, is unwilling to exclude the opposite of love in
his coal-hole vision, or to discount hell in his arrival at Paradise. He
is not reticent. He is, rather, volubly cosmic—in the human cosmos.
The word known to all men is in the cosmos ineffable, I suspect.
It might come fairly close to being "Shantih," or perhaps even
Justius's "Awmawm," but, as I can dimly see it now, it is not merely
"love."

But to return to Joyce's image, the various Eucharists which touch
the high points of its development deepen from the villanelle's
"chalice flowing to the brim" through Buck's shaving mug, Bloom's
tub, Molly's chamber-pot, until it reaches Shem's seemingly degraded
yet amazingly elevated Grecian urn, in which he makes his
eucharistic ink. The contrast of the two literary imagined
chalices, Stephen's and Shem's, shows something of the increasing
profundity of the image. Stephen's villanelle chalice, a fancy, somewhat romantically inflated vessel too eagerly fulfilling the re-
quirements of the consecration of the Mass, recalls the "Araby"
chalice borne so ineffectively through the Dublin streets. And the
villanelle chalice, too, gathers about itself perverse, unhealthy

vibrations, sounding with what I have elsewhere referred to as a Dracula tonality. The urn of Shem, once consecrated to sadness, more naturally receives the effusion from the bowels of his misery, and takes on its human ("consubstantial") rather than blood-brimming werewolf ("subsubstantial") tonalities especially in the context of Bloom's tub and Molly's pot.

Ellmann perceptively suggests that Buck, in his difficulty about "those white corpuscles" on the opening page of *Ulysses*, is looking down at the white beads of lather in his mug, beaded bubbles which could recall those presumably winking at the brim of the diseased beaker of the villanelle. Yet the tonality of Buck's relatively genial blasphemy is much healthier, by conventional norms at least, than Stephen's, if less profound. Buck the scientist is poking fun at dogma, but he is also out to dominate, to use, and perhaps to destroy the artist, as the prelatial patrons of the arts in the middle ages often did. His eucharist will be useful in cleansing and shaving, but will not be in any sense nourishing. Stephen's will have potentialities both for nourishing and, in its enchanting, baneful alchemical and diabolical aspects, poisoning ("and in the porches of their ears I pour" [*U* 196]).

Bloom's pleasant imagined tub, holding his body consecrated by nature to life ("the father of thousands"), offers the most humanly attractive eucharistic image that Joyce presents—pleasant to acquiescent Bloom as well as to the race which could, potentially, spring from his willing loins—willing, at least, in this eucharistic image. It is Bloom as priest, after all, who, having brooded over the Eucharist in the Mass he witnessed, says of himself in his imagined clean trough of water, "This is my body" (*U* 86). He can give, if not romantic ever-living life, real human life to others, which Stephen, priest of the eternal imagination, aiming to give a romantic reflection of the life his own twisted experience has revealed to him, cannot do, since, like another Prodigal, he squanders his substance among whores. Bloom's eucharist, less inflated than Stephen's, would indeed be human only and mortal, but it would be complete. Stephen's literary sacrament of ever-living life, mixed with the seraphic and diabolic, surges either upward with Michael or downward with Lucifer in its Icarian effort to escape this mundane planet, this limited crystalline world. In its fear of and exclusion of earth and water, of death and urine, Stephen's frustrated soul wants both heaven and hell at once, and is satisfied with neither. If his eucharist could be mixed with Bloom's, the results might be good—or they might not.

Molly does a pretty good job of mixing the two. I cannot yet clearly

see, as Tindall long has, that Stephen and Bloom become a satisfactory Bleephan in the eucharistic meal Bloom confects for Stephen.
Maybe so, but far more satisfactory, as I can now perceive the matter,
is the union that results from the chalice Molly confects of blood and
urine. Here Ellmann's great insight into the mixing of the Dublin
consecrations and the Dublin menstruations must be quoted:

> But Joyce is establishing a secret parallel and opposition: the body of God and
> the body of woman share blood in common (*UL* 171).

And here too Molly brings in all that is good in the Eucharists of
Stephen and of Bloom—the allure of woman and the potentiality for
sharing life in the human body—and partially tends to correct what is
bad—the destructive, cannibalistic voraciousness of female blood-
sucking bat and sow and the fearful paralysis of the timid hedonist.
She alone of the eucharistic confectors has no idea at all, consciously at least, that she is involved in any sacrament, which may
be one important reason why, as "only natural," she expresses most
fully the "human only" experience of our race and, as the *clou* to
immortality, best defies time. One surely must not leave out, in trying
to perceive Joyce's whole vision, the complicating elements which
make Molly share the diabolical (or quasi-diabolical) negative things
in the previous Eucharists, but Ellmann's emphasis on love, if not
carried too far, seems to me surely the right one. At least it operates
in the book, and in me, as in Ellmann, with great force.

The fullest development of the eucharistic image, with all its
possibilities and all of its positive and negative elements operative,
can be found on pages 185-86 of *Finnegans Wake*. First the preparation of the materials, echoing faintly the instructions for the
preparation of the host, emerges from the Latin passage on page
185, which may be translated thus:

> First of all, the artificer, the old father, without any shame and without per-
> mission, when he had donned a cope and undone the girdles, with rump as
> bare as on the day of birth, squatting on the viviparous and all-powerful
> earth, weeping and groaning the while, defecated into his hand; and secondly,
> having unburdened himself of black air, while he beat out the battle-signal,
> he placed his own faeces, which he entitled his "purge," in a once honorable
> vessel of sadness, and into the same, under the invocation of the twin brothers,
> Medardus and Godardus, he pissed happily and melodiously, continuously
> singing with a loud voice the psalm which begins, "My tongue is the reed of a
> scribe swiftly writing." Finally, from vile crap mixed with the pleasantness
> of the divine Orion, after the mixture had been cooked and exposed to the
> cold, he made for himself imperishable ink.[3]

This and the following paragraph describe the confection and effect of Shem's Eucharist. Analogous to Molly's chamber-pot, Shem's

urn, now degraded (and, as it turns out, elevated) to receive the human waste which will, miraculously, provide "the radiant body of everliving life," brings in among other things cosmic Hellenic myths, astrological personages, canonized saints controlling the passing of waters, Old Testament prophets using their tongues as swiftly producing pens, Dublin editors rejecting Joyce's writing, epic and Miltonic and Uranian contexts, the wealth and power of the United States, the whole nineteenth century literary effort to determine rather than to reflect reality as in Balzac and Wilde, the impact of Christianity, the domination of priest and king and their doom, and the squid's great miracle in black ink:

> Then, pious Eneas, conformant to the fulminant firman which enjoins on the tremylose terrian that, when the call comes, he shall produce nichthemerically from his unheavenly body a no uncertain quantity of obscene matter not protected by copriright in the United Stars of Ourania or bedeed and bedood and bedang and bedung to him, with this double dye, brought to blood heat, gallic acid on iron ore, through the bowels of his misery, flashly, faithly, nastily, appropriately, this Esuan Menschavik and the first till last alshemist wrote over every square inch of the only foolscap available, his own body, till by its corrosive sublimation one continuous present tense integument slowly unfolded all marryvoising moodmoulded cyclewheeling history (thereby, he said, reflecting from his own individual person life unlivable, transaccidentated through the slow fires of consciousness into a dividual chaos, perilous, potent, common to allflesh, human only, mortal) but with each word that would not pass away the squidself which he had squirtscreened from the crystalline world waned chagreenold and doriangrayer in its dudhud. This exists that isits after having been said we know. And dabal take dabnal! And the dal dabal dab aldanabal! So perhaps, agglaggagglomeratively asaspenking, after all the arklast fore arklyst on his last public misappearance, circling the square, for the deathfete of Saint Ignaceous Poisonivy, of the Fickle Crowd (hopon the sexth day of Hogsober, killim our king, layum low!) and brandishing his bellbearing stylo, the shining keyman of the wilds of change, if what is sauce for the zassy is souse for the zazimas, the blond cop who thought it was ink was out of his depth but bright in the main (*FW* 185-86).

The black ink of the frightened squid-artist squirted into this chaos, available to the individual creator because he has penetrated through the shell of self to the dividuality in which humanity shares, the *quidditas* common to allflesh, may, at least in its epiphanic defiance of Time, be allied to Shakespeare's more conventional challenge in Sonnet 65:

> Oh, none, unless this miracle have might,
> That in black ink my love may still
> shine bright.

My friend Richard Kain, from his vast knowledge of Joycean materials, referred me to the review of *Ulysses* from which Joyce draws his squid image, N.P. Dawson's "The Cuttlefish School of Writers." The relevant passage is:

> For given a degree of talent, there is an increasing school of writers who imitate the cuttlefish, and conceal their shortcomings by 'ejecting an inky fluid,' which is the definition the dictionary gives of a cuttlefish. The Cuttlefish school would not be a bad name for these writers who perhaps not being as great genuises as they would like to be, eject their inky fluid, splash about and make a great fuss, so that it is difficult to tell what it is all about, and it might as well be genius as anything else.[4]

The "crystalline world" of Joyce's passage might conceivably be influenced by Dawson's question, "Would we even find 'Ulysses' under glass in a museum?,"[5] though the major source, as I now see the matter, is Milton's rational crystal universe hanging in chaos.

Thus Joyce's black ink like Shakespeare's will by a miracle have the extraordinary power of bringing immortality (of a sort) to the artist's love (perhaps both subjective and objective genitive). Shem's ink goes through the shades of the Irish flag ("chagreenold [green and gold] and doriangrayer ["or" and off-white]') to reach its black dudhud, implying, I judge, that Shem's love, among others, is Ireland, even paralyzed, colorless, and dead. But mainly here, it seems to me, the Eucharistic image indicates two things: the concealment, sublimation perhaps, of the creating artist in his art, and the quasi-sacramental victory over time and space. The squid, in sending out into Miltonic chaos, among the United Stars of Ourania, its protective ink, does screen itself effectively from the crystalline world, but it also gives a message that it is there somewhere, a fact ("this exists") that we then know. As we know that God the Creator exists when we see his creation, though we cannot directly know what he is in himself, so we know that the artist-creator exists when we see his carefully formed ink. But we cannot—and the busy, busy Joycean psychoanalysts could well note this—with certitude tell what he is in himself.

More important, the image indicates that the artist is now transaccidentated under the accidents of ink, as Christ is under the accidents of bread. Now the Word that will not pass away (*U* 391; *FW* 186) can be carried to true believers, and through the mystery of himself we can share life more fully than Bloom can transmit it or Molly can assent to it. Stephen's image has reached a new cosmic depth, not divine but human only and mortal, but probably, the image implies, the best we are likely to find. Matthew Arnold might look up from his trimming of A. Lawn Tennyson in pleased delight, one guesses. And we can see now better Joyce's own attitude toward himself as the essential individual opening into that primitive dividual human chaos where the androgynous artist's creative efforts can bring forth his literary race to carry life, livable and unlivable, into the world.

Through his development of the Eucharist image, then, Joyce manages to reflect in Stephen the Romantic and Victorian fluctuations between the Shelleyan ineffectual angel and the Wildean, or perhaps better, Swinburnean perverse and rebellious devil, with their common abhorrence of ordinary humanity. In Buck he suggests along with some good qualities, an expedient common-law union of science and Catholicism, destructive not only of both of those but of humanity as well. In Bloom and Molly he does, through his uses of Catholic belief, far more than D. H. Lawrence could to justify sex's ways to man, and to set forth, without denying the human basis for hell, the tremylose terrian's drive toward some kind of heaven. In Shem he combines all that he has had before in his eucharistic image with a deeper imaginative apprehension of literature's cosmic worth to the human race. With this image Joyce reveals to us who choose to see that we are both gods and doggone clods, and then, faced with the ultimate question about the word known to all men, Joyce, without reticence or embarrassment, in his own prudent dudhud, imitates both Old Man River and Elijah's God: "Our Mr President, he twig the whole lot and he ain't saying nothing" (*U* 508).

Marquette University

APPENDIX

Transubstantiation:	Stephen, who in *Portrait* prefers "transmutation"—aiming to make the divine (and diabolical) human.
Subsubstantiation:	Buck as scientist-priest, Boylan as stud, Bella as enchantress—all aiming to make the human bestial.
Consubstantiation:	Bloom and Molly—aiming to make the human human, in flesh. Molly tends to bridge the human and at least some secular or humanistic "divine."
Transaccidentation:	Shem—making the human share the divine aspects of the Eucharist as well as the diabolical aspects of the Black Mass, in carrying the living human artist throughout human time and space, under the accidents of ink rather than those of bread.

NOTES

1. *Ulysses on the Liffey* (New York: Oxford University Press, 1972), p. 139. Hereafter *UL*.

2. *Allusions in "Ulysses": An Annotated List* (Chapel Hill: University of North Carolina Press, 1968), p. 48.

3. For a detailed discussion of this translation, see my article "*Finnegans Wake*, Page 185: An Explication," *JJQ*, 4 (Fall 1966), 3-16.

4. "The Cuttlefish School of Writers," *Forum*, 69 (1923), 1182.

5. Ibid., p. 1184.

Leo Knuth

JOYCE'S VERBAL ACUPUNCTURE

The halo effect as well as its opposite are pitfalls for critics which are hard to avoid. In the case of Shakespeare it can't do much harm: he is canonized by now, and rightly so—people have been canonized for less. Joyce's reputation is as yet less secure. No other modern writer has suffered more from the wide lunatic fringe of uncritical admirers for whom nothing the master has written is random, and from the insensitive crowd of hidebound, heavyhanded, or hostile critics who refuse to believe that *Ulysses* and *Finnegans Wake* are strong enough to stand on their own false bottoms, and who suspect Joyce of graphorrhea. As long as we do not know what it is that causes readers to feel attracted to or repelled by Joyce, it is hard to assess the wide divergences in rating scales. Since few critics clearly define their analytic and evaluative disciplines and procedures (or precommitments) it is generally difficult to form an estimate of the reliability or relevance of the guiding idea (or bias) which directs a certain approach or appraisal. When we find a useful book such as *Surface and Symbol* saying that there is a regrettable tendency among Joyceans to seek large structural symbols in small verbal correspondences,[1] this may sound reasonable enough at first, until we remember that Joyce said: "I've put in so many enigmas and puzzles that it will keep the professors busy for centuries arguing over what I meant, and that's the only way of insuring one's immortality"(*JJ* 535). When we discover that Adams himself is sometimes inaccurate, our confidence in him is seriously undermined, and we begin to wonder what he means by "large" and "small." *Ulysses* (not to speak of *Finnegans Wake*) is a book that *should* be subjected to detailed analysis: Adams himself has set a good example, and if his book contains errors it is because he has not been painstaking enough and should have paid even more attention to tiny details than he did.

Joyce, although averse to sensationalism in the ordinary sense, was inclined to enigmatography and paradoxism. This tendency, which is in the best Irish tradition, is by no means limited to Irish writers. It is also found in non-Irish geniuses, including Jesus and Shakespeare. The riddle is, after all, the oldest form of literature. The modern attitude to regard it as inferior is mere prejudice. Even though it is not *en vogue* today, and many critics tend to frown upon it, one should bear in mind that literature is in the future as well as in the past. It is a regrettable circumstance that, for better or for worse, it is the critic who determines what literature is. He should be aware of his humble position, and realize that literature is an empty page until a writer comes along and fills it. Joyce, with his yen for mystification, chose to fill it with multivalent words, i.e. with ambiguities; he was in search of simultaneity of effect. Readers who have no taste for his peculiar mixture of levity and gravity, or who emphasize either the naturalistic outer form or the symbolic inner form had better leave Joyce alone. The fact that our modern culture has relegated the riddle to the nursery should not blind us to the fact that other times and climes see the reading of riddles as an art not indulged in merely for fun. The riddle is an essential feature of Joyce's art. He called his *alter ego* after the artifex who built the labyrinth, and labyrinths are to direction what riddles are to unambiguous denotative language.

There are critics who, needled by Joyce's verbal acupuncture and by his allowing strings of association to depend upon the know-ledge of comparatively esoteric facts, appear to be insensitive to his resolve to create an all-embracing archetypal pattern in the Homeric parallels, the correspondences and the other symbolic trappings of the schema of *Ulysses*. Some of them, strangely attracted by his writing, have sought to save Joyce from himself by extracting the naturalistic "novel" from the book, thereby remolding it nearer to their hearts' desire. This is an unscholarly attitude. It reduces *Ulysses* to the level of other novels. It is a denial of one of Joyce's greatest merits, the discovery of a mimetic form, a form that mimics the *quidditas* of the message. It ignores the reason why, in *A Portrait*, the language changes with the growth of the protagonist; why, in *Ulysses*, the "style" and the "technic" change as the subject changes. The windy metaphors in "Aeolus," the culinary and alimentary allusions in "Lestrygonians," the Shakespearian phrases in the Library episode, the false clues in "Wandering Rocks," the verbal equivalents of musical devices in "Sirens," the I-form and the bombastic style parodies suggesting the bulging muscles of "Cyclops," the nine-part structure suggesting embryonic growth in the "Oxen of the Sun," the flabby style of "Eumaeus," suggesting mental and physical fatigue, the purely denotative language of "Ithaca," which massacres all emotions, the "gynomorphic" structure of "Penelope," are all obvious examples of Joyce's mimetic form which have very little to do with the paraphrasable content of the "story." But since they were important to Joyce, they should be important to the student of Joyce.

There are even more subtle instances of the "many enigmas and

puzzles" which are to "keep the professors busy for centuries."
Sometimes enigmatic signs and hints, apparently dissociated from
the realistic texture, generate images which provide important
structural clues. An example is the SOS signal I see concealed in
Sweets of Sin (*U* 237), which reflects the SOS shape of the book—the
O emblematizing the theme of cyclic recurrence and also serving as
a pictograph of Bloom, the "allroundman" (*U* 235), flanked by the
first and last letters of the novel. The idea on which the title of
the book and the Homeric parallels rest is the concept of metempsychosis. The key word is first introduced in "Calypso," and
rightly so, for metempsychosis is the most economical soul-saving
device, and the "art" of "Calypso" is "economics." Molly's "O,
rocks!" after Bloom has explained the term as "the transmigration
of souls" (*U* 64) contains an allusion to the episode of the
"Wandering (=transmigrating) Rocks," as does the "orangekeyed
chamberpot" with its collar of esses encircling its rim. For in the
exact center of this labyrinthine episode we find the section dealing
with Bloom's acquisition of *Sweets of Sin:*

> The shopman lifted eyes bleared with old rheum.
> —*Sweets of Sin*, he said, tapping on it (*U* 237).

The "tapping" of the shopman, and the persistence of the letters
SOS,[2] combined with the "capital esses" which Miss Dunne is
scribbling on her jotter like an automatist (*U* 229), and the "round
o and crooked ess" in Miss Kennedy's book (*U* 262) are all tiny
verbal hints of the central message of the book, a message which
ties in with the importance of Mark 8:36 and Hebrews 10:39 in
the central chapter of *A Portrait:* "One thing alone is needful, the
salvation of one's soul" (*Portrait* 110).

Bloom, as we know, is not only the avatar of Odysseus. He has
also messianic dimensions, which are frequently hinted at in the
text, but which are also suggested by the number of chapters. In
Hebrew the characters that spell the number 18 also spell the word
chai (life),[3] and in Greek the number 18 is spelled *iota* plus *êta*,
which is also used as an abbreviation of *Jesus*. The *clou* which rivets
the two interpretations together is found in "Hades," when Mr.
Kernan quotes John 11:25—"*I am the resurrection and the life*"
(*U* 105).

We encounter the ideas triggered by the associations engendered
by 18 in the recurrent description of a figure consisting of a
circle and a cross. It occurs for the first time in the opening sentence
of the book, which mentions the shavingbowl on which a mirror and
a razor lie crossed. To see mirror and razor as symbols of art and

medicine, and associate them with the protagonists of the first chapter is quite feasible—although the mirror also refers to Mulligan as Narcissus—but underlying this kind of symbolism there is the image of the circle and the cross, which recurs a few pages later when the two shafts of light form a cross in the circular domed room of the tower (*U* 11). In "Aeolus" the image reappears in a somewhat different form. Here it is the layout of the ad which Bloom is trying to arrange for Alexander Keyes: two crossed keys surrounded by a circle. The suggestive power of the image (which does not invalidate the key symbolism) becomes evident when we recognize it as one of the figures of the imago mundi and of the Buddhist mandala. It is also the shape of the Celtic cross. (The word "cross," by the way, is one of the two most important Irish loanwords in English, the other one being "whisky.") A curious manifestation of the mandala figure appears in chapter X. This time the reader needs a map of Dublin in order to see it. Dublin is the locale and the subject of chapter X. With the North and South Circular Roads and the Royal and Grand Canals encircling it, Dublin appears on the map as a disk. The routes of the representatives of Christ and Caesar with which the chapter opens and closes form an "X" on the disk of Dublin. (The Clongowes Wood flashbacks serve to complete Father Conmee's part of the "X.") Bloom, who finds himself at the topographical center (under Merchant's Arch, or near it), appears in the central section (section X). He is a microcosmic replica of the figure: he is called an "allroundman" (*U* 235), and "crucified" by the Citizen. The reader, like Stephen at Sandymount Beach, is expected to read the signatures of all things, both *nacheinander* and *nebeneinander*. Joyce has left plenty of clues. One such clue is the snippet of Bloom's interior monologue in "Lotus Eaters,"

> Crown of thorns and cross. Clever idea Saint Patrick the shamrock. Chopsticks? (*U* 80).

It is immediately followed by a reference to Father Conmee, whom we do not meet until chapter X. The reference serves as a link tying one mandala allusion together with another. To dismiss such small verbal correspondences as coincidental and irrelevant is to ignore a feature which differentiates Joyce's art from that of other writers. In the fragment quoted above Bloom compares and contrasts Christianity and Buddhism. The traditional emblem of Christianity is transfigured into a hedonistic image: two chopsticks set athwart on a plate. It is an instance of Joyce's delight in crossing the thin line between irreconcilables, in finding the points where apparently unrelated things coincide. Why should we in our peevish opposition (as cross as two sticks) take it to heart?

I do not intend to deal exhaustively with Joyce's enigmatography, nor to classify the different kinds of riddles. I merely wish to show that the chasing of clues is a rewarding exercise. It is also functional in terms of the main theme of *Ulysses*. The theme of the *Odyssey* is the quest. Joyce's mimetic version of it allows his readers to become fellow adventurers, questing for the answers to the "many enigmas and puzzles" which he has strewn in their paths. The riddles are functional, because there can be no *Aha Erlebnis* unless there has been concealment first. One can only seek what is hidden.

One such riddle involves the function of Molly's chamberpot. Like all receptacles it is clearly a feminine symbol, but why does it figure in the metempsychosis scene? It is obviously more than a realistic detail on the existential surface level. I will return to this question later, but first I should like to say something about metempsychosis. Its importance can hardly be overestimated. The very title of *Ulysses* would be meaningless without it. A full treatment lies outside the scope of this article. But it should be obvious that this concept must be related to the idea of change, of history repeating itself, of time and space, of mind and matter, ideas which play such an important part in Joyce's *oeuvre*.

The idea of metempsychosis ties in with the recurrence of certain key words in varying contexts, whereby a déjà vu sensation is created in the mind of the reader, at first probably only in the marginal field of consciousness. The moment the reader becomes aware that he is undergoing new experiences as if they had happened before, he will realize that this device serves a special purpose, that this device is functional in terms of the basic concept of the book. When the reader, on page 154, 182, or 269, or 653, is conscious of having met them pikehoses before, this awareness is in the nature of what Joyce calls an epiphany.

A comparatively simple illustration.[4] In "Nestor" there is a flashback in which Stephen relives an experience in the library of Saint Geneviève:

> By his elbow a delicate Siamese conned a handbook of strategy. Fed and feeding brains about me: under glowlamps, impaled, with faintly beating feelers . . . (*U* 25).

In "Calypso" Bloom is watching the cat lapping up the milk:

> He watched the bristles shining wirily in the weak light as she tipped

three times and licked lightly. Wonder is it true if you clip them they can't
mouse after. Why? They shine in the dark, perhaps, the tips. Or kind of
feelers in the dark, perhaps (*U* 56).

The two passages are linked by the word "feelers." As soon as
this "feeler" is recognized as a hint, we notice the other parallels:
a delicate Siamese/a cat; strategy/a mousing cat; fed and feeding/a
feeding cat; glowlamps/they shine in the dark. Quite apart from
the question whether Joyce did or did not mean to suggest some kind
of mental telepathy between Bloom and Stephen (in which case this
example should be listed with other instances of the thoughts of one
protagonist being telepathically communicated to the other, and we
shall have to note the differences between the interior monologues of
the sender and the recipient), the example shows how the reader is
affected by what I call Joyce's verbal acupuncture. The déjà vu
sensation in the reader rests on what psychologists call the persevera-
tion factor: the tendency of an impression to leave an influence on
subsequent experiences. By a skilful blending of certain key words
Joyce succeeds in integrating them into fragments of ever widening
scope. Thus, apropos of the tapping bookseller mentioned earlier
in this article, it may be observed that a study of the contexts in
which the word *tap* occurs will reveal how Joyce plays on the
reader's readiness to accept suggestion. On page 30 we read: "He
tapped his savingsbox against his thumbnail." Both "tapped" and
"savingsbox" prepare the reader for the hidden SOS signal in the
central section of "Wandering Rocks." The word "thumbnail"
appears again in the metempsychosis scene of "Calypso":

—Met him what? he asked.
—Here, she said. What does that mean?
He leaned downwards and read near her polished thumbnail.
—Metempsychosis? (*U* 64).

After Bloom's patient explanation about "the transmigration of
souls" and Molly's impatient exclamation, "O, rocks!",
the word "thumbnail" has become part of the "Wandering Rocks"
cum SOS cluster. In "Sirens," as if to remind the reader of this
cluster, we find: "Chips, picking chips off rocky thumbnail,
chips" (*U* 256) and, a little later, "Chips, picking chips off one
of his rocky thumbnails" (*U* 261). The code signal of distress,
suggested by "—*Sweets of Sin*, he said, tapping on it" (*U* 237) is
adumbrated by Martin Cunningham's *mea culpa* gesture in "Hades":
"He tapped his chest sadly" (*U* 95), while the word "*Tapping*"
on page 528 is immediately followed by a paragraph containing the
words "rocks" and "peccadillo" on page 529. The kind of reading

I advocate would be meaningless if Joyce were just a writer of naturalistic prose. It is the kind of reading, however, which is indispensable for *Ulysses* and *Finnegans Wake*, where verbal echoes are designed to guide the reader to the solution of certain tantalizing riddles. Although Bloom is unaware of his role as an avatar of his Greek and Semitic prototypes, his bookhunt guides him to the book whose title synthesizes the two opposing forces in the intellectual climate of our culture: the Hebraistic consciousness of sin and the Hellenistic awareness of beauty. The reader, by listening to certain verbal echoes (*tap, sin, rocks*), is guided to the center of the labyrinthine "Wandering Rocks" episode where he is allowed to experience an epiphany, which Joyce, in *Stephen Hero*, defined as "a sudden spiritual manifestation, whether in the vulgarity of speech or of gesture or in a memorable phase of the mind itself." What could be more vulgar than the sight of a blear-eyed keeper of a porn-shop, tapping on a book called *Sweets of Sin*, and saying "That's a good one"?

Homophonic wordplay is an important ingredient in Joyce's technique. A good example is the paronomastic use of the Hebrew letter *Sin* in the first section of "Wandering Rocks." In a way it points forward to the *Sweets of Sin* in the central section. Joyce knew, however, that *sin* is Hebrew for "tooth." Throughout the chapter teeth are very much in evidence. Boylan, for instance, who appears several times in this chapter, is always seen with a flower between his smiling teeth. He becomes an emblem of Bloom's castration complex, because the legend of the Symplegades, which is the classical parallel of "Wandering Rocks," is an example of what folktale specialists call the *vagina dentata* motif. Viewed against this background Molly's "I was cracking the nuts with my teeth" (*U* 750) acquires a special dimension, and turns her into a veritable *Síle-na-bhfiacal*. Whether the references to Elijah in "Wandering Rocks" are intended as another allusion to teeth ("Elijah the Tishbite," I Kings 17:1) is doubtful, but Stephen's "Agenbite" (*U* 243) and Father Conmee's "ivory bookmark" (*U* 224) most probably are. More interesting, however, is the sub-surface influence exercised by the "flock of muttoning clouds" in Father Conmee's Clongowes Wood flashback(*U* 224). Since this kind of sky is called a "mackerel sky" in English, and since Bloom is repeatedly compared to a sheep[5] and his college nickname was "mackerel" (*U* 162, 548), the words, appearing in the first section of this labyrinth chapter, serve as a signpost to its center, the section with Bloom functioning as the *Agnus Dei* (note, in passing, that the

theme of the legend of the Symplegades is the quest of the Argonauts
for the fleece of the sacrificial ram, and that a labyrinth symbolizes
the quest for the center). At the same time Father Conmee's phrase
puts us in mind of Song of Songs 6:6: "Thy teeth are as a flock of
sheep"—more teeth, and SOS again. The reader who has become so
far enmeshed in his (or Joyce's) associative processes will find it
hard to resist the potential double entendre in Molly's "he [Boylan]
must have eaten a whole sheep" (*U* 742).

Joyce's use of transparent names is too well known to require
extensive treatment. It may be worth while, however, to remind the
reader of the pseudonym Bloom uses in his clandestine correspondence with Martha: Henry Flower. The name Henry, which means
"Home Ruler," is important in connection with Bloom's plight, and
with a recurrent phrase which appears for the first time in
"Calypso": "homerule sun rising up in the northwest" (*U* 57;
compare also *U* 164, 376, 482). As Bloom turns into Eccles Street,
"hurrying homeward,"

> Quick warm sunlight came running from Berkeley Road, swiftly, in slim
> sandals, along the brightening footpath (*U* 61).

A glance at the map will show the reader that Berkeley Road is
northwest of Eccles Street. The curious effect is caused by the grey
cloud that temporarily covered the sun (*U* 61). It is the same cloud
that is mentioned on page 9. The cloud is referred to again in
"Ithaca": "a matutinal cloud . . . at first no bigger than a woman's
hand" (*U* 667). The phrase is molded in a matrix borrowed from the
story of Elijah in I Kings 18:44. Here it is the cloud which will
break the drought. Another "small verbal correspondence" is found
in the third section of "Wandering Rocks," when Molly throws a
penny to the one-legged sailor: "A woman's hand flung forth a coin
over the area railings" (*U* 226). At this stage the cluster of associations begins to thicken. Since the "onelegged sailor" is singing
The Death of Nelson, the reader is reminded of "the onehandled
adulterer," as the one-eyed Nelson is called by Stephen (*U* 148), and
this phrase in its turn reminds us of Molly's chamberpot, "that
absurd orangekeyed utensil which has only one handle" (*U* 547).
Thus we see how verbal correspondences succeed in tying the themes
of adultery, usurpation, and homerule together. Most of these
correspondences are, of course, only noticed in a "retrospective
arrangement," to borrow Mr. Kernan's favorite expression, which
is repeated seven times in *Ulysses*.

There are other correspondences which are situational rather
than verbal, such as the Homeric parallels, which were elaborated

upon by Stuart Gilbert, and Bloom's association with Christ and Moses, commented upon by others. Bloom also re-enacts several incidents in the life of Elijah, which I do not remember having seen discussed, except for his Elijah-like ascent to heaven at the end of the "Cyclops" episode (*U* 345). Like Elijah, he consoles a widow. A humorous situational and color inversion occurs when Bloom, after receiving the Elijah handbill, feeds the gulls on O'Connell bridge (cf. I Kings 17:6). These situational correspondences are perhaps less conspicuous than the verbal ones, such as the obscene innuendo of "is coming" and "throwaway" in the Elijah-is-coming throwaway—which becomes obvious in the masturbation scene of usicaa"—but they are no less characteristic, and often inextricably interrelated with the verbal ones. When Bloom refers to this incident as "My fireworks" (*U* 371) we are reminded of the fact that Elijah is the prophet of fire, but here again the correspondence is verbal rather than situational.

Besides these echoes and correspondences, verbal and situational, Joyce employs other associative devices. Some of them are reminiscent of orthodox allegory. The Gold Cup, for instance, is to Sceptre and Throwaway what Molly is to Boylan and Bloom. Others are harder to pinpoint, less categorical and restrictive, more plurisignal and dynamic. A good example is the orange-keyed chamberpot in "Calypso." I have touched on its Greek fret and related it to the SOS signal. I have also discussed the implications of its having "only one handle." On the symbolic level it is closely linked up with other receptacles mentioned in the book, such as Mulligan's shavingbowl, which reminds Stephen of his mother in the first chapter. Its symbolic relationship with Molly rests partly on the fact that, like Molly, the "Pride of Calpe's rocky mount" (*U* 319), it reminds one, through etymological association, of Gibraltar (*Kalpe* = pot). Its color, orange, facilitates association with the Gold Cup, another container which emblematizes the weaker vessel. But why does it figure in the metempsychosis scene? Its realistic function on the existential level would seem to make it a suitable symbol of waste. Viewed in this context it is symbolic of our throw-away age, and is closely connected with Throwaway-Bloom. In that case it is the symbolic antithesis of the "art" of the "Calypso" chapter ("economics") and of the concept of metempsychosis—the most economical way of preserving psychic energy through the ages. On the other hand, it may embrace the opposite idea. Urine is a waste product, but it may be put to good use as a fertilizer. We return to nature what we have received. As a symbol of metabolism—the preservation of matter—it parallels metempsychosis. It serves the same purpose as the commode in "a commodius vicus of recirculation" in the opening sentence of *Finnegans Wake*. In that case the orange-keyed chamberpot links directly with metempsychosis (the soul-saving device) and with SOS.

Enough, I think, has been said to show that a highhanded dismissal of "small verbal correspondences" is unwarranted, and that, in dealing with Joyce, a micro-detailed analysis of reverberations is often a rewarding experience. Joyce's verbal acupuncture will cure the reader of over-involvement in the social aspects of *Ulysses* by increasing the distance between the reader and the surface realism of the story, and of the notion that Joyce's artistic mode is essentially nonhumorous. The boundary line between levity and gravity is irrelevant in dealing with Joyce. It is better to avoid the dichotomy, and accept both aspects of his art simultaneously, even if it involves a paradox. For the paradox was precisely what he sought. It resolves the conflict between opposites. His work shows an increasing awareness of the importance of the *coincidentia oppositorum*, until it reached the stage where his favorite preoccupation became the erasing of antinomies. Hence, also, his predilection for wordplay. The lancet of his art has a *puntiglio*. It is the pun that establishes a meaningful relation between ideas that normally refuse to combine. Again, it should be borne in mind that a paradox is the verbal equivalent of what in theology is called a miracle. And to work miracles was his desire: "that's the only way of insuring one's immortality."

In the last analysis, however, the reading of *Ulysses* (and this holds good for *Finnegans Wake* as well) is not just the study of an artifact. It is a confrontation with the writer; a conflict of the reading public with Joyce's ego—the ego of an Irish Catholic humorist, who may seem insensitive, dehumanized, too cerebral, arrogant, ironical, cunning, and deceitful to those who prefer some honest crusader.

The University of Utrecht
The Netherlands

NOTES

1. Robert M. Adams, *Surface and Symbol: The Consistency of James Joyce's "Ulysses"* (New York: Oxford University Press, 1962), p. 225.

2. SOS, the telegraphic code signal of distress, suggests itself to the mind of the reader in the reference to the Seal of Solomon, in the many quotations from Song of Songs, in "The Sorrows of Satan" (*U* 184), and in "Secret of all secrets" (*U* 242). SOS is also found in the opening paragraph of "Lestrygonians": "Save. Our. Sitting..." (*U* 151). The ludicrous juxtaposition of the Christian brother and His Majesty the King adumbrates the Christ-Caesar opposition of "Wandering Rocks," where the SOS motif finds its culmination in the central section. John Gross (although he does not appear to have noticed SOS) has some interesting observations on Joyce's delight in playing with letters (*James Joyce* [New York: Viking Press, 1971], pp. 75f.). I have dealt with the SOS theme at greater length in "A Bathymetric Reading of Joyce's *Ulysses*, Chapter X," *JJQ,* 9 (Summer 1972).

3. David Toor has pointed this out in a note in *The Explicator*, 24 (Apr. 1966), item 65.

4. For this example I am indebted to Simona Verdin of Brussels.

5. Bloom is called "old sheepsface" (*U* 345), "a black sheep" (*U* 461); mention is made of his "sheepish grin" (*U* 527); in the account of his quarrel with the Citizen we read: "What properly riled them was a bite from a sheep" (*U* 658).

Mark Shechner

THE SONG OF THE WANDERING AENGUS:
JAMES JOYCE AND HIS MOTHER

But thou has suckled me with a bitter milk: my moon and my sun thou
hast quenched for ever. And thou hast left me alone for ever in the dark ways
of my bitterness: and with a kiss of ashes thou hast kissed my mouth.

—Stephen Dedalus

The great danger against which mankind has evolved culture is that of
object loss, of being left alone in the dark.

—Géza Róheim

I The Theory

Caught as he is between two roaring worlds, Stephen Dedalus
knows something about dialectics. Without contraries, he might tell
us, there is no progression, and the Shakespeare he invents for
his enemies in the library is a triumph of the dialectical imagination.
The transforming power of art has made William the conquered
into William the conqueror by converting those failures that are
uniquely human into virtues that are appropriately godlike.
Shakespeare's powers, it seems, are reconstructed flaws, his bows,
erstwhile wounds. His godlike androgyneity is the apotheosis of
his sexual confusion; his divine autonomy a version of his human
aloneness. His life becomes art according to a syllogism: if real loss,
then symbolic gain. Thus: if cuckold, then avenger; if victim, then
victor; if lost son, then eternal father; if a victim of the family, then
creator of his own family. All things that oppress him are grist
for his mill, because as an artist, *loss is his gain*. This dialectic of
loss and gain in *Ulysses* is only one of the book's thematic doublets
but it is crucial both to Stephen's theory of art and Bloom's rumina-
tions on love. Loss is a dilemma that goes to the roots of Joyce's
creative imagination, an enabling condition or irreducible cause that
insinuated its way into everything he wrote. But the dilemmas of
Joyce the man were both motives and exploitable ground for Joyce
the artist. Like the Church Stephen explains to his baffled opponents
in the library, Joyce's art is founded irremovably because it is
founded upon a void, a gap, an absence.

The syllogism of loss and gain that Stephen invents for Shakespeare inhabits as well a central place in psychoanalytic speculations
upon creativity. Indeed, as Géza Róheim and other like-minded
anthropologists have insisted, nothing less than all of human
culture is founded upon absence. "Civilization," argues Róheim,
"originates in delayed infancy and its function is security." He adds,

"It is a huge network of more or less successful attempts to protect mankind against the danger of object-loss, the colossal efforts made by a baby who is afraid of being left alone in the dark."[1] In recent years, particularly among the British or "object-relations" schools of psychoanalysis, the idea has grown up that creativity especially is arrayed against loss by restoring what is absent, re-constituting what is damaged, atoning for what has been injured.[2] Hanna Segal, for example, has proposed that art partakes of a ritual of mourning, being an internalization and re-representation of whatever has been lost, ruined or destroyed. She quotes with approval Proust's view that art is a response to loss, and declares that "all creation is really a re-creation of a once loved and once whole, but now lost and ruined object, a ruined internal world and self."[3] Similar conclusions have been drawn by William Niederland, an American analyst who observes, "The mystery of death, the sudden disappearance of a more or less ambivalently-loved object, e.g., the death of a sibling in childhood, seems to provide a powerful stimulus for fantasies and strivings of a restitutive character."[4] He quotes from K.R. Eissler's psychoanalytic study of Goethe to the effect that "the first spurt in Goethe's writing of *Wilhelm Meister* . . . was initiated or precipitated by news from home . . . that his father was a dying man."[5]

In a word, artistic creation makes abundant sense as *re*-creation. What is made by the artist is a substitute object which bears a significance, not its own, that has been displaced onto it from something that is lost, ruined or otherwise unavailable. The elegance of such a theory for the study of Joyce is self-evident, for it organizes the categories of "art" and "exile" into a luminous, intelligible whole. It tells us plainly what we have always understood intuitively: that what Joyce did with his art was to recreate a lost world in order to restore, preserve, protect, preside over and control it. It proposes also that the theme of sundering, which hovers about the end of *Chamber Music* and invades all of Joyce's books thereafter, is not just another leitmotif in *Ulysses*, but a necessary psychological condition for the book's existence. For Joyce as for Shakespeare, loss was gain, and may indeed have been the single necessary condition for the lifelong gain of his creativity.

II 1903-04 and the Sources of Art

When the twenty-year-old James Joyce went auspiciously forth to encounter the reality of Parisian experience in December 1902, no real father nor fabulous artificer stood him in good stead. Nor need

they have, for that flight was not so much an exile's departure as
a bohemian's excursion: a young man's tentative surrender to the
spell of arms and voices from abroad. And to the extent that
he did take his household gods with him, they were not images
of the father. As Ellmann has said of the Stephen Dedalus who
prepares to leave Ireland at the end of *Portrait*: "He buys his
own ticket for Holyhead, but claims to have been deported. Yet
his mother prepares his clothing for the journey; she at any rate
does not break with him. Of this young man it may be safely
predicted that he will write letters home" (*JJ* 302).[6] And those
letters, we know, will be answered by a mother's admonitions not
to drink unboiled Parisian water (*Letters* II, 20) or wear the soul
out with tears (*Letters* II, 22). *Amor matris*, as Stephen concludes
desperately in *Ulysses*, may be the only true thing in life, and the
lesson, it seems, was well taught by a mother who wrote to a son,
scarcely eighteen days in Paris, "I only wish I was near you to
look after and comfort you but we will be united very soon again
thank God for *home you must come* if only for a week (*Letters* II, 22).
Home he did come, for one final Christmas in the bosom of the
family, before departing again to Paris, by way of London, near the
end of January. More letters home, telling of literary ambition and
personal anxiety, creative asceticism and noble poverty ("Today I
am twenty hours without food" [*Letters* II, 29]), in a tone more
dutiful than desperate, known by parents everywhere as the
filial-heroic. "Do not despair though", she assures and advises
him, "for I still feel full of hope for you and this month will tell
a great deal keep all your friends and in a suitable time call on
Mrs. McBride who received you well . . ." (*Letters* II, 32).

In one letter home, after announcing his literary timetable for the
next fourteen years (his "book of songs," 1907; his first comedy
and his "Esthetic" in subsequent five-year intervals), he begs her to
respond to his adventures and schemes: "You will oblige me very
much if you will write to me and tell me what you think of me.
I shall read your letter with great anxiety" (*Letters* II, 38).

That anxiety was, if anything, understated. Alone and hungry in
Paris, he dreamed of her, and because all events brought grist to
his mill, even at twenty, he memorialized the dream in his growing
collection of epiphanies.

> She comes at night when the city is still; invisible, inaudible, all unsummoned.
> She comes from her ancient seat to visit the least of her children, mother
> most venerable, as though he had never been alien to her. She knows the inmost
> heart; therefore she is gentle, nothing exacting; saying, I am susceptible
> of change, an imaginative influence in the hearts of my children. Who has

pity for you when you are sad among the strangers? Years and years I loved
you when you lay in my womb.'

This mother most venerable who had come to him at night was
not only Mary Joyce but her blessed and virginal namesake as well.
The tone of her reproach was gentle, for the alien son who had
left Ireland, Church and mother for Paris, art and isolation, was not
in mortal sin—merely in danger of offending his mother. But
early in 1903, May Joyce was alive and a life in Dublin for her
son still seemed a possibility. During this same sojourn, under
the pressure of more violent dreams he drafted a decidedly uncourtly
poem which, in later form he made the capstone of *Chamber Music*.
The trauma of separation, of sundering, emerges suddenly from a
vision of violent and irresistible masculinity. Joyce transcribed the
poem in a letter to Stanislaus:

I hear an army charging upon the land
And the thunder of horses plunging, foam about their knees,
Arrogant, in black armour, behind them stand,
Disdaining the reins, with fluttering whips, the charioteers.

They cry amid the night their battle-name;
I moan in sleep, hearing afar their whirling laughter.
They ride through the gloom of dreams, a blinding flame,
With hoofs clanging upon the heart, as upon an anvil.

They come triumphantly shaking their long green hair,
They come out of the sea and run shouting by the shore—
My heart, have you no wisdom thus to despair?
Little white breast, O why have you left me alone? (*Letters* II, 27-8).

The version that was published in *Chamber Music* in 1907 ends
with the incantatory "My love, my love, my love, why have you
left me alone?" a powerful but "nicer" expression of loss and
despair than the naked and embarassing "little white breast, O"
of the original. What the later line lacks in specificity and, perhaps,
honesty, it gains in rhetoric. The image of the lost breast, it seems,
has been suppressed, and the affect associated with it invested in
the language itself.

This anxious idyll of sympathetic alienation was interrupted by
John Joyce's Good Friday telegram, "Mother dying come home
father," which drew his son back to the center of paralysis to
await, through an agonizing summer, his mother's death on August
13, 1903. We know from Stanislaus' account of the deathbed scene
that Stephen's obsessive recollections of the event in *Ulysses*
somewhat distort what really happened.⁸ Contrary to Stephen's
memory, it appears that both James *and* Stanislaus were ordered to

kneel and pray, and that it was not their mother but a hated maternal uncle, John Murray, who gave the order. It appears also that both brothers refused to make what they felt to be a gesture of false piety at this uncle's behest and that their mother was quite unconscious throughout this curious struggle. However that may be, Joyce's guilt over his mother's death and the circumstances surrounding it was every bit as great as his sense of loss. He later confessed to Nora, "My mother was slowly killed, I think, by my father's ill-treatment, by years of trouble, and by my cynical frankness of conduct (*Letters* II, 48). *Exiles* and *Ulysses* independently support the same inference: that Joyce's already well-developed sense of guilt was augmented by his feeling of having failed or betrayed his mother, and that this conviction, if anything, grew more intense rather than less during the years in Trieste.[9]

Soon after his mother's death, Joyce wrote a poem which may have been a epitaph for her. It was first entitled "Cabra," later "Ruminants," and was still later rewritten as "Tilly."[10] It was a laconic, anxious and moody poem, quieter than "I Hear an Army" but bearing imagistic similarities to it. Because its music was somber and wintry, Joyce held it out of *Chamber Music* in 1907, proclaiming to Stanislaus that his "dancing days" were over (*Letters* II, 181). It remained unpublished until it appeared in 1927 as "Tilly" in *Pomes Pennyeach*. The early "Cabra/Ruminants" version reads:

> He travels after the wintry sun,
> Driving the cattle along the straight red road;
> Calling to them in a voice they know,
> He drives the cattle above Cabra.
>
> His voice tells them home is not far.
> They low and make soft music with their hoofs.
> He drives them without labour before him,
> Steam pluming their foreheads.
>
> Herdsman, careful of the herd,
> Tonight sleep well by the fire
> When the herd too is asleep
> And the door made fast.

Despite the apparent lucidity of the surface, the poem is a mystery. The cattle drive is affectively neutral and thematically nonsuggestive; the final apostrophe to the herdsman is ominous but nonspecific. Something threatens from without, but one can sleep before a fire within behind a door made fast. There is no obvious allusion to a mother's death and yet, *and this is axiomatic, we may assume its presence throughout*. The apparent date of composition would argue that. "Cabra" is a winter poem and winter 1903 is our best bet. Moreover, the poem's objectless anxiety, its joyless music in the context of Joyce's otherwise gayclad lutanist verse of the period and its non-publication for twenty-three years call special attention to its mysteries. But the imagery of the poem is scrupulously noncommittal. If the image of the cattle drive bears elegaic import, it is not obvious. We are met by a seemingly real herdsman driving real cattle along a real red road in a poetic setting that does not appear metaphoric or symbolic. But again, it is impossible for one who knows Joyce not to seek out the autobiographical, and specifically the familial, in such a poem. The tone invites speculation, as does our limited knowledge of the poem's circumstantial background. *We know Joyce;* he was always an "occasional" poet. And we know too that loss, or the threat of it, was his characteristic occasion. For myself, I cannot suppress the suspicion that it is John Joyce and the multitudinous children of his wifeless household who trudge here gloomily toward the house Stanislaus Joyce nicknamed "Bleakhouse," 7 St. Peter's Terrace, Cabra.[11]

All available evidence argues that the version we know as "Tilly" did not exist before 1916, and may be dated even later than that. And it is not improbable that the rewriting represents a response to a different situation and that "Tilly" is therefore a different poem. Nevertheless, if we take the precarious liberty of reading "Tilly" as a gloss upon its predecessor, we get some interesting results. For if the family drama was ever there in "Cabra" to begin with, it has surely been illuminated in "Tilly."

> He travels after a winter sun,
> Urging the cattle along a cold red road,
> Calling to them, a voice they know,
> He drives his beasts above Cabra.
>
> The voice tells them home is warm.
> They moo and make brute music with their hoofs.
> He drives them with a flowering branch before him,
> Smoke pluming their foreheads.
>
> Boor, bond of the herd,
> Tonight stretch full by the fire!
> I bleed by the black stream
> For my torn bough!

The mourning which we had to infer from the mood and rhythm of "Cabra" is now manifest in the image of the tree bleeding for its torn bough. Given the economy of Joyce's art, that torn bough is surely the same branch that flowers in the herdsman's hand. That torn bough also, so blatantly and self-consciously a "Freudian" proclamation of castration, is perhaps a measure of Joyce's familiarity with the more obvious principles of dream interpretation and of his willingness to mythologize himself according to a prearranged program of symbolic meanings. And if I am right in seeing the imprint of the Joyce family upon the enigmatic cattle drive, what we have in "Tilly" is a lament for the loss of maternal care as well as a dreary portrait of the Joyce family after May Joyce's death, and an acknowledgment of a son's sense of castration by a malignant, boorish father.

But even if that is correct, it makes of "Tilly" at best, a retrospective lament. The 1903 "Cabra/Ruminants" may be built upon loss but it is not, on the face of it, a lament. No wailing poet bleeds there for his torn bough, which is the real point of this digression. For what we have is not a young man's complaint but a young artist's work; a tough, controlled and lucid poem. Joyce's mother dies and he epiphanizes a random local event which appeals to his unconscious sense of his own situation. He experiences a deep loss and creates an image of Ireland. If that is in fact what happened, then "Cabra" was indeed auspicious. For it was precisely out of a sense of castration and abandonment, it seems to me, that Joyce's creativity finally and most suddenly emerged.

On January 7, some five months after his mother's death, Joyce wrote in one day his narrative essay, "A Portrait of the Artist," in which the central fantasy is one of ecstatic oral merger with an omnibus whore/Virgin/saint/muse/temptress whose very ambiguity is emblematic of the missing mother. He submitted it to W.K. Magee (John Eglinton) and Frederick Ryan for their new journal of "free thought,"*Dana*. Predictably, Ryan and Magee (whom Joyce had nicknamed "the horrible Virgin" [*CDD* 14]) rejected it because of its overt sexuality. Almost on the moment, Joyce began to expand it into the autobiographical novel, *Stephen Hero*. This burst of creative labor by a young man who, until then, had little more than the Dedalian "capful of light odes" to call his genius father, was stupendous. He finished the first chapter of *Stephen Hero* by February 10 (*JJ* 153) and by the end of March had written eleven chapters (*CDD* 19-20). Nor had he completely abandoned poetry. Though the greater part of *Chamber Music* was complete, he added, in April, three more poems to the collection (*JJ* 155) and may have added yet others in the fall. Later that summer, he was to write his Swiftian satire on the Irish literary scene, "The Holy Office," and begin work on *Dubliners*. In short, in the period between his mother's death and his flight into exile with Nora, Joyce was not the guilt-paralyzed Stephen Dedalus of *Ulysses*. Rather, he had discovered or had been discovered by that spring of creative energy that, with rare exceptions, stood him in good stead the rest of his life. If anything, he became like Stephen's Shakespeare who transformed himself into the creator-God of the Elizabethan stage after his flight from Ann Hathaway, and who, as if in imitation of the earlier sundering, wrote *Hamlet* in the months following his father's death. Whereas for Stephen, the final separation from mother leads to guilt, melancholia, and paralysis, for Joyce, in reality, it seems to have yielded a creative mixture of desperation and hard work.

It does seem that May Joyce's death released her son from some long-standing inhibition against exploring the past in writing. One suspects, on the basis of Stephen's sullen and irritable relations with his mother in *Stephen Hero*, that the gentle tyranny of maternal disapproval constrained Joyce from beginning the task he had to undertake and finally did undertake in *Stephen Hero*, *Portrait*, *Ulysses* and *Finnegans Wake*; the task of descending into the nightmare of personal history in order to forge some durable sense of himself from the brittle and painful fragments of childhood.

But he was not just liberated to work, it seems. He was compelled to. His writing makes sense as the effort to reconstruct in symbolic form what had been lost in reality: his mother and an entire environment that was infused with her presence and invested with maternal significance. Despite the disappointments of life in Ireland and the squalor and apparent disorder of the Joyce household, Joyce's ego and his sense of reality were no doubt stabilized and made coherent by his mother's ordering presence. Her death affected him, not only as a loss of that ambiguous *amor matris*, but as a threat to his psychic integrity as well as his trust in the reliability of a stable, supportive reality. After her death, the center no longer held. For that reason, it seems that Joyce, starting in January, 1904, gave up plans for the projected "comedy" and "esthetic" and set out instead to shore up the threatened inner and outer worlds by reconstructing them symbolically in the form of autobiography. If this is in fact the case, then Stephen Dedalus' magniloquent promise in *Portrait* to forge in the smithy of his soul the uncreated conscience of his race is no mean adolescent boast, but a statement of what he must do in order to survive.[12] Moreover, since Joyce's project of reconstructing the soul of Ireland went hand in hand with the remaking of his own, we find him, in the first "*Portrait*" sketch, entertaining fantasies of nympholeptic

oral union with a maternal "dearest of mortals" *and* vowing to return
to the past in order to plot the curve of his own emotional growth.[13]
Later that year, Stanislaus wrote in his diary that his brother
spoke admiringly of Ibsen as a "self-made man" (*CDD* 52). That
phrase, we now know, describes a formula for genius that Joyce
took in desperate earnest in the midst of the institutional and
familial failures of Irish life.

To what extent too this sudden creative activity is an act of
restitution or atonement toward the dead mother for hostile acts or
wishes against her we can only guess. We have Joyce's own confession to Nora that his own cynical frankness of conduct had killed
his mother (*Letters* II, 48) as well as Stephen's and Richard Rowan's
overwhelming guilt in *Ulysses* and *Exiles* respectively that could
hardly have been fabricated out of whole cloth by Joyce's "dis-
interested" imagination. "He kills his mother," accuses Mulligan,
"but he can't wear grey trousers" (*U* 6). Some sixteen hours later
Stephen cries out a denial to the mother herself, "Cancer did it,
not I. Destiny" (*U* 580). Atonement and undoing as manifested in
creative activity are difficult motives to identify in an author's
life. Theory urges us to seek them out and if we are lucky some
of our discoveries may fit and provisionally confirm our theory.
Joyce's first published prose fiction, for example, "The Sisters,"
a story by one Stephen Daedalus, appeared in *The Irish Homestead*
on August 13, 1904, the first anniversary of May Joyce's death.
Coincidence? Possibly.

Joyce's disposition to seek out symbolic solutions to real dilemmas
did not always preclude his discovering in the world without as
actual what was in his world within as possible. Thus his drive
to restore through fantasy and art losses suffered in reality did not
prevent him from falling in love with Nora Barnacle and transferring
onto her the burden of his need. As the 1909 letters demonstrate in
detail, she was, willy-nilly, the lost mother come back, but ever on
the brink of being lost again, and thus ever to be wooed, chided,
loved, admonished, injured and wooed once more.

All evidence suggests that Joyce's commitment to Nora was
instantaneous. Their courtship was troubled but it demanded of him
none of the agonizing, unending preliminaries that had soured his
flirtations with the chaste beauties of middle-class Dublin. Their
first date took place on June 16, 1904. Within a week, Nora was
addressing him confidently as My Precious Darling," (*Letters* II, 42)
and he was discovering, more slowly, his own self-embarrassed
language of endearment. The combination of Joyce's emotional
and sexual isolation and Nora's openness to his advances allowed

his libidinal trademarks to surface instantly. From the very beginning, Nora was cherished as something less than the sum of her parts. His first note to her reads, "I may be blind. I looked for a long time at a head of reddish-brown hair and decided it was not yours" (*Letters* II, 42). Another concludes with the synecdochic, "Adieu, dear little brown head" (*Letters* II, 43). He appropriates from her a glove for a bed-partner and teases, "Your glove lay beside me all night—unbuttoned—but otherwise conducted itself very properly— like Nora" (*Letters* II, 43). Again with a sartorial eye, he entreats, "*Please* leave off that breastplate as I do not like embracing a letterbox," and elsewhere, with a rare attention to physical detail, croons, "I kiss the miraculous dimple at thy neck" (*Letters* II, 43,44).

The filial theme develops also. Nora is, predictably, the refuge of sinners and comfortress of the afflicted. The poet who had written, perhaps to her, "I would in that sweet bosom be/ . . . Where no rude wind might visit me"[14] anxiously writes to his beloved that he must see her because "I have been in such a whirl of trouble that I want to forget everything in your arms" (*Letters* II, 45). But she is not only his mother come back to take him in her arms, she is even more surely an object of that cynical frankness of conduct which, he confided to her, had contributed to his mother's death. "There is something also a little devilish in me that makes me delight in breaking down people's idea of me and proving to them that I am really selfish, proud, cunning and regardless of others" (*Letters* II, 51-2). Object lessons abound: "How I hate God and death!" he proclaims to her. "How I like Nora! Of course you are shocked at these words, pious creature that you are" (*Letters* II, 50). Such offense predictably yields to remorse. The dialectic of attack and atonement appears early in their relationship and often. "My dear, dear Nora I suppose you have been very much upset since last night," (*Letters* II, *51)* is a standard greeting. "I will not speak of myself for I feel as if I had acted very cruelly." The sentence might stand as their insignia, their coat of arms: vert, an artist couchant proper, bearing apologies. Like her prototype, whom a restive son had cruelly dazzled with his erudition and accused of stupidity,[15] she can only puzzle at such complexity of emotion and subtlety of thought, and is forced once to confess, "I read that long letter over and over again but could not understand it I think I will take it to you to morrow eve—and perhaps you might make me understand it" (*Letters* II, 52). Both discover in short order that talk is not their *métier*. More and more he finds himself wearily and regressively silent with her. In

one letter, which sounds like a confession of marital boredom cast
as a lover's homage, he writes, "The mere recollection of you over-
powers me with some kind of dull slumber. The energy which is
required for carrying on conversations seems to have left me lately
and I find myself constantly slipping into silence" (*Letters* II, 56).

Whatever it was that had brought and held James and Nora so
firmly together may have been both physical and spiritual but it
was hardly intellectual. A marriage of bodies and souls, as they
came quickly to understand, need not be a marriage of minds as
well. But James did not want a marriage of minds. Intellectually
he felt himself to be autonomous. His intellectual nourishment,
moreover, was gotten from masculine sources which he preferred to
encounter indirectly, in libraries, "painted chambers loaded with
tilebooks." Nora's virtues were the maternal ones: a fragile
constancy, honesty, lack of education, a minimum of ideas, a simple
Catholic piety, a readiness to condescend to him upon demand, and
the possession, however trivial, of a secret life.

The ambiguous fate of this project to install Nora in that ancient
seat vacated by May Joyce is revealed not only in the 1909 letters
from James to Nora but in his books, most especially *Ulysses*. The
measure of its success is the relative stability of James Joyce's
life: he stayed with Nora, raised a family and wrote his books.[16]
The measure of its failure is more omnibus and encompassing, for
its inscription is everywhere on his life, his "marriage," his art.

The 1909 letters remain the clearest expression of the project
and of its insufficiency.[17] Nora, the woman into whose "soul of
souls" he would return in order to become the "poet of his race,"
whose death he mourns though she is very much alive, whom he
calls "my strange-eyed Ireland" and "my little mother" was always
a substitute figure.[18] Thus the attempt to refashion her, to deck
her in furs, to brighten her hair, to develop her breasts by having
her drink cocoa, was a twofold and paradoxical project. On the one
hand, it proposed to make manifest the restitution wish by making
of Nora an appropriate mother. But Joyce's attempt to do so
made him, in effect, her mother as well, a paradox Joyce may
well have understood. The fantasy that she would be his handiwork,
a slow and painful creation of his own,[19] even as he retreated for
emotional nourishment into the warm secret gloom of her flesh,
represents marriage as a job of mutual mothering. If she would
nurture him, he, in return, would do no less than create her: he
would become her mother in order that she might remain his.
Thus it appears, everywhere in his letters to her, that his filial

supplications are laced with parental condescension. From the beginning, she is his "Little Pouting Nora" (*Letters* II, 43), "My dear little Goodie-Brown-shoes" (*Letters* II, 43), "My particularly pouting Nora" (*Letters* II, 44). Even at her most maternal, she was always his "little Nora." The phrase "little mother" which appears in the 1909 correspondence is an epiphany. In the circularity of such maternal mutuality lies its economical wonder, since as the circle of co-maternity contracts about its thematic center, Nora disappears and the allotropes of the mother whom he would recreate in art: Mary (May) Joyce, Ireland (Kathleen), the Church, the BVM, Gretta, Bertha, Molly, ALP, dissolve into the masturbatory splendor of Dedalian self-sufficiency. The unconscious proposition: "I will make you in order that you can nurture me," becomes, "I will create myself in order to become self-nurturing." In the totalistic universe of the self-made man, maternity may take its place alongside paternity as a legal fiction. Yet, in Joyce's case, the maintenance of this fantasy of self-generation and oral self-sufficiency which repeals motherhood in favor of total autonomy, required a real, quasi-maternal presence. The satisfactory introjection of the "idea" of the mother into the ego of the son required at all times the presence of some external analogue or simulacrum, for the dream of self-sufficiency would not work unless it was anchored to something in the real world. Nora had to exist in order that her husband could become self-sufficient.

III Come Thou Lost One!

Attempts to restore lost objects by introjection or internalization or by recreation or substitution are, at best, imperfect psychic stopgaps and it is the very irreparability of loss that lies at the heart of *Ulysses*. The deepest movements in the book are the paired tropisms of Stephen and Bloom: the former's radical drive toward isolation and autonomy, and the latter's need to be reconciled with all he has lost: his past, his present, his future, all of which is handily symbolized by Molly's afternoon tryst with Boylan. The isolation, or the threat of isolation against which Joyce's art is arrayed, is reflected in *Ulysses* in the general alienation of all his dishevelled, wandering Dubliners. Their condition is the thematic heart of *Ulysses*. Beneath the mock-heroism, fetishism, nationalism, oedipal drama, irony, anticlericalism, sexual perversity, stylistic virtuosity, cloacal obsessiveness, fraternal rivalry, guilt, wit, shame, messianism, masochism—beneath all other thematic, stylistic and deep-psychic materials, is the fact of sundering. Sundering is the ineluctable void upon which *Ulysses* is built. *Ulysses* is a book of distances in which all things proclaim their isolation. There is the distance of the exile from home, of the prophet from the promised land, of husband from wife, of father from son, brother from brother, Dubliner from Dubliner, present from past, comet from sun. Joyce's characters inhabit a universe from which satisfactory human connections have been excluded. The marriage of Poldy and Molly would seem to be the most enduring and gratifying of relationships in *Ulysses*, and we know the price at which its sad and fragile stability has been bought. In Dublin, breakup is more than a habit; it is a cosmology. Dubliners meet briefly like particles in space, reconnoiter in a formal astral dance, then fly off into solitary orbit in the Irish void. The very indiscriminateness of human dissociation argues for the existence, somewhere, of a primal flaw or flaws, a core of dislocation that invests all human possibilities with the assurance of failure. Somewhere at the heart of this universe is a deep-psychic equivalent of Original Sin.

We seem to be confronted by a breakdown of what Erik Erikson calls "mutuality."[21] Trust in the possibility of fruitful interaction between persons has been foreclosed and we find ourselves in a universe of defensively self-enclosed actors: autoerotics, automystics, automobiles, autodidacts. The interior monologue in Joyce's books is no gratuitous device of style; it is the stylistic correlative of the self-enclosed mode of existence it represents. Such a massive failure of mutuality in favor of total narcissism can only be regarded as an oral failure, and it is indeed around the ramifications of such an oral failure that the thematic core of *Ulysses* is organized.

I believe it is fair to say that the book's variegated and encyclopedic surfaces and symbols are set down in sedimentary layers upon a psychic base of oral need and oral insufficiency. Moreover, if this claim errs at all, it is on the side of tautology, inasmuch as psychic development itself can be so described.[22] However, in the case of *Ulysses*, this self-evident theorem has special critical usefulness for without it we could hardly winnow meaning out of the chaos of conflicting psychic materials. For example, in Bloom's case, it enables us to see clearly that Bloom, despite his preference for anal sexual fantasies and (presumably) acts, is a classic oral character. His basic condition is his isolation and his all-pervasive and indiscriminate hungers. Bloom leaves 7 Eccles St. in the morning in search of spiritual, emotional, sexual and alimental nourishment. His passivity and dependency upon Molly testify to the same oral insufficiency, as do his voyeurism and his tendency to think of loving (as does Stephen) in terms of eating. But beyond Bloom's needs and tastes, one finds the multiple ramifications or displacements of "the mother" projected everywhere into the ambience of Joyce's Dublin. As catastrophic mother she is Bella Cohen, the ghost of May Dedalus, and the Aunt Dante of *Portrait*. As betrayer, she is Eve, Ann Hathaway, Helen, Devorghil, Kitty O'Shea, Molly. As temptress, she is the *Photo Bits* nymph, Josie Breen, Nurse Callan, Gerty MacDowell and, of course, Molly. As savior, she is Gerty and Molly; as whore she is Bella, Zoe, Kitty, Florry, Cissy, Edy, perhaps Gerty, and, in some ways, Molly. The lost mother is numinous and mythic—she expands into every category of experience, investing an entire universe with promises of love, abandonment, punishment and an aura of bitter mystery. She is the Church, Stephen's Italian master, "A crazy queen, old and jealous," as well as the Virgin. She is present under the various aspects of Ireland: the old sow that eats her farrow, Kathleen ni Houlihan, the peasant milkwoman. She is the promised land toward whom all voyages tend: Ithaca, Agendath Netaim, Penelope, Molly's melonous buttocks, a lost, Druidic Ireland. She is the white breast of the dim sea upon which Stephen broods all day, the scrotum-tightening sea itself, or, as Algy calls it, the "great sweet mother."

The apparently overwhelming contradictions in the image of this polymorphous mother are not unresolvable. The psychoanalytic schedule of psychic developmental events confirms what our intuitions tell us about the mother in *Ulysses*. It insists that the level at which she operates as a betrayer and threat to her son does not run as deep as that upon which she is felt to be home, paradise, the promised land, our great, sweet mother. As we have seen, the ambivalence toward Molly is resolved at the end of her soliloquy, albeit at the cost of some dramatic credibility. But it should be clear from Molly's casual demolition of Dante Riordan, from her recitation of finer poetry than the lame temptress, Gerty MacDowell, and from her ceremonial position at the end of the novel, that we are in a universe that is essentially comic, one in which we may expect the good mother to drive out the bad. In this universe, when the intra-psychic dilemma over the identity of the mother moves toward its regressive solution, the nurturing mother wins out over the catastrophic, the numinous over the ambiguous.

In *Ulysses*, as in the *Odyssey*, the grand dramatic movement, the exile's return, is an archetypal oral theme. The hero's situation is the same in each: he is an isolated, separated, incomplete man. It is this situation and the quest that issues from it that bound the *Odyssey* to Joyce's purposes, beyond any abstract formulas about historical parallelism or historic change. Whether the modern world recapitulates the ancient or represents its debasement is not to the point. Both epics are an expression of a universal, *individual* struggle—the struggle of the lost son to get back to the infinitely-removed mother. And this may be the most primitive and universal literary theme of all, for its psychological origins antedate the oedipus complex, and its ramifications, correspondingly, are more pervasive. Thus, what lies at the heart of this correspondence of epics also goes beyond the recurrence of discreet Homeric themes and events in *Ulysses*, which, as S. L. Goldberg has observed, "nowhere [seem] to emerge *of necessity*, dramatically realized in, and an integral part of, the action."[23] What moves us dramatically is the single Homeric parallel, the lonely exile and the agonizing return, the isolation from and quest for the nurturing mother. *Ulysses* extracts from its prototype the epic of regression. It yearns after a lost homeostasis and idealizes the pastoral. *Ulysses* highlights the oral paradigm in the *Odyssey*, which is why a passive and dependent middle-aged man seems an appropriate hero. Bloom's character is the sign of his quest. He wants only to be reattached to what has been taken from him: wife, son, daughter, the halcyon days of his childhood, mother, father, his people, Jerusalem. In short, Bloom would be restored to the entire nurturing reality that has fallen away from him. Such a passive hero in any other epic mode could only be a fool, or a satiric butt. But a regressive hero can be a serious figure of sorts in a regressive epic. Joyce could not have recreated Achilles or Aeneas as oral-passive characters without satiric intentions, but an oral-passive Odysseus is only comic, and is not without his measure of dignity.

Bloom and Stephen may not be the most errant of the many wandering Irish rocks in *Ulysses* but they are the ones that hold our attention. S. L. Goldberg, using Joyce's own vocabulary of isolation and drift, describes the heroes as they appear in "Ithaca" as "wanderers like the stars at which they gaze."[24] And that does seem to describe their situation. Wandering Aengus meets Wandering Jew, and after a brief communion of coffee, cocoa, philosophy, and co-urination, they drift apart, dishevelled, wandering stars. But this wandering is directed, purposive motion. Like the stars at which they gaze, Bloom and Stephen are in orbital flight. As they take leave of each other, Bloom stays on the inside of the threshold at 7 Eccles St., a "centripetal remainer," and bids farewell to Stephen, the "centrifugal departer." Bloom, the regressive hero, is on the homeward leg of his daily orbit; Stephen is outward bound. This mutual orbital motion presumes a center of attraction, and in fact, Stephen and Bloom do navigate about a common center. Schematically, in "Ithaca," it would have to be Molly, though more abstractly, and correctly, it is the idea of the mother, of which Molly is but one incarnation. Bloom's path has been homeward tending since he left Eccles St. in the morning, for, as he puts it, "the longest way round is the shortest way home." Stephen, in radical flight from an internalized ghostwoman with ashes on her breath as well as an external crazy queen, old and jealous, is also homeward tending via the same circuitous route. His path leads backward from the catastrophic mother to the primal oral ideal. He had told Davin at the end of *Portrait* that "The shortest way to Tara was *via* Holyhead," and we may guess that Stephen, as he leaves Bloom's house, is Holyhead bound, having travelled that route once before in search of Tara. And Tara, to risk being tiresome, is one and always the same, the arms of the Druidic past, the bosom of Celtic Ireland, the heart of Kathleen, the womb of the mother.

Of course this persistent fantasy of being restored to the lost mother is *not* a simple consequence of May Joyce's death in 1903. That event alone, coming when Joyce was already a young man of 21, was not in itself likely to have given rise to a career of plaintive longing such as we find everywhere in *Ulysses*. Rather, we have to look backward to more fundamental losses and separations—the loss of primal oral unity that is the common experience of all children, and those subsequent serial losses of daily love and daily attention that are especially attendent upon growing up in a large family. Exile is built into childhood. In "Proteus," Stephen reflects on his mother's death as one of a succession of losses, each of which involves a bed: "Bridebed, childbed, bed of death" (*U* 47-8). For both Stephen and Bloom, that bed is the place of betrayal, never the place of love.

May Joyce's death, then, has to be regarded, not as the cause of those lonely searches for love and anxious efforts toward restoration we discover in her son's books, but the special occasion for them. Her deathbed confirmed for him what her bridebed and a succession of childbeds had threatened: you can't go home again. The first loss, the loss of the primal mother, is the real one; regard all others as imitations. It follows that the creative response called up in Joyce by his mother's death was there from the beginning, biding its time and awaiting its occasion.

Who, then, is really lost? If loss, as a psychic condition, precedes loss as reality, then we must ask who is real and who has faded into impalpability to become a ghost by separation: mother or child?

What we know about the desperate dependence of ego-identity upon this often fragile relationship jusitifies the question. As Simon Dedalus sings the plaintive aria from Flotow's *Martha* in the Ormond Bar, the listening Bloom silently identifies. *"Co-me, thou lost one!"* (*U* 275) the aria leaps, *"Co-me thou dear one!"* It holds its flight as it soars towards its resplendent climax *""Come! . . . . To me!"* and plummets downward into smiles and applause. One reflects on lovelost Si Dedalus and lovelost Leo Bloom and recalls the chilling question Stephen had put to Cranly in *Portrait* after the latter's discourse on the wages of aloneness: "Of whom are you speaking?"

State University of
New York at Buffalo

NOTES

1. *The Origin and Function of Culture* (1943; New York: Anchor Books, 1971), p. 131. It was originally published as Nervous and Mental Disease Monograph, No. 69, 1943.

2. See the panel discussion on creativity of the 27th International Psychoanalytic Congress, Vienna, July 29, 1971 in *International Journal of Psychoanalysis*, 53 (1972), 21-30. See also Melanie Klein, "Infantile Anxiety-Situations Reflected in a Work of Art and in the Creative Impulse" and "Mourning and its Relation to Manic Depressive States," in *Contributions to Psychoanalysis*, 1921-1945 (London: Hogarth Press, 1948.

3. "A Psychoanalytical Approach to Aesthetics," *International Journal of Psychoanalysis*, 33 (1952), 196-207. See also Sigmund Freud, "Mourning and Melancholia," in *Standard Edition*, vol. 14.

4. "Clinical Aspects of Creativity," *American Imago*, 24 (Spring-Summer 1967), 6-34.

5. Niederland, p. 9. K. R. Eissler, *Goethe: A Psychoanalytic Study* (Detroit: Wayne State University Press, 1963).

6. Ellmann, as usual, has dealt with these events most thoroughly. I repeat them merely to underscore patterns of mother-son relations that appear to be important.

7. *The Workshop of Daedalus: James Joyce and the Materials for "A Portrait of the Artist as a Young Man,"* ed. Robert Scholes and Richard M. Kain (Evanston: Northwestern University Press, 1965), p. 44. See also mention of it in Stanislaus Joyce, *My Brother's Keeper: James Joyce's Early Years* (New York: McGraw-Hill, 1958), pp. 29-30. Hereafter *MBK*.

8. There is, of course, always a question about Stanislaus's accuracy. See *MBK*, p. 234.

9. See especially Sheldon Brivic, "James Joyce: From Stephen to Bloom," in *Psychoanalysis and Literary Process*, ed. Frederick C. Crews (Cambridge: Winthrop, 1970).

10. There are two manuscripts of the "Cabra/Ruminants" version; one in the Lockwood Memorial Library at SUNY, Buffalo, the other at Cornell. Though the Cornell typescript is entitled "Cabra" and the Buffalo manuscript "Ruminants," the texts are identical. Both are signed Dublin: 1904, though both are undoubtedly later transcripts, perhaps done in Zürich. The dating and meaning of all versions of the poem are presently in question. See Chester G. Anderson, "James Joyce's 'Tilly,' " *PMLA*, 73 (June 1958), 285-98; Robert Scholes, "James Joyce, Irish Poet," *JJQ*, 2 (Summer 1965), 255-70; John T. Shawcross, " 'Tilly' and Dante," *JJQ*, 7 (Fall 1969), 61-4; and Robert Scholes "Letter to the Editor," *JJQ*, 8 (Winter 1971), 192-93.

The earliest indication we have of the existence of "Cabra/Ruminants" is at the beginning of Stanislaus's diary, which was begun in late August or early September 1903. See *The Complete Dublin Diary*, p. 2 and George H. Healey's note about the beginning of the diary, p. x. The "Cabra/Ruminants" poem may have been in existence in September 1903, the month after May Joyce's death, and while it is indeed possible that it actually antedates her death, it surely does not antedate the final stages of her illness.

11. Stanislaus Joyce, *The Complete Dublin Diary*, ed. George Harris Healey (Ithaca: Cornell University Press, 1971), p. 39. Hereafter *CDD*.

12. Niederland has observed appropriately: "In exploring the lives—and ills—of creative personalities, one becomes increasingly aware of the great amount of energy available to them. Their energies appear to converge on the creative process and seem to be regression not so much in the service of the ego, as in that of ego restoration, sometimes even ego survival" (Niederland, p. 21).

13. See the opening proclamation of the "Portrait" essay.

14. *Chamber Music*, VI. Ellmann thinks it likely that the poem was inspired by Nora (*JJ* 171).

15. See letter from May Joyce to James Joyce, Dec. 18, 1902? (*Letters* II, 22).

16. John Gross, in his excellent introduction to Joyce's work, *James Joyce* (New York: Viking Press, 1970), makes just this point. It cannot be overemphasized that Joyce could and did manage his life and his work admirably, and that the abundant "evidence" of psychopathology must be weighed against his hard won successes.

17. I have discussed the 1909 letters at some length in an unpublished essay, "A Correspondence of Joyces."

18. See Gross, p. 19.

19. See *Exiles* 62, 67.

20. See Freud, "Mourning and Melancholia," and Melanie Klein, "Mourning and its Relation to Manic Depressive States," n.2.

21 *Childhood and Society* (New York: Norton, 1963), pp. 68ff.

22. The sedimentary metaphor for psychic development was suggested by Freud in the first chapter of *Civilization and its Discontents*, in *Standard Edition*, vol. 21.

23. *The Classical Temper: A Study of James Joyce's "Ulysses"* (London: Chatto and Windus, 1961), p. 149.

24. Ibid., p. 196.

Bernard Benstock

ULYSSES WITHOUT DUBLIN

"Mr Joyce's book has been out long enough for no more general expression of praise, or expostulation with its detractors, to be necessary; and it has not been out long enough for any attempt at a complete measurement of its place and significance to be possible." In this manner T. S. Eliot opened his brief, directional essay, "*Ulysses*, Order and Myth," in the November 1923 *Dial*,[1] marking a momentary pause at which the swirling waters of contemporary reception of *Ulysses* ended and the magnitude of its conception plunged it into literary history. Not that *Ulysses* was not already a legend in its own time—and before. Serial publication in the *Little Review* whetted appetites and axes, but nothing regarding its hectic publication in book form could be said to be anticlimactic. The core of admirers waited in the wings to extol the finished product, while those who knew that they were obligated to be offended honed their imprecations in advance. A year and a half after the date of publication, Eliot's quiet words of homage and discreet nod in the direction of the book's mythic scope concluded a short and turbulent era. Waves of belated adulation and horror were yet to come, but the initial period of hasty evaluation and reaction had had its momentum and critical perspective became on the whole more reflective.

Those must have been wonderful months in 1922-23 when over-reaction set the tone for the ephemeral book review of James Joyce's Blue Book of scatalogical eschatology. That the Shakespeare and Co. volume was the same size and color as the London telephone directory provided several reviewers with their opening quip; that its price was exorbitant proved a source of relief to many holier-than-thou commentators who apparently operated under the traditional assumption that the poor were greater consumers of prurience, while those who could afford expensive pornography were the least defilable. Yet what united both the attracted and the detractors was a general sense of awe in the face of a momentous accomplishment: genius was acknowledged by many on both sides of the fence, while the size, shape, scope, dimension, and even enormity of *Ulysses* humbled many of its admirers. The offended swore that they had a glimpse of the Devil writ large! No one foresaw much of a reading public for the monster: no one predicted its general sales half-a-century later, much less its fixed position in college curricula. The coterie assigned it to the realm of coterie literature, while the Comstocks breathed a sigh of relief that its difficulties would make it inaccessible to the masses.

If revulsion is not literary criticism, neither is enthusiasm: both engender excesses and misconceptions that literary criticism ventures forth to correct. Eliot seems somewhat peeved that Valéry Larbaud should have anticipated him, dismissing the April 1922 article in *Nouvelle Revue Française* (*CH* I, 252-62) as "rather an Introduction than a criticism" (*CH* I, 268), and becomes bouyant when he has so astute a critic as Richard Aldington to correct. That *Ulysses* is a "libel on humanity" (*CH* I, 188)[2] now seems a serious misreading of the basic tone of the work, and Eliot exonerates it of libel, although he gives little stress to the point. Instead he accentuates his correction of Aldington's designation of Joyce's "great *undisciplined* talent" (*CH* I, 269), finding order and logic and structure where few had hitherto seen anything but chaos, enormity and all-inclusiveness. And although several others had suggested that the title *Ulysses* is a purposeful invocation of Homer's *Odyssey* and some even claimed to have been privy to notebooks of schematic parallels with the Greek epic, it is Eliot who pronounced that "Mr Joyce's parallel use of the *Odyssey* has a great importance" (*CH* I, 270). For T. S. Eliot this mythic structure creates order out of the massive accumulations of contemporary materials in *Ulysses*: "Instead of narrative method, we may now use the mythical method. It is, I seriously believe, a step toward making the modern world possible for art" (*CH* I, 271).

Aldington's pre-publication problem with the unfinished *Ulysses* in 1921 was deciding between fish and flesh in determining the nature of the work: on one hand he comments that "from the manner of Mr. Joyce to Dadaisme is but a step, and from Dadaisme to imbecility is hardly that" (*CH* I, 186), while on the other he asserts that "Mr. Joyce is a modern Naturaliste, possessing a greater knowledge of intimate psychology, but without the Naturaliste preoccupation with *l'écriture artiste*" (*CH* I, 187). (Joyce is of course neither: *Ulysses* is actually good red herring.) The dada assumption is based on an inability to make order out of the seeming chaos of the book's bulk: that Joyce was random in his selectivity and himself freely associative and automatic in his undisciplined writing. His residence in Paris was suspect, as was his friendly alliance with many of the word-revolutionaries there. In fact Joyce allowed a degree of misconception to perpetuate, maintaining his contacts with *transition* and its editorialists and assuming that time would succeed in sifting his wheat from their chaff. The naturalist tag was based on historical development. Joyce's own apologia for *Dubliners* acknowledged it as "a chapter in the moral history" of Ireland, while its style of "scrupulous meanness" gave close attention to the minute details of the very ordinary and the very real in everyday life. Nor is it difficult to understand how readers for decades could have interpreted the trapped and paralytic existences studied in *Dubliners* as examples of a coldly deterministic universe. An occasional "queer old josser" and an instance of "smugging" in the square, Corley squeezing a sovereign out of a slavey and Stephen succumbing to a whore with "frank, uplifted eyes" were enough to posit a case for the early Joyce's preoccupation with the seamier side of life. The critics and reviewers, including Aldington, had the "naturalist" label ready to slap onto the blue cover of *Ulysses* long before its appearance, and the final product must have seemed naturalistic beyond their wildest expectations. Aldington explained:

> But I did hope to see him write real tragedy, and not return to the bastard genre of the Naturalistes who mingle satire and tragedy, and produce something wholly false; I hoped to see his characters emerge into a clearer air from the sordid arena in which they were subdued by Fate in a debris of decayed vegetables and putrid exhalations.
> Clearly I hoped the wrong thing. *Ulysses* is more bitter, more sordid, more ferociously satirical than anything Mr. Joyce has yet written. It is a tremendous libel on humanity . . . (*CH* I, 187-88).

Aldington's description of naturalism contains an interesting stress on satire, hardly a commonly acknowledged concomitant of the movement. That Aldington sees the satirical thrust of *Ulysses* somewhat redeems his otherwise myopic view, and perhaps his definition of naturalism derives a posteriori from Joyce's work. By way of contrast one finds Edmund Wilson's *New Republic* review of July 1922 (one which Joyce reputedly appreciated as one of the best); despite his overwhelming appreciation of the book, Wilson nonetheless finds fault with the overall structure: "What is wrong is that Mr. Joyce has attempted an impossible genre. You cannot be a realistic novelist in Mr. Joyce's particular vein and write burlesques at the same time" (*CH* I, 229). If a consensus between Wilson and Aldington were necessary to establish *Ulysses* within the naturalistic mold, Joyce would escape without the label. When the Kilkenny cats finished mauling each other, all that remained were their tails, and all that remains of the specter of naturalism is Joyce's microscopic accuracy in capturing verisimilitude, his careful delineation of the city of Dublin and its denizens. Even Arnold Bennett, the subject of Virginia Woolf's attack on mundane commitment to realism, reviewed *Ulysses* in 1922 by asserting, "I would not accuse him of what is absurdly called 'photographic realism'" (*CH* I, 220). The specter of naturalism had varying effects in various cultures: the English had rarely known its excesses and settled for the pallid "realism" of Bennett, Wells and Company instead; the Irish considered it a foreign, Continental horror destined to spoil the purity of Celtic mysticism if allowed in (and therefore never let it in; they let George Moore out instead); but the French were able to take it in their stride and had long since learned to live with the phenomenon. Consequently a critic like Larbaud is capable of suggesting in 1922 that Joyce's affinities for naturalism were relatively mild and subtle. Larbaud in a short parenthetical paragraph gently separates Joyce from Zola and other extremists, dissociates him from the Russian and English novelists of the nineteenth century, keeping him for France instead, asserting that "it is with our Naturalistes that Joyce, from his first prose work, has the most affinities" (*CH* I, 255). He is careful, however, to retrace his steps after this statement of influence and add: "It is always necessary to keep from considering him as a late naturalist" and "even the epithet of neo-naturalist would not suit him" (*CH* I, 255). And although Larbaud's conclusion may seem to beg the question, it at least has the virtue of detachment and cool observation: "For even while admitting that he departs from naturalism, one is obliged to recognize that he has not tried to break away from this discipline, but to perfect it and to mold it in such a way that in *Ulysses* one further recognizes the influence of a naturalism that one would rather consider from Rimbaud and Lautremont, whom Joyce has not read" (*CH* I, 255).

Irish criticism in the twenties groaned under the weight of the newly-arrived super-realism. Such strange bedfellows as Joyce, O'Casey, and Liam O'Flaherty were discovered under the bed and constituting a literary movement, if not actually an international conspiracy. AE was benign in his comment on this trio, claiming that their works were "more intimate, intense, and daring than any other realism in contemporary literature,"[3] while Y.O. in the *Statesman* bemoaned the unfortunate change in Ireland: "From the most idealistic literature in Europe we have reacted so that with Joyce, O'Flaherty, and O'Casey, the notables of the movement, we have explored the slums of our cities, the slums of the soul."[4] In effect, the Irish were prepared to pass Alien and Sedition Acts in order to prevent their native son and prophet-without-honor from corrupting them, and soon rioted against O'Casey's *Plough and the Stars*, forcing him too into Joycean exile. (O'Casey ironically insisted that even his Dublin plays were not examples of "photographic realism" and went on to denounce the "Green Goddess of Realism," although like Joyce he utilized himself and aspects of his own life as basic material and recorded the conversations of his contemporaries for literary use.) By coming into contact with Joyce in Paris, Valéry Larbaud, Mary Colum, and others could have access to firsthand information from the author himself and feel a distancing between themselves as readers and the realistic subject matter of *Ulysses*. But the stay-at-home Irish found themselves to be that subject matter, and unable to see the smile on the author's face they were horrified to see the warts on their own. C. C. Martindale, S.J., for example, in a paragraph that begins with a perceptive acknowledgement that Joyce's Ulysses is both "Everyman" and "No Man," ends that same paragraph by complaining that "Mr. Joyce has . . . the offensive habit of introducing real people by name. We know some of them. One such person (now dead, it is true) we knew well enough to see that Mr. Joyce, who describes him in no unfriendly way, yet cannot *see*. We absolve him of wilful calumny. But we realize that he is at least more likely than not to have mis-seen not only one person, but whole places, like Dublin, or Clongowes; whole categories, like students; whole literatures, like the Irish, or the Latin" (*CH* I, 205-06).

Father Martindale, whose absolution should have delighted Joyce, has made the obvious mistake of confusing realism with reality. He assumes that Dublin exists as an absolute reality and that John Eglinton or John Howard Parnell were actually "real" people, that once he himself fixed their existences permanently in his own mind, all other versions of them must correspond precisely with his own. The city and its citizens, Clongowes Wood and Father Conmee were rescued by Joyce from their nebulous state of flux and "fixed" within a literary framework in order to transmute them from protean possibilities into reality. Arthur Power claims that Joyce told him in 1921: "In my Mabbot Street scene I have, in my opinion, approached reality closer than anywhere else in the book (except perhaps for the last chapter) since sensation is the object heightened even to the point of the hallucination which is the exalted vision of the mystics" (*CH* I, 182). Art does not follow life in *Ulysses*; it subsumes life. When Stephen walks along the strand in "Proteus" he contemplates stopping at the Goulding household in Strasburg Terrace: the tone of his father's voice sets the key for his speculations and he hypothesizes making his visit, apparently combining aspects from previous stops there into a "heightened" vignette. His deft ear reproduces the uncle Richie and cousin Walter; his literary vocabulary culled from his reading of the Elizabethans provides the descriptions of the scene; and his father's mocking voice contributes editorial comments until Stephen concludes with his own rejection of the idea of a visit: "This wind is sweeter" (*U* 39). His preference is for the sea breezes along the strand in lieu of his uncle whistling Ferrando's aria. It seems apparent that by the time Stephen has finished his imagined stay with the Gouldings, he has passed Strasburg Terrace, and the recreation of the scene in his mind is the greater reality than the random visit would have been. When Simon Dedalus sees Stephen walking toward Dublin, he assumes that his son has actually been to the Gouldings's and vents his mocking disdain upon his in-laws in actual duplication of Stephen's fabricated echo of his father's voice. For Simon the visit by Stephen is a *real* event: his conjecture allows for no contradiction. But the reader knows that Simon's version of reality is fallacious; Stephen's heightened version is singularly authentic.

As "Domini Canis," Shane Leslie reviewed *Ulysses* for the *Dublin Review* in September 1922. He found that "the entire setting of the book is Catholic Dublin" and it "contains a fearful travesty on persons, happenings and intimate life of the most morbid and sickening description" (*CH* I, 200-01). Leslie is grateful that the prohibitive price will keep it out of the hands of those travestied, yet choosing his words carefully he eventually comments: "We will give the devil his due and appreciate the idyll of Father Conmee, S.J., who with most people mentioned in the course of the book, is really a Dubliner. Many pages are saturated with Catholic lore and citation, which must tend to make a book more or less unintelligible to critics, who are neither of Catholic or Dublin origin" (*CH* I, 202). The initiate's usurpation of Joyce's Dublin as his own will become a chronic condition during the fifty years of *Ulysses*, and even an occasional outsider who walks the streets of bulldozed Dublin looking for Mabbot Street or Barney Kiernan's will echo the assumption that the native Catholic Dubliners are a chosen people ideal for the reading of Joyce's Blue Book. Yet a careful examination of Conmee's idyll should dispel any envy of Leslie's proximity to Joyce's source material. Through the "Wandering Rocks" Conmee carries the responsibility of personifying the Irish Catholic Church in apposition to Lord Dudley's position as exemplar of imperial Britain. The Jesuit is on a mission, to secure a berth for one of the Dignam orphans at a school in Artane, yet the tone of his idyllic revery as he heads north is full of condescension, He interprets the venture as a casual outing

("Five to three. Just nice time to walk to Artane") and has a moment's difficulty remembering his beneficiary's name ("What was that boy's name again?") which soon provides him with a bit of witty Latin punning: *"Vere dignum et justum est"* (*U* 219). Conmee is a plethora of smiles and salutes, as he greets and is greeted by anyone he passes. Charity proves a dead end since he has only a silver crown in his purse, and so the lame sailor (whom Molly blesses with a coin) receives cold comfort from the priest who blesses him "in the sun" (*U* 219). Piety is serviced by a tardy reading of his breviary, since its regular time had been pre-empted by a visit from Lady Maxwell. And spirituality is replaced in Conmee's thoughts by constant references instead to prosaically secular matters.

Forty years after Shane Leslie blessed Father Conmee's idyll, Robert M. Adams expertly dissected it and found it suspect,[5] despite Joyce's kind words for the *real* Conmee who had indeed been his benefactor at Clongowes and Belvedere. While the surface of the priest serves well enough to suggest both courtliness and kindliness, his function in the novel is deeper. His condescension is pervasive (toward schoolboys, war veterans, women, old men, non-whites, Protestants, and even Father Bernard Vaughan, whom he both condones and patronizes), but beneath his demeanor lurks the absurdity of his naiveté: he accepts Mrs. M'Guinness's superficially queenly mien as real despite his awareness of her profession as a pawnbroker and concludes by blessing the "flushed young man" and his "young woman" emerging from a gap in a hedge (*U* 224). Vincent Lynch and his Kitty, as we later learn, have been having the real idyll, tumbling in the hay, but Conmee could hardly be expected to surmise such goings-on from the twigs clinging to Kitty's skirts. If he knows of Mrs. M'Guinness's profession, perhaps he also knows the families of the three boys who are entrusted with his letter as far as the posting box: Adams's detective work reveals the sons of bookmakers and pawnbrokers and the nephew of journalist Gallaher. If Leslie recognizes Conmee as a "real" Dubliner, he does not indicate that he also recognizes the Lynams, Sohans, and Gallahers as his fellow citizens as well. Despite Leslie's rare moment of praise for Joyce's treatment of the benign rector ("his reign was mild," notes Conmee in self-congratulation [*U* 224]), the idyll may well be mock-pastoral instead.

Two other aspects of the Jesuit Superior are worth attention. In his thoughts he sinks into a nostalgia for the past that reveals his true vocation: it is not as Father John Conmee that this courtly gentleman fulfills himself, but as "don John Conmee," performing the marriage ceremony between a noble bridegroom and his noble bride in the aristocratic past of "oldworldish days." The free-associative process moves from his physical presence on Malahide Road to a recollection of Lord Talbot de Malahide to a reverence for "old times in the barony," the title that connotes to him the history of the Belvederes. Conmee was born too late and now yearns for the "beeswaxed drawingroom, ceiled with full fruit clusters" (*U* 223). The other characteristic is Conmee's role as the benefactor of youth, since his present concern is with placing young Dignam in Brother Swan's institution for destitute boys. Conmee's services as rectifier in Clongowes for the unjustly punished Stephen and in his placement of Stephen in Belvedere are recalled here by Conmee's efforts for the dead Dignam's indigent son. Therefore it is important to remember that Conmee had also served as young Stephen's betrayer, that he revealed to Simon Dedalus the joke at Stephen's expense that he shared with Father Dolan over Stephen's manly act of seeking redress from the rector: "—Father Dolan and I, when I told them all at dinner about it, Father Dolan and I had a great laugh over it. *You better mind yourself, Father Dolan,* said I, *or young Dedalus will send you up for twice nine.* We had a famous laugh over it. Ha! Ha! Ha!" (*Portrait* 72). Of all of Stephen Dedalus's betrayers, real or imagined, Conmee is ·the subtlest. Although Joyce never reveals Stephen's immediate reaction to his father's narration, it soon becomes apparent how deep the wound has been for him. When a vocation in the Society of Jesus is suggested to Stephen the director at Belvedere is viewed as having "deeply grooved temples" and the waning sunlight touches the "curves of the skull" (*Portrait* 154). That Stephen sees the priest's head as a "skull" (or that Joyce intrudes the word into his narrative as if deriving from Stephen's unverbalized perception) recalls the skull on Father Conmee's desk, alluded to no less than three times during the brief interview between Stephen and the rector. As he leaves the director's office and wanders out of Belvedere College, Stephen turns onto Gardiner Street: "He was passing at that moment before the jesuit house in Gardiner Street, and wondered vaguely which window would be his if he ever joined the order" (*Portrait* 161). The decision to reject the offer is made by Stephen without the reader being privy to his thoughts but the link between Conmee's skull and the director's skull, supported by the subtle betrayal by the rector/provincial, may well have had its subliminal impetus. And now in *Ulysses* the benign and courtly Conmee, "of saint Francis

Xavier's church, upper Gardiner street" (*U* 222) leaves his presbytery
to help another little boy, and while reading his breviary under
the Hebrew letter *Sin* blesses the fornicator who will soon become
Stephen Dedalus's Judas. Perhaps it is not in Shane Leslie's Dublin
that the roots of Joyce's *Ulysses* run deep, but in the reality fixed
in the previous Joyce works, in *Dubliners* and *A Portrait of the
Artist as a Young Man.*

Robert Adams is also correct in noting the way in which Joyce
employs his style against Conmee, especially in those numerous
sentences throughout "Wandering Rocks" which monotonously
begin with "Father Conmee," setting up a silly litany. In addition
there is the absurd repetition of Conmee's smiles and salutes (the
smiles in particular are suspect because of the priest's awareness of
his dentifrice, marking the smile as a public gesture). Father Conmee
is socially successful where Leopold Bloom is not, in catching the
eye and earning the greeting of every Dubliner he meets. Yet the
snubbed Bloom is an important counterpart to Conmee, since his
generosity toward the Dignam family, revealed by Martin Cunningham in this chapter, is tangible and sincere (Conmee considers
Cunningham with his usual condescension: "Good practical catholic:
useful at mission time" [*U* 219]). Just as Mrs. Bloom is the lame
sailor's obvious benefactress, Bloom has served as the good
samaritan for the Dignam children:

> I see Bloom put his name down for five shillings [John Wyse Nolan said].
> —Quite right, Martin Cunningham said, taking the list.
> And put down the five shillings too.
> —Without a second word either, Mr Power said (*U* 246).

And during the early evening hours Bloom makes his journey to
the Dignam home in Sandymount in the company of Martin
Cunningham, duplicating Father Conmee's trek to Artane on the
boy's behalf.

In a second review of *Ulysses* Shane Leslie (this time under his
own name without recourse to his doggy-god *nom de plume*) in the
Quarterly Review for October 1922 repeats his basic view of the
book as dependent upon the accuracy of its depiction of the Irish
capital. He sees the sole purpose of *Ulysses* as being "to bless the
wondering world with an accurate account on one day and one night
passed by the author in Dublin's fair city, Lord Dudley being
Viceroy (the account of his driving through the streets of Dublin
is probably one of the few passages intelligible to the ordinary
English reader)" (*CH* I, 208). His mention of Lord Dudley acciden-
tally suggests just how little intelligibility Leslie is deriving from this

particularly easy chapter. "Wandering Rocks" significantly opens with Father Conmee and closes with the Lord Lieutenant: the former begins his trek in the northeastern quadrant of the city and moves further northeast out of Dublin; the latter begins his ride from the Phoenix Park in the northwestern quadrant and cuts the city in half heading southeast. At no point do their paths intersect in either time or place. Rather than being at opposite ends of the spectrum of good and evil, Conmee and Dudley seem to confidently claim their jurisdiction over Dublin and are in fact the two masters that Stephen claims have him in servitude. Another analogue for Conmee in "Wandering Rocks" is the Reverend Hugh C. Love, the Anglican landlord obsessed with Irish history, who delves into the bowels of Dublin to investigate the historic site under St. Mary's Abbey. As is another Protestant, one whose path does intersect Conmee's: as Conmee at Newcomen bridge stepped on to an outward bound tram, "off an inward bound tram stepped the reverend Nicholas Dudley C. C. of saint Agatha's church, north William street, on to Newcomen bridge" (*U* 222). This embarrassment of Dudleys in the chapter is a further example of Joycean reality: the Protestant clergyman is yet another "real" Dubliner pressed into service by James Joyce for ironic parallel. The established Church and the imperial State function under one name and represent the English master; although Conmee can keep so free of the Lord Lieutenant during the course of their dual trips through Dublin, Lord Dudley's emissary and namesake tracks him down nonetheless.

If verisimilitude equals reality for Shane Leslie, and Joyce's accuracy in his depiction of Dublin one of the few values of *Ulysses*, there still remains the critic's horror of the excesses of such realism. And so "the practice of introducing the names of real people into circumstances of monstrous and ludicrous fiction seems to us to touch the lowest depth of Rabelaisian realism. When we are given the details of the skin disease of an Irish peer, famous for his benefactions, we feel a genuine dislike of the writer" (*CH* I, 209). Ignoring such oxymora as "Rabelaisian realism," we are nonetheless confronted by the genteel concept that the limits of realism are governed by propriety. If an Irish peer is both generous and diseased, the author may only mention his generosity; improper disclosure of the disease perverts good realism into the Rabelaisian kind.

Yet Joyce's Dublin of 1904 was almost two decades away from the Dublin of 1922, and Leslie is aware of the distancing in time that must necessarily change the rules of the game: "Certainly it takes

a Dubliner to pick out the familiar names and allusions of twenty
years ago," he comments, "though the references to men who have
become as important as Arthur Griffith assume a more universal
hearing" (*CH* I, 209). Which raises the question of how real is the
Arthur Griffith of *Ulysses*. I have asserted elsewhere that the
Arthur Griffith accepted by critics Robert Adams and Robert Tracy
bears little resemblance to the Irish political leader that walked the
streets of Dublin in 1904.[6] Joyce has created his own Griffith for
literary purposes in juxtaposition to the Leopold Bloom who never
saw the light of real day in that real Dublin. Griffith's presence
in Dublin on 16 June 1904 adds to the appearance of reality which
is operative throughout the book, and it is logical that a quasi-
political Bloom should be aware of his presence. He apparently has
noticed Griffith and knows something about Griffith's political
stance, and has pointed him out to Molly as "very intelligent
the coming man" (*U* 748) (Molly is unimpressed of course and
notices that Griffith has no neck). Griffith's witticism regarding the
geographical inaccuracy of the headpiece over the *Freeman Journal's*
leader has also reached Bloom and he finds it amusing, although
on its second time around in his thoughts it begins to pale. The
knowledge among Bloom's fellow Dubliners that Bloom's origins are
vaguely Hungarian compounds the speculation about the mysterious
foreigner in their midst; Griffith's pamphlet on "The Resurrection
of Hungary" drew the analogy between Irish hopes for home rule
from Britain and Hungarian success in achieving such autonomy
within the Austro-Hungarian Empire. The association between
Bloom and Griffith is therefore based on an absurd coincidence,
but when John Wyse Nolan feels compelled to defend Bloom
against the anti-semitic Citizen, he makes the connection a valid
one by asserting that Bloom provided the idea of home rule to
Griffith. And Martin Cunningham finds it convenient to corroborate
this fantasy in a moment of good will toward the magnanimous
donor of five shillings. It is within the framework of this
fanciful context that Shane Leslie accepts the reality of Griffith's
"presence" in *Ulysses*, but the Griffith that Leslie knows and the
one conscripted for off-beat service by Joyce could hardly be
expected to know each other. Even when he retained the real names
and accurate descriptions of individual Dubliners for his novels
James Joyce was creating fictional characters. His sense of reality
was expected to overwhelm mundane reality (and certainly the
polite reality of his Dublin critics).

Ulysses is no more about Dublin than *Moby Dick* is about a whale—although no less. Joyce's boast to Frank Budgen that "if the city one day suddenly disappeared from the earth it could be constructed out of my book" certainly attests to Joyce's penchant for accuracy whenever possible, but he could hardly have expected such reconstruction to have taken place from the reality he credits most, the Mabbot Street scene and Molly's soliloquy. Mary Colum's review, however, strictly emphasizes the lesser reality when she views *Ulysses* as a "kind of epic of Dublin. Never was a city so involved in the workings of any writer's mind as Dublin is in Joyce's; he can think only in terms of it. In his views of newspaper-offices, public houses, the National Library, the streets, the cemetery, he has got the psychology of that battered, beautiful eighteenth-century city in its last years of servitude" (*CH* I, 232). By the choice of her adjectives Mary Colum has imposed upon *Ulysses* aspects and attitudes never incorporated by Joyce. It is the critic not the author who claims that Dublin is battered and beautiful (Joyce never even tells us that it is eighteenth-century, much less that it is in its last years of servitude). Mrs. Colum is editorializing on the basis of her own preconceptions: *Ulysses*, by reminding her of the city she knew, is awakening her feelings about Dublin. And although she is far more perceptive about the literary value of the book than Shane Leslie, she shares his Dubliner's self-congratulatory appreciations of the reality of the work: "It hardly seems possible that it can be really understood by anybody not brought up in the half-secret tradition of the heroism, tragedy, folly and anger of Irish nationalism, or unfamiliar with the philosophy, history and rubrics of the Roman Catholic Church; or by one who does not know Dublin and certain conspicuous Dubliners" (*CH* I, 232). In contrast, however, there is the review by Gilbert Seldes in the *Nation* (August 1922)—which Mrs. Colum alleges was one of the three Joyce was most pleased with, along with Wilson's and her own: "More important still," Seldes admits, "are the interests associated with 'the uncreated conscience of my race'— the Catholic and Irish. I have written this analysis of *Ulysses* as one not too familiar with either—as an indication that the book can have absolute validity and interest, in the sense that all which is local and private in the *Divine Comedy* does not detract from its interest and validity" (*CH* I, 238).

Too much familiarity with Joyce's Dublin might indeed be dangerous in attempting a balanced reading of *Ulysses*, and perhaps a reader with the detachment of a Seldes has a distinct advantage over Mary Colum—and certainly Shane Leslie. Few people at this time could have been aware of Joyce's statement to the prospective publisher of *Dubliners* that his stories were intended as a "chapter in the moral history" of Ireland. Many were involved, however, in analyzing the moral content of Joyce's work, and those for whom the term suggested what it meant to Joyce (a critical view of the ethical values of the Irish people subjected as they were to the political realities of British rule, the religious control of the Catholic Church, and the demands and conditions of their social and economic class) found in *Ulysses* a continuation of a sociological examination. Even Leslie then acknowledges that "it contains some gruesome and realistic pictures of the Irish capital," but insists on judging the moral value of the book itself: "it also contains passages fantastically opposed to all ideas of good taste and morality" (*CH* I, 206). Joyce himself used the word "moral" without qualms: it was significant to him in describing the condition of life in Dublin, not as a value judgment to be imposed on literature. To many of the Irish, *Ulysses* set up a mirror to their Caliban images, and the rage this engendered proves self-revealing. Joyce's intention as a gadfly remained consistent throughout his literary career, although by the writing of *Ulysses* it has somewhat slackened in intensity. About *Dubliners* he wrote in 1906: "It is not my fault that the odour of ashpits and old weeds and offal hangs round my stories. I seriously believe that you will retard the course of civilisation in Ireland by preventing the Irish people from having one good look at themselves in my nicely polished looking-glass" (*Letters* I, 63-4).

It is certainly no surpirse, therefore, that so perceptive an Irishman as Bernard Shaw would assume that this remained a major intention in *Ulysses*, and his letter to Sylvia Beach also assumes that this intention forms the major purpose of Joyce's new work. Shaw sounds amazingly like the Joyce of 1906 when he notes:

> I have read several fragments of *Ulysses* in its serial form. It is a revolting record of a disgusting phase of civilisation; but it is a truthful one; and I should like to put a cordon round Dublin; round up every male person in it between the ages of 15 and 30; force them to read it; and ask them whether on reflection they could see anything amusing in all that foul mouthed, foul minded derision and obscenity. . . . to me it is all hideously real: I have walked those streets and know those shops and have heard and taken part in those conversations. . . . It is, however, some consolation to find that at last somebody has felt deeply enough about it to face the horror of writing it all down and using his literary genius to force people to face it. In Ireland they try to make a cat cleanly by rubbing its nose in its own filth. Mr. Joyce has tried the same treatment on the human subject. I hope it may prove successful (*CH* I, 189-90).

Shaw's letter, brief as it is, is a masterpiece in what it reveals. He discerns the "moral" purpose of Joyce's work of art so well that he considers it the sole function of the novel. The foul obscenity that he comments on is not Joyce's (as Leslie and *The Pink Un'* would have it) but that of the Dubliners being evaluated. The accuracy of Joyce's perceptions is corroborated by Shaw's own experiences and "moral" vision. And consequently he views *Ulysses* as a didactic work of literature, a necessary corrective to Irish hypocrisy and cynicism to be employed as a weapon. He makes it compulsory reading, and even exults in the potency of the purgative (medicine must taste bad in order to be of medicinal value). And as one of the major Irish humorists of the age he fails to discover what is "amusing" in the work of the other major Irish humorist. He notices neither humor nor satire in *Ulysses*, suggesting that the tract will teach by its shocking accuracy rather than by any satiric exaggeration.

Without accepting any aspect of *Ulysses* as didactic, Jackson Holbrook nonetheless parallels Shaw's designation of the book as a "record." In his June 1922 review in *To-Day* Jackson claims: "He is not even out to amuse, like George Moore and the storytellers, or to criticise, like Meredith, or satirise, like Swift. He simply records like Homer, or, indeed, Froissart" (*CH* I, 198). Amuse-criticize-satirize: these now seem so close to what apparently were Joyce's intentions in *Ulysses*, while the habit of merely recording like a mechanical apparatus seems furthest from anything Joyce had ever intended. To view Joyce as a "recorder" has a distinct advantage for Jackson: it relieves Joyce of the onus of immorality in his literary intentions since the objective apparatus that registers the seismographic shocks of daily life in Dublin cannot be accused of ulterior motives. *Ulysses* then "is neither moral nor immoral. Mr. Joyce writes, not as though morals had never existed, but as one who deliberately ignores moral codes and conventions" (*CH* I, 198). This credits Joyce with the scientific objectivity that the naturalists had hoped to find in themselves, an objectivity that Zola could not claim without realizing the limitations it imposed upon his literary creativity.

The specter of naturalism colors a reading of *Ulysses* to a serious extent by tarring all the elements in the work with the same brush. Acknowledging the precision of Joyce's power of description is the advantageous aspect of the view, but not seeing all of the characters in the novel (especially its central character) as the victims of the naturalist's objective record. Not only can Jackson not differentiate between Bloom and (say) Simon Dedalus or Lenehan or the Citizen, but he focuses on this "modern *Ulysses*" as the central target of the naturalistic vivisection. He asserts that the recorder's method "has its dangers. Mr. Joyce has faced them, or, rather, ignored them. He has been perfectly logical. He has recorded everything—everything in a single day of the life of an uninteresting and, to me, unpleasant, and, if we forget the parable of the sparrows, negligible human being" (*CH* I, 198-99). Bloom may indeed be negligible (it is only to God that the fall of a sparrow is of concern; to the naturalistic writer it is only a phenomenon to be observed and recorded), but once Jackson sees him as unpleasant or even uninteresting he is imposing a value judgment that his own interpretations of Joyce's intention cannot allow him. If Joyce's view of Bloom is unimpassioned, where does Jackson's unease derive from? Either the critic brings his own prejudice to bear upon the character whom he labels "the Twentieth Century Yahoo" (*CH* I, 199) or Joyce has done something other than *record*, has indeed criticized and satirized (but failed to amuse). Jackson has impaled himself on the horns of *two* dilemmas when he insists about Bloom: "you are introduced to his friends and enemies; you learn what he thinks of each; every action and reaction of his psychology is laid bare with Freudian nastiness until you know his whole life through and through; know him, in fact, better than you know any other being in art or life—and detest him heartily" (*CH* I, 199). To know Bloom apparently is to detest him: the scientific purpose of a Freudian analyst is not objective but willfully *nasty*. Such assumptions (in what is generally a favorable review of *Ulysses*) are self-defeating. The shared objectivity of design which informs the work of the pure naturalist and the Freudian scientist belies Jackson's over-reaction to Leopold Bloom. Nor does Jackson (or any other reader, for that matter) know all there is to know about Bloom: there remain hundreds of questions about him, his past, his habits, his preferences, his reasons for various actions and reactions. Bloom is still and always will be the "Mystery Man on the Beach," the mysterious stranger of the modern *Ulysses*.

But one does not have to view Freudianism as nasty to adhere to the persecution of Leopold Bloom. For Joseph Collins, reviewing *Ulysses* in the *New York Times Book Review* (May 28, 1922) Bloom is "a moral monster, a pervert and an invert, an apostate to his race and his religion, the simulacrum of a man who has neither cultural background nor personal self-respect, who can neither be taught by experience nor lessoned by example" (*CH* I, 225). And Collins's credentials as a reviewer are revealed at the end of the piece: "I am probably the only person, aside from the author, that has ever read it twice from beginning to end. I have learned more psychology and psychiatry from it than I did in ten years at the

Neurological Institute" (*CH* I, 226). His perspective is that of a practicing analyst, and he is overwhelmed by the accuracy of Joyce's psychoanalytical viewpoint. Like an Aesopian blindman he has his hands on the one and only valid interpretation of *Ulysses*, that of Joyce's contribution to psychological literature: "There are other angles at which *Ulysses* can be viewed profitably," Collins admits, "but they are not many" (*CH* I, 226). Bloom is outflanked: an objective recording reveals him as detestable although we know him "through and through," while psychoanalytical probing reveals "the vile contents of that unconscious mind" (*CH* I, 225). Collins, however, denies deliberate recording by the author. He maintains that Joyce "is the only individual that the writer has encountered outside of a madhouse who has let flow from his pen random and purposeful throughts just as they are produced. He does not seek to give them orderliness, sequence or interdependence" (*CH* I, 224).

Although many reviews during that year of befuddlement, 1922, acknowledge that the author of *Ulysses* had previously written *Dubliners* and *A Portrait of the Artist as a Young Man*, there is a marked ignorance of the possibility that Joyce's intentions in his new work in some way derive from professed ideas exposed by his young artist in *A Portrait*. Could the same Joyce who painstakingly developed for Stephen Dedàlus a complicated theory of aesthetics allow himself to present random throughts without order in the minds of his characters? And can such a literary consciousness deny itself so completely as to allow only what the eye sees on the surface of reality to be recorded without a governing attitude? Even when one separates the young potential artist from the mature writer it seems impossible to expect that Joyce regressed into photographic naturalism or automatic writing. For Arnold Bennett, the creator of "the dailiest day possible," absolved of the accusation of "what is absurdly called 'photographic realism,' " was instead writing a book that "is more like an official shorthand writer's 'note' than a novel" (*CH* I, 220-21). Bennett finds no aspect of selectivity in *Ulysses*, but is hardly as sanguine about this free-form method as Joseph Collins. He insists that Joyce is wrongheaded because he "is resolved at any price not to select, not to make even the shortest leap from one point of interest to another. He has taken an oath with himself to put it all down and be hanged to it" (*CH* I, 221). Admitting extravangance in both praise and blame (but allowing negative extravagance of the lion's share, despite exultations over Molly's soliloquy), Bennett scored *Ulysses* for its fourfold deficiency: "The author seems to have no geographical

sense, little sense of environment, no sense of the general kindness
of human nature, and not much poetical sense" (*CH* I, 221). In this
summary then not only is the familiar libel on humanity repeated, but
Joyce is also denied his poetic style and his naturalistic strengths.
The Dublin that natives like Shaw and Mary Colum and even Shane
Leslie found so convincingly real is seen by Bennett as devoid of
its geographical and environmental exactness: "the uninstructed
reader can perceive no form, no artistic plan, no 'organization' . . . in
the chosen day," Bennett insists (*CH* I, 220).

Yet Bennett concedes that he has already read Larbaud's comments
on *Ulysses* and cannot bring himself to doubt that Larbaud has
seen Joyce's drafts for the novel. This knowledge does him no
good, however, since it prevents him from dismissing *Ulysses* as a
leg-pull without giving him any advantage over what he has read
in Joyce's book. Even Larbaud's suggestion of Joyce's debt to the
Odyssey does not help him much. He notes that "the spirit of
Homer presided over the shaping of the present work, which is
alleged to be full of Homeric parallels," but all he can add is:
"It may be so" (*CH* I, 220). Bennett's shyness at undertaking a full
investigation of these possibilities in *Ulysses* is only an extreme
example of the relatively little attention given to the allegorical
levels by reviewers between Larbaud's initial statement in April
1922 and Eliot's distinct nudge a year-and-a-half later. Larbaud put
it in the form of a warning, "The reader who approaches this book
without the *Odyssey* clearly in mind will be thrown into dismay"
(*CH* I, 258), but Bennett and others opted for dismay. Reviewers
found enough to worry about in their reading of Joyce without
having to reread Homer as well. It is hardly surprising that Leslie
would do little with the possibility, although he could not ignore that
as a title *Ulysses* must have its specific meaning: "In spite of a thin
parallelism with the movement of the Odyssey, for the episodes of
Circe, Æolus, Nausicaa, are visible amongst others less easily
traceable, there has been an abandonment of form and a mad
Shelleyan effort to extend the known confines of the English
language" (*CH* I, 211). Nor do Mrs. Colum and Mr. Wilson over-
exert themselves in this area of investigation. Wilson is in fact
discomforted by the Homeric superstructure, accepting the
realization that "the major theme of the book is to be found in its
parallel with the Odyssey," but complaining nonetheless: "Yet I
cannot but feel that Mr. Joyce made a mistake to have the whole plan
of his story depend on the structure of the *Odyssey* rather than on
the natural demands of the situation" (*CH* I, 229). It is apparent that
Wilson does not read *Ulysses* as a novel governed by the reality of

its Dublin milieu but as a highly symbolic work that depends to an exaggerated extent upon its "plan." His objection is quite specific: "I feel that though his taste for symbolism is closely allied with his extraordinary poetic faculty for investing particular incidents with universal significance, nevertheless—because it is the homeless symbolism of a Catholic who has renounced the faith—it sometimes overruns the bounds of art into an arid ingenuity which would make a mystic correspondence do duty for an artistic reason" (*CH* I, 229).

Wilson's attitudes toward *Ulysses*, therefore, could hardly be shared by the Mary Colum who was so aware of her city of Dublin dominating the fabric if not the structure of Joyce's book. Her opinion of it as "a kind of epic of Dublin" precludes her observation of another epic informing and perhaps even subsuming *Ulysses*. Consequently she takes a dim view of those who overconcern themselves with Homeric parallels:

> One of the chief occupations of critics of this book is making parallels between the sections and characters of *Ulysses*, and the *Odyssey*. The chief reason for this performance is that the author exhibits a notebook with all these parallels and many other symbolical explanations. When it comes to symbolizing, authors have from all time talked the greatest nonsense; think of the nonsense that Goethe achieved when explaining the second part of *Faust*! Just as plausible correspondence could be made between *Faust* and *Ulysses* as between the *Odyssey* and *Ulysses* (*CH* I, 233-34).

On the mere hint from Larbaud that a notebook exists Arnold Bennett pulls in his claws and begrudgingly allows the possibility of a super-structure for Joyce's book, yet Mary Colum, having seen the note-book, dismisses it and the symbolic correspondences it delineates as the fanciful product of the author's wishful thinking, preferring her own *Ulysses* as a portrait of her battered and beautiful city. Wilson accepts the parallels as there but regrets that they obfuscate what could have been—and apparently should have been—a novel about the real Dublin somehow lost in the Homeric shuffle. How catholic was Joyce's taste to accept these two as among the three best reviews of *Ulysses*—or how ironic was the catholicity of his taste.

Although concerned with the physical setting of the city of Dublin, *Ulysses* is by no means a parochial book: instead it strives to rise far above the parochial by viewing the city and its inhabitants with irony and detachment. It is to this end that the *Odyssey*, valuable in giving form and structure to *Ulysses*, also serves to lift the work out of its literal context. Joyce presses Homer into service in order to universalize *Ulysses* in historic time. As I have

demonstrated in "*Ulysses*: The Making of an Irish Myth,"[8] Joyce
marshals the salient facts of Irish history and legend to weigh
the events of 16 June 1904 with a full complement of the Irish past:
dependence upon the *Odyssey* adds the dimension of a universalized
and mythic past that is fundamental to Western civilization, while
Bloom's Semitic heritage and role as the Wandering Jew, Moses,
and Elijah supplement the New Testament with the Old, Greek
culture with Hebraic. (With a nod to Victor Bérard and his *Les
Phéniciens et l'Odyssée*, Joyce cemented his two-part under-
structuring.) Stuart Gilbert's weighty Homeric reading in *James
Joyce's "Ulysses,"* replete with Joyce's imprimatur, carries the
Larbaud-Eliot suggestion of the parallel with Homer to its finite
extension, positing a *Ulysses* intricately involved with its source
material. The *Odyssey* certainly serves as the best single corrective
to the parochial reader who saw in Joyce's work an exact replica
of his own Dublin, and to the naturalist who mistook the carefully
sketched layer of reality as the essence of *Ulysses*.

Joyce's use of Homer, however, reveals the same sort of detachment and irony as his use of his native city: literary parody follows
hard upon the parallels, not in the pejorative sense of mockery
(the "Oxen of the Sun" chapter is a testament both to the grandeur
of English literary prose and to Joyce's skill in encapsulating that
grandeur with a touch of self-glory) but in a contemporary awareness that too literal a parallel would in itself be a mockery. Joyce's
Telemachus is not Odysseus' son: he has somewhat succeeded in
denying his own father, whom he relegates to the condition of mere
consubstantiality. His quest for a spiritual father takes place in the
remote region of his unconscious yearnings, and it is Mulligan
ironically enough who voices the idea: "O, shade of Kinch the elder!
Japhet in search of a father!" This is in response to Haines's misconception that Stephen is the ghost of his own father, and Haines
undercuts Stephen's Hamlet theory (as yet unexpounded to him)
by adding, "I read a theological interpretation of it somewhere . . . .
The Father and the Son idea. The Son striving to be atoned with the
Father" (*U* 18). It is from this germinal suggestion that Stephen
Dedalus has his first incarnation in *Ulysses* as the father-seeking
Telemachus, and if after several hours spent with Bloom late that
night he is still unaware of any spiritual affinity with his overly
friendly and solicitous host, it must be remembered that Homer's
Telemachus never does succeed in his search: he is apprehended
instead by an Odysseus that he at first fails to recognize.

The Jewishness of Joyce's Odysseus is of course an invented

fiction which makes Bloom far from typical as an Irish Dubliner, and removed from the literal Dublin seen by Mary Colum and others. That Joyce discovered in Bérard a possible Semitic source for his version of Odysseus was only one of those happy accidents that Joyce loved and courted: parallel and parody play hide-and-seek— or chicken-and-egg—with each other. If there is an anticipation in the Greek wanderer of the Phoenician merchant, positing Semitic roots in Homer's Ithacan, then Semitic Bloom has his own Jewishness mitigated by his never having been a Jew. On one hand he can rail at the Citizen, "Your God was a jew. Christ was a jew like me" (*U* 342), while on the other he can speculate on whether Stephen assumes that he is Jewish:

> What, reduced to their simplest reciprocal form, were Bloom's thoughts about Stephen's thoughts about Bloom and Bloom's thoughts about Stephen's thoughts about Bloom's thoughts about Stephen?
> He thought that he thought that he was a jew whereas he knew that he knew that he knew that he was not (*U* 682).

Yet in this "Ithaca" chapter of homecoming and recognition the Son that is presumably seeking atonement with the Father inexplicably sings the "Hugh of Lincoln" song of ritual murder soon after Bloom, the non-Jew, has recited in Hebrew from the Song of Solomon and chanted in Hebrew from the Zionist anthem. Joyce has constructed an enigma that defies solution: Bloom accepts and rejects his Hebraic origins, even accepting-in-rejection. And as Odysseus he attempts to claim Stephen as his son, offering a quasi-permanent hospitality with definite rights and privileges within his household. The Homeric parallel, however, can be extended even further: not only is Stephen fulfilling the role of Telemachus with which the novel opens, but is also doubling as the chief suitor found by Odysseus occupying his palace. Blazes Boylan has escaped unharmed and unchallenged, while Stephen is being groomed by Leopold Bloom as his replacement. Three times during the course of the day Bloom has seen Boylan; he first ignores him, and finally pursues him into the Ormond, curious why at 4 p.m. Boylan is not where he is expected to be, at 7 Eccles Street. And three times during the day he sees Stephen, moving progressively closer until on the fourth occasion, at the hospital, he begins his solicitous guardianship of the drunken youth. On the conscious level he seeks to replace the son he will never have with the intellectual companionship of an intelligent young man (like the Sinclair he searches for at the Burton). By Joycean irony the relationship Bloom hopes for may have to be paid for by satisfying a possible Oedipal desire that Bloom assumes Stephen would have: Odysseus tacitly accepts the inevitability of retaining his Telemachus by having him as his replacement in Penelope's bed.

Stephen's polite rejection of Bloom's offer of a night's lodgings has often been interpreted as his inability to perceive the implied relationship that makes Bloom the father he has been searching for. It is consistent with his self-image as a prospective exile that Stephen, now friendless, homeless and soon to be jobless, must refuse the new ties suggested by Bloom and continue his pilgrimage. But in so doing he is also establishing a mystic bond with the same Bloom that he is obviously rejecting. In the language of the catechism chapter the offer and refusal read:

> Was the proposal of asylum accepted?
> Promptly, inexplicably, with amicability, gratefully it was declined (*U* 695).

A dozen years earlier the ten-year-old Stephen had inadvertently invited the older man to dinner at his parental home. As the question-and-answer format presents it:

> Did Bloom accept the invitation to dinner given then by the son and afterwards seconded by the father?
> Very gratefully, with grateful appreciation, with sincere appreciative gratitude, in appreciatively grateful sincerity of regret, he declined (*U* 680).

Even in the negative these two isolated instances create a parallel system of relationships between Stephen and Bloom, Telemachus and Odysseus, but only in the *language* of the novel. It is only in the style of Joyce's presentation that the actual bond exists, tenuous as it is.

Most mysterious of all is the character of Joyce's chosen Penelope. The early estimates of the bed-sodden Mrs. Bloom insisted that Joyce's parallel was not just parody but actual travesty, that the perfidious Molly could not hold a candle to the faithful Penelope. Many of the earlier reviewers tended to ignore Molly, although those who praised *Ulysses* often commented on the excellence of the writing in the "Penelope" chapter. A reviewer in the *Evening News* (8 April 1922) summed it up as being "730 pages—all about the doings, within 24 hours, of two Dublin journalists, Stephen Dedalus and Leopold Bloom. Bloom 'Ulysses' and Dedalus 'Telemachus' " (*CH* I, 194). This capsule presents a book *without* a Molly in it, much less a Penelope. Father Martindale bemoans the misuse of Joyce's talent for writing "exquisite prose-music" in being "at his most convincing in his chosen line when murmuring through half a hundred pages the dream-memories of an uneducated woman"

(*CH* I, 206). (Dismissing Molly as merely an "uneducated woman" may be the most extreme insult of all!) In true male-chauvinist fashion Arnold Bennett and Joseph Collins (and of course Carl Jung) expressed their awe that Joyce could capture "feminine psychology" so magnificently, making Molly Bloom a mysterious creature of that other world, uncomprehendable to men—except in this rare instance. Not to be outdone by male critics in this area, Mary Colum washes her hands of Molly: "The revelation of the mind of Marion Bloom in the last section would doubtless interest the laboratory, but to normal people it would seem an exhibition of the mind of a female gorilla who has been corrupted by contact with humans" (*CH* I, 233). The laboratory has already been heard from: they cannot prove it, but they are willing to accept Joyce's word for it that this is female psychology. Mrs. Colum consigns it to the laboratory because it is *not* representative of the human female. Nor of course would it bear any relationship to Homer's Penelope for Mrs. Colum, since she denies any real involvement of the Homeric epic in Joyce's. It remains for the singular Gilbert Seldes among the initial purveyors of *Ulysses* to say what so obviously needs saying: "in the thoughts of Mrs. Bloom something coarse and healthy and coarsely beautiful and healthily foul asserts itself. Like the Wife of Bath, she can thank God that she has had her world, as in her time" (*CH* I, 237).

But Molly/Penelope could not be ignored for long, and since it was consistently assumed that the adulteress of 16 June 1904 was no neophyte at the trade, that Blazes was indeed the most recent in a series that has been continuous, it was assumed that Joyce was at his most devastating in parodying the fidelity of Homer's model wife. Bloom is certainly no voyager, never having been out of Ireland except for a day's trip to Holyhead and an excursion on the *Erin's King* (and the W. B. Murphy of the *Rosevean* is a *true* Odysseus, howbeit vulgarized into a travesty). By analogy Molly is no true Penelope, but a converse paragon of infidelity. The existence of post-Homeric versions of the story, particularly Roman examples of an unfaithful Penelope, added new parallels to the existing Joyce parody: the title is a Roman *Ulysses* rather than a Greek *Odyssey*, with an emphasis on the man instead of his voyage. And once the critics belatedly arrived at the realization that Molly Bloom was after all a woman like any other female character in fiction, several were aghast at how basically unpleasant she really was: Erwin Steinberg and J. Mitchell Morse[9] stripped her of her role as earth-mother, denied her lineage from the legendary Penelope, and refused to have her sloughed off as an example of "feminine psychology." Consequently they were all the more repelled by her unhealthily human foulness. Several gentlemen have rushed forth with cloaks and kisses, and an appreciative eye for voluptuously ample breasts, to protect Molly from such detractors.

It has taken almost half-a-century for readers to become aware that Molly has been accused and convicted without a shred of evidence against her. Bloom's list of the basic 24 post-marital lovers (plus Mulvey as precursor) will not stand up for a moment in court. Bloom is masochistically rubbing his nose in stoic self-pity: he cannot possibly believe in the totality of his list, much less in a majority of the hypothetical lovers. Molly's reverie has the sanctity of confession: she cannot be lying to herself, and when she mockingly dismisses 18 of Bloom's candidates it is obvious that she could never have considered them as worthy of her favors. At worst she could have forgotten; but what validity has a lover to her if he has left no residue in her private thoughts, especially when she enjoys licentious thoughts with such relish? When she luxuriates over Boylan's potential and performance she is being absolute in her admiration, not comparative. If Stanley Sultan and David Hayman[10] are correct, and they have the power of negative evidence very much on their side, we are left with the difficult prospect of having to accept the unfaithful Molly as a faithful Penelope after all.

This true parallel may then be greater parody than the travesty that was formerly accepted. Bloom has had his Calypso, Circe, and Nausicaa during the course of the day (his memory is not very specific regarding the infidelities of the previous decade, during which he has not fulfilled sexual involvement with his wife) and Molly has maintained herself, against her will and her nature, without having been unfaithful. Irony then is supplemented by the prosaic realities of Dublin life: her opportunities for such liaisons would have certainly been limited—although not impossible, even with Milly in the house. If 16 June 1904 proves to be the first day on which Molly had completed an adulterous affair, then she loses her title as "faithful Penelope" after all, and for her at least it is anything but "the dailiest day possible." But Joyce insists upon even one more possibility in the presence of Stanley Gardner in Molly's thoughts. Although he is absent from Bloom's list (so that unlike Mulvey he has not been mentioned by Molly to Bloom) he looms as a definite possibility considering the emotion with which Molly remembers him: his death in South Africa, although not of war-inflicted wounds but of disease, makes him a romantic figure in her thoughts. He is a lineal descendant of the first-love Mulvey (whose first name Molly has some difficulty in recalling, however) since Molly has given him Mulvey's ring. But in a book that has multiple mysteries and several mystery men (from M'Intosh to Bloom on the beach), Gardner cannot be pinned down too precisely either. His significance in Molly's thoughts is great, but she never credits him with having been in her bed. And if he is to be seen as an avatar of Mulvey, he too may have had to settle for kisses and embraces and manual manipulation. And the ultimate irony of Molly's position as a true/false Penelope comes with the closing moments of her soliloquy: near sleep at least she regresses to romantic recollections of the past, blending first kisses with Mulvey under Moorish walls in Gibraltar with the first seduction by Bloom on the Hill of Howth. It was apparently Bloom that she credits with calling her "a flower of the mountain" among the rhododendrons of Howth, and Mulvey who called her "a Flower of the mountain" (*U* 782-83) in Gibraltar: or if the two incidents have been confused in her drowsy mind, Molly may be returning to a state of innocence that predates her womanly experience and makes her more chaste than even Homer's Penelope.

Joyce's *Ulysses* can hardly be accepted as a rewriting or updating of Homer's *Odyssey*: the handling of the Homeric materials is willfully idiosyncratic (with the inclusion of the "Wandering Rocks" episode Joyce rushes in where Homer feared to tread), depending entirely upon the suitability of Odyssean aspects for Joyce's larger scheme. Nor is a literal recapitulation of his own Dublin sufficient basis for more than the setting of his *Ulysses*: the Dublin of 1904 cannot be reconstructed from the book, only the Dublin that had its origins in Joyce's creative imagination. The reader who has never seen the licensed premises of David Byrne at 21 Duke Street as it was in 1904 can never experience it as it was then by either visiting it as it is now or by reading the "Lestrygonians" chapter. The present pub is a place called Davy Byrne's (the Joycean use of the proprietor's nickname has now been shifted to designate the place itself, and even Joyce's comment that it is a "moral pub" has been added to its sign and advertising); its modern fixtures are quite different from its past decor, and just as Joyce had immortalized the pub, the pub has subsumed him as well: his likeness is part of a mural and a room called the "Ulysses Bar" has been added. Conversely, little descriptive material is available in the "Lestrygonians" chapter, hardly enough to even sketch in the pieces for a reconstruction. Instead, Davy Byrne's moral pub exists only in what it means to Bloom, a decent alternative to the horror of the Burton. The latter had been his first choice for lunch, primarily because it is inexpenseive and then because of the possibility that "young Sinclair," a clerk at Harris's around the corner, might be there. (For a while the false lead had directed readers to assume that the Burton was Joyce's renaming of the Bailey, across the street from Davy Byrne's, but Thom's Directory locates the Burton at 18 Duke Street; besides, Bloom "turned back towards Grafton street" [*U* 170] to get to Byrne's, something he could not have done from the Bailey.) Despite the disgust welling up within him at the sight of the gorging going on in the Burton, Bloom lingers on in the doorway; a chat with young Sinclair would have justified patronizing the awful place: "—Not here. Don't see him./ Out. I hate dirty eaters" (*U* 170). For Bloom the choice is between a cheap, slovenly eatery and the clean, decent setting for a light lunch. The tension established by Joyce between the Burton and Davy Byrne's is comprehendable to almost any reader. One can have disappeared completely and the other changed radically, but the contrast that exists in Bloom's mind transcends the literal reality of the previous existences.

Attention to detail remained an obsession with Joyce nonetheless: the Dublin that he knew provided the important materials for the life of his novel. A persistent memory, access to newspapers and Thom's Directory, and questions answered by mail from Dublin kept the city as it was in 1904 permanently fixed in mind, although he began the work a decade after that date and had last visited the city several years before. If his Sirens were to be barmaids they would have to be at the Ormond Hotel, one of the few places in Dublin that employed females to tend bar, since most Irishmen still insist that only a man can "pull a good pint." A perfect setting for the accidental encounter of Bloom and the Citizen suggests itself as the pub near the law courts, one that had retained its connections with the legal profession: Bernard Kiernan's on Little Britain Street (both the pub and the street name have now passed into history, although a faint, blackened street sign, "Britain Street Little," may still be seen on one of the corner buildings). No sooner was *Ulysses* published in 1922 than the whole political climate of the book became obsolete as British Ireland was replaced in the 26 southern counties by the Irish Free State. And one of the first official results was the demolition of Nighttown even to the extent that street names were purposely changed to obliterate any memory of the unsavory quarter whose reason for being supposedly was as a service to British troops. Joyce's Nighttown was opened to the world just as the "real" Nighttown ceased to exist, and official banning of Joyce's book eventually proved to be just as futile as the banning of the red-light district in Dublin.

It is the "Circe" chapter that indicates how feeble the surface reality of *Ulysses* actually is in relation to its literary reality, what Joyce himself suggested as the "exalted vision of the mystics." The Circean metamorphosis of men into swine is only a grace note to this enormous segment of *Ulysses*, and the psychological explanation of Stephen's drunkenness and Bloom's fatigue can hardly account for the unrealistic phenomena of the chapter. Allowing for the hallucinatory effect of drink and weariness in the human brain barely covers the situation in "Circe." Some of the long, detailed, and extended hallucinations take place during brief intervals of recorded time, at times even within the natural sequence between a spoken comment or question and its resulting retort. And although it is almost always possible to separate hallucination from reality, there are fragments within the context that are inexplicable. Residual bits of hallucinatory material continue to intrude even after reality has been restored. And psychologically untenable are those elements of hallucination that change places of origin: Stephen hallucinates with Bloom's background material; Bloom with Stephen's; and on occasion they share the impossibility of a mutual vision, as both Stephen and Bloom see the beardless face of Shakespeare in the mirror. The Nighttown destroyed by official decree after 1922 provides only the marginal surface for the Nighttown that Joyce's artistic sense of reality created in *Ulysses*.

Joyce's Dublin persists as a microcosm of the modern city. Joyce had commented that the city was both a national capital and yet a relatively small community in which the citizens knew each other well enough for him to create the interaction of his characters. The Dublin of *Ulysses* represents the urban scene of the twentieth century with an even greater impact than the New York of Dos Passos, or the Chicago of James T. Farrell, or even the London of Virginia Woolf's *Mrs. Dalloway*. Its actual residents are transformed into rounded fictional characters. Some like John Eglinton already have dual existences (in real life as W. K. Magee), existing fictionally within their pseudonyms even before Joyce redeploys them. For Joyce's purposes John Howard Parnell exists primarily as the ghost of his dead brother ("poached eyes on ghost" [*U* 165]) and his non-existence at the council chamber causes the assistant town clerk to ask, "Where was the town marshall, he wanted to know, to keep order in the council chamber" [*U* 247]). In reality Joyce has the town marshall seated in the D.B.C. playing chess and observed by Mulligan and Haines, so that his absence from the council makes him his own ghost as well. (His chess-playing is predicted by Bloom who has seen him two hours before: "Drop into the D. B. C. probably for his coffee, play chess there. His brother used men as pawns" [*U* 165]). Those in the funeral carriage who see Reuben J. Dodd assume that he is Jewish; Joyce of course knew that he was not, but allowed his characters the misinformation of Dublin rumor, a greater reality. Even George Russell undergoes a Joycean trans-formation: already existing in self-fictionalized form as the mystic AE, his appearance in the National Library episode occasions Stephen's thoughts on the money that he owes Russell. Stephen, however, sees himself as the epicenter of his own universe and contemplates the multiple facets of his own self ("I, I and I. I'") before absorbing his creditor into his scheme of things: "A. E. I. O. U." The George Russell who has lent money to Stephen Dedalus is a fictional character existing exclusively in his mystic relationship to Stephen.

The real Dublin of 1904, transmuted into everliving life by James Joyce in *Ulysses*, has receded in time—and, considering the effects of bulldozers, in space as well. For the many readers, even those who read *Ulysses* in the original, that Dublin is unknown: it is the fictional city that has its major reality for Joyce's constant parade of readers. The city Joyce constructed is a microcosm of the urban scene that is becoming progressively more familiar to the modern world, and the individuality of the characters borrowed and created ("forged") by Joyce depend upon their existences within the framework of the novel. The Homeric parallels provide them with additional universals, but when those parallels disintegrate into parodies the universality is not lost, their humanity is un-diminished. *Ulysses* is a self-contained universe in which the author, unable to rely on any shared system of values with his prospective readers and unable to guarantee the realism of his fabricated city to more than a few who remember its streets and some of its citizens, chose to make all the values significant within his work self-reliant. Within a given urban center a host of residents live their ordinary lives, speculating freely and at times wildly about a stranger in their midst who has resided there all of his life. Relegated to the role of scapegoat he carries his humanity a notch higher; unable to redeem them he constantly redeems himself instead. And that other resident-stranger, the lonely and determined artist, may on this one occasion capture sufficient recognition of that basic humanity to record for the world outside Dublin and the span of time after 1904 the single encounter that makes 16 June 1904 a day charged with the significance to transform it from the "dailiest day possible."

Kent State University

NOTES

1. For early reviews of *Ulysses* see Robert H. Deming, *James Joyce: The Critical Heritage*, Vol. I (London: Routledge and Kegan Paul, 1969). Hereafter *CH* I.

2. It has been suggested that Aldington's comments were purposely set up for Eliot's refutation—??

3. See John Zneimer, *The Literary Vision of Liam O'Flaherty* (Syracuse, N.Y.: Syracuse University Press, 1970), p. 18.

4. Ibid., p. 19.

5. *Surface and Symbol: The Consistency of James Joyce's "Ulysses"* (New York: Oxford University Press, 1962), pp. 13-8.

6. "Arthur Griffith in *Ulysses*: The Explosion of a Myth," *English Language Notes*, 4 (Dec. 1966), 123-28.

7. *James Joyce and the Making of "Ulysses"* (1934; Bloomington: Indiana University Press, 1960), p. 68.

8. "*Ulysses*: The Making of an Irish Myth," in *Approaches to "Ulysses": Ten Essays*, ed. Thomas F. Staley and Bernard Benstock (Pittsburgh: University of Pittsburgh Press, 1970), pp. 199-234.

9. Erwin R. Steinberg, "A Book with a Molly in It," *James Joyce Review*, 2 (Spring-Summer 1958), 55-62; J. Mitchell Morse, "Molly Bloom Revisited," in *James Joyce Miscellany, Second Series*, ed. Marvin Magalaner (Carbondale: Southern Illinois University Press, 1959), pp. 139-49.

10. Stanley Sultan, *The Argument of "Ulysses"* (Columbus: Ohio State University Press, 1964), pp. 431-33; David Hayman, "The Emprical Molly," in *Approaches to "Ulysses,"* pp. 103-35.

William M. Schutte

LEOPOLD BLOOM: A TOUCH OF THE ARTIST

In the fifty years since the appearance of *Ulysses* in Sylvia Beach's Paris bookshop there has been a general recognition that Leopold Bloom stands at the center of the book, that in Joyce's words, "As the day wears on Bloom should overshadow them all."[1] Nonetheless, in critical discussions he has all too often been shoved firmly, if usually politely, into the background while discussions have raged about the structural patterning and the manifold techniques of the novel, the uses of irony, or the roles of Molly and Stephen.

Most critics seem to have felt much more comfortable discussing Stephen than Bloom. As Leslie Fiedler's comments at the Second International Joyce Symposium suggest, Stephen is a figure with a special attraction for the academic mind. He is what we were, or what we like to think we were, when we were young, before we made our decision, conscious or not, to write about imaginative literature rather than create it. So, like Fiedler's, our "first uses of James Joyce . . . were essentially a relationship to and uses of the figure of the insufferable Stephen."[2] Of course, he was not insufferable for most of us when we first read *A Portrait* or *Ulysses:* he epitomized, especially in *A Portrait*, our own aspirations, our own sensitivities, our own hatred of the forces whose nets *we* were determined to fly past. And when we grew older and came to understand our limitations better, we turned quite naturally to the explication of Stephen and of his ideas, a congenial task and a significant one, since Stephen is immersed in aesthetic and scholarly problems both in *A Portrait* and *Ulysses* and is modeled in part on Joyce's own youthful self. He is "our kind of person," and especially in the first quarter century after the publication of *Ulysses*, he received a disproportionate amount of attention.

We have come somewhat more slowly to appreciate Leopold Bloom. Probably this is as Joyce anticipated. Bloom was not to overshadow the others until the day wore on. Whereas Stephen has all of the qualities attractive to the scholar and literary critic—intellect, learning, the ability to synthesize and generalize, and more than a touch of pedantry—Bloom has none of these in any significant quantity. Yet in the end, his creator insisted, he should prevail—and much recent criticism suggests, I believe, that he does. From the pioneering, and still highly relevant, studies of Richard M. Kain and Harry Levin we have been moving toward a clearer understanding of Bloom as a character and of his place in the complex tapestry of *Ulysses*, of how he becomes the heart of the book.

There has also been increasing concern in recent *Ulysses* criticism about the relationship of the early "realistic" episodes to the later sections, which are clearly intended to move the narrative out of a representational mode for ends which seem clear enough to each critic but on which no two seem to be in full agreement. Most do emphatically agree, however, on the importance of the early episodes. Essential, according to Arnold Goldman,

> is the recognition that the symbolist techniques in *Ulysses*, with which Joyce had little to do for six chapters, begin in Aeolus to gather head, initiating a process by which we are to be progressively *detached* from the mimetic action of the novel, from the primacy of the Dublin scene. But because of the preparation [provided by the early episodes] we do not thereby reject the reality of that scene.[3]

S. L. Goldberg is equally emphatic in insisting on the importance of the representational, but he does not make a firm distinction between sections:

> The common assumption that *Ulysses* is a complex, symbolic poem, to which the ordinary interests and techniques of the novel are irrelevant, is justifiable only so long as we do not forget that it is also—and rather more obviously—a representational novel, and much, if not most, of its meaning is expressed through its representational mode. It contains "probable" and significant characters in a "probable" and significant setting, doing and saying "probable" and significant things, so that it inevitably calls into play those expectations and assumptions we bring to the novel . . . and which control the way we seek its meaning.[4]

A. Walton Litz makes much the same point in a somewhat different way:

> Most criticism of *Ulysses* is founded on the assumption that the essential life of the novel lies in the elaborate scheme of correspondences which Joyce revealed to his early commentators; but anyone who has examined the work-sheets will realize that many of the correspondences represented for Joyce a kind of "neutral" order. They provided frames which could control his diverse materials without merging into them . . . . It would be a grave mistake to found any interpretation of *Ulysses* on Joyce's *schema*, rather than on the human actions of Stephen, Molly, and Mr. Leopold Bloom.[5]

Although there has been essential agreement on the importance of the early scenes and on the primacy of Mr. Leopold Bloom—Litz's manner of listing the three main characters is significant—much of what has been said about the early Bloom episodes has been hurried and inconclusive. They are usually discussed briefly and in terms of the information they provide about Bloom's situation and interests, before the critic moves on to the more "controversial" episodes. Today the technique of the early episodes seems so relatively transparent and the portrait of Bloom so clearly defined that they do not attract extensive discussion. Yet if the book *is* a representational novel (as well as "a complex, symbolic poem" perhaps) and depends for its essential meanings on the human actions and reactions of the major characters, if, in other words, our interpretation of the symbolic content is to be validated by the human actions, it would seem important to know precisely what happens in those early episodes.

I should like here to consider in detail the materials of one early episode in order to determine how Joyce presents his central character and what the essential elements of that character are. I have chosen to concentrate on one episode both because of space limitations and because a survey of the early Bloom sections has convinced me that to deal with all of them would add much evidence but would not materially affect the conclusions I have reached.

"Lestrygonians" is as close to a "typical" Bloom episode as we have. Unlike "Calypso" and "Lotus Eaters," it is not much affected by Joyce's need to establish themes and relationships. Unlike "Hades," it presents Bloom in his natural habitat, the streets of Dublin, with their constant reminders of his most pressing concerns, notably the impending invasion of his bed by Blazes Boylan; in "Hades," on the other hand, Bloom is unusually contemplative and undisturbed. Furthermore, "Lestrygonians" is the last complete Bloom episode which is relatively unaffected by non-representational techniques,[6] depending for its effects on realistic dialogue, brief narrative passages which indicate what actions are taking place, and stream-of-consciousness passages designed to simulate what is going on in Bloom's mind. Before we consider "Lestrygonians" in detail, however, a few general observations may be helpful.

In his recent book on *Ulysses* Richard Ellmann has told us that "Joyce's intentions regarding Bloom have sometimes been misconstrued. Bloom is exceptional rather than average."[7] He is indeed exceptional, quite as exceptional in Dublin as Stephen Dedalus and far more so than the Gibraltar-born Molly. He is exceptional, we know, in his social isolation. In a city in which every man seems to have a score of cronies, Bloom has none.[8] With no man does he seem to be at ease. Socially, therefore, he is an outsider. But he is an outsider, too, in a far more significant way: unlike other Dubliners—and unlike Stephen—he has never felt the tug of the nets flung "when the soul of a man is born in this country . . . to hold it back from flight" (*Portrait* 203). Nationality, language, and religion have had little impact on his life; he cannot be excited by them. He can see them with an objectivity denied to those around him, and especially to Stephen, the other camera eye through which we see the Dublin scene.[9]

Thus, as has often been pointed out, Bloom is well suited to the traditional role of commentator. Insofar as *Ulysses* is a study of Dublin, "the center of paralysis" as Joyce once called it,[10] Bloom's perceptions of what goes on around him should be taken seriously. Like those of other commentators, however, they must be evaluated in the light of the limitations which Bloom's creator has placed on him, particularly his lack of knowledge about and understanding of certain aspects of Irish culture. He is, after all, the product of a particular environment and set of circumstances. He is largely self-educated, and he does not always recall accurately all of the facts which he more or less assiduously collects from his observation, reading, and conversation. Later on in *Ulysses*, Bloom may achieve another status and take on other roles: he will become, if most modern critics are correct, a principal agent of affirmation. But his achievement of that role is based on his earlier role as denizen of the Dublin habitat and commentator on it. It is this role which is central in the episode we shall examine. And we shall find, I think, that he is something more than an ordinary commentator.

At the end of the ninth section of "Wandering Rocks," the voluble Lenehan regales McCoy at considerable length with the story of the liberties he claims to have taken with Molly ten years before as they rode back from the annual dinner at the Glencree Reformatory. At the end of his recital he is "weak" with laughter at his own story. But suddenly he becomes solemn and says "seriously": "He's a cultured allroundman, Bloom is. He's not one of your common or garden . . . you know . . . There's a touch of the artist about old Bloom" (*U* 235).

If one considers the placing of this comment and its somewhat unlikely source, it is difficult not to interpret it as a reminder from the author that Bloom may in fact be something more than the common vulgarian that he seemed to some early readers. We are reminded, too, by Richard Ellmann that "Joyce was Tolstoyan, he respected simplicity, he thought simple people were not divorced from artistic capacity" (*UL* 130). Ellmann is speaking here not of Bloom but of Gerty McDowell. Earlier, however, he has said: "It might appear that Bloom, however Odyssean, lacks Stephen's prime characteristic, the artistic sense. But Joyce implies otherwise" (*UL* 30-1). Ellmann then speaks of Bloom's "untutored interest in drama" (he likes both *Lear* and *Hamlet* but does not feel compelled to evaluate them), of his rejection of "Matcham's Masterpiece" (he was not moved or touched by it), and of his thoughts about writing for *Titbits*. Of Bloom's jotting down bits of his wife's conversation to be worked into a story, Ellmann says: "In fact these entries bear a crude resemblance to the inch-by-inch naturalism which Stephen Dedalus at moments practices, and also the the jumpiness of the internal monologue" (*UL* 31).

This appears to be Ellmann's case for Bloom's having an "artistic sense." And a very weak case it is. Ellmann, it seems to me, has gone to the wrong place for his evidence. Bloom does have an artistic sense—though he is not, of course, an artist—but it is revealed, not in his conscious thoughts about writing, but in the nature and content of his stream of consciousness. It is there, not in his vague plans—more mercenary than literary—for publishing titbits, that Bloom displays a touch of the artist.

What are the qualities traditionally required of the literary artist? An interest in words and in language, certainly. (We may remember the recurrent emphasis in the early sections of *A Portrait* on Stephen's reactions to the sound and meaning of words.) Keen perceptions of events and of the meanings which underlie them. (We think of Stephen's epiphanies: "Copies to be sent . . . to all the great libraries of the world, including Alexandria" [*U* 40].) Compassion for his fellow men and an understanding of the nature of their strengths and weaknesses. And finally, architectonic skill, the ability to shape his perceptions with the aid of the "right" words into a unified and meaningful whole. This last skill Bloom manifestly does not have; organization is not apparent in any aspect of his life, and there is nothing to suggest that he has ever produced in writing anything more substantial than the lines he submitted in 1877 at the age of eleven in competition for a prize offered by the *Shamrock* (*U* 677-678). But, as I shall show, he is as keenly interested in words as Stephen, his perceptions about the world around him are usually penetrating and often unconventional, and his compassion encompasses not only his acquaintances but all mankind. "For Joyce's purposes," as Ellmann has said, "an unimaginative Bloom would not have done at all, since so much of the book was to take place in his mind" (*UL* 31).

I have suggested that Bloom has an artist's appreciation for words. In "Lestrygonians" there is a surprising amount of commentary on words and on their use. Most obvious, and most naive because they concern poetic technique, are Bloom's remarks on poetry called up by his observation of the gulls:

The hungry famished gull
Flaps o'er the waters dull.

That is how poets write, the similar sounds. But then Shakespeare has no
rhymes: blank verse. The flow of the language it is. The thoughts. Solemn.

Hamlet, I am thy father's spirit
Doomed for a certain time to walk the earth (U 152).

Unfortunately at this point Bloom's meditations are cut off by the
applewoman's cry, and his thoughts move to other matters. However, he returns to the subject later in the episode after seeing a
woman walking with AE whom he assumes to be the poetess Lizzie
Twigg—"My literary efforts have had the good fortune to meet with
the approval of the eminent poet A. E. (Mr Geo Russell)" (U 160).
He also assumes that she is a vegetarian.

Her stockings are loose over her ankles. I detest that: so tasteless. Those
literary ethereal people they are all. Dreamy, cloudy, symbolistic. Esthetes
they are. I wouldn't be surprised if it was that kind of food you see produces
the like waves of the brain the poetical. For example one of those policemen sweating Irish stew into their shirts; you couldn't squeeze a line of poetry
out of him. Don't know what poetry is even. Must be in a certain mood.

The dreamy cloudy gull
Waves o'er the waters dull (U 166).

Bloom's notions about the origins of the poetic impulse may
strike us as comic—he himself prefaces his suggestion with the words
"I wouldn't be surprised if . . ."—but the notion that brain power
and artistic talent are affected by the food we eat has often been
seriously advanced by scientists, and the genesis of talent is still
obscure. His comments on the lady's dress are sharp and to the point.
We can understand his unhappiness with esthetes whose stockings
are rumpled. And his comment on the absurdity of imagining that
poetry could come from one of the burly policemen he has seen a
few minutes earlier (U 162) is expressed in a characteristically
appropriate way: "You couldn't *squeeze* a line of poetry out of him."
(Italics mine.) Bloom's revision of the couplet hardly raises the lines
to a high level of poetic achievement, but the impact of the lines is
effectively altered. And he does recapitulate the process which a poet
uses in making revisions.

In "Lestrygonians" Bloom has still other comments to make on
language. In the midst of his effort to recall the limerick about
Mr. McTrigger he remarks not unperceptively that writing
limericks is "easier than the dreamy creamy stuff" (U 172).[11] During
his consideration of the problems of Mrs. Purefoy and the need for

family planning, he gives the *coup de grace* to the inflated rhetoric
of Dan Dawson's speech, a recitation of which he has heard in the
newspaper office: "Time someone thought about [solving the
problem] instead of gassing about the what was it the pensive bosom
of the silver effulgence. Flapdoodle to feed fools on" (*U* 161).[12]
Bloom is not to be taken in by empty rhetoric, whether in political
speeches or advertising copy: "What is home without Plumtree's
potted meat? Incomplete. What a stupid ad!" (*U* 171). And recalling Molly's reaction to his explanation of the meaning of
metempsychosis ("O Rocks!"), he concludes: "She's right after
all. Only big words for ordinary things on account of the sound"
(*U* 154). He savors, too, the irony in vegetarians serving nutsteaks
"to give you the idea you are eating rumpsteak" (*U* 166).[13]

If Bloom's views on formal poetry are unsophisticated, then, he is
nonetheless a shrewd judge of rhetoric. In establishing Bloom's
artistic credentials, however, what he says about words is far less
important than what he does with them. Like all good writers—and
certainly like his creator—he is an incurable tinkerer with language.
Not by him are proverbs and other common sayings to be used in the
solemn Polonian manner. His active intelligence transforms them. An
innocent cliché slightly altered becomes a sardonic and genuinely
witty comment on some aspect of Dublin life. Again and again in
"Lestrygonians" (as in the other Bloom episodes) this process occurs.
A brief meditation on Pat Kinsella, whose Harp Theatre has become
a pub and who has become a beggar, as Bloom supposes, is topped
off by: "The harp that once did starve us all" (*U* 168), a transformation which like all witty remarks sets the mind going in several
directions. His comment on communal dining is, "Never know whose
thoughts you're chewing" (*U* 171); on upper-class manners, "Know
me come eat with me" (*U* 175); and on not knowing what's in the
food one is served, "Too many drugs spoil the broth" (*U* 175). He
sees Mrs. Purefoy as sentenced to "life with hard labour" (*U* 161),
and Nosey Flynn's mouth as being so large that he "could whistle
in his own ear" (*U* 172). Of Professor Goodwin's numerous
"positively last" appearances, he says, "May be for months and may
be for never" (*U* 156).[14]

Bloom's wit expresses itself in other ways as well. "There he is:
the brother. Image of him. Haunting face," he says as John Howard
Parnell walks by. "Look at the woebegone walk of him. Eaten a bad
egg. Poached eyes on ghost" (*U* 165). Only a moment earlier he had
passed the Provost's House of Trinity College: "Provost's house.
The reverend Dr Salmon: tinned salmon. Well tinned in there.

Wouldn't live in it if they paid me" (*U* 164). Perhaps one should
have some notion of the forbidding entrance to the Provost's house
to appreciate this pun fully. But there is no problem with his comment on "Nobleman proud to be descended from some king's
mistress. His foremother" (*U* 167). Bloom's inventiveness is further
evidenced by what he has to say about Tom Moore's statue, pointing
its "roguish finger": "They did right to put him up over a urinal:
meeting of the waters" (*U* 162). (In Ireland Moore's poem "The
Meeting of the Waters," about the confluence of the Avonmore and
the Avonbeg in the Vale of Avoca, has long been extremely popular.)
Toward the end of the scene Bloom's mind brings together two
normally unrelated activities: watching a terrier choke up "a sick
knuckly cud on the cobble stones" and then lap it up "with new
zest," he applies a business cliché, "Returned with thanks having
fully digested the contents" (*U* 179). A loafer gnawing on a bone
inspires an appropriate Want Ad: "Handy man wants job. Small
wages. Will eat anything" (*U* 180). And as he himself considers what
to have for lunch, he muses, "Sandwich? Ham and his descendants
mustered and bred there" (*U* 171).

As one finds more and more of these choice titbits, far more
choice than anything Bloom will ever commit to paper, one wonders
how some critics could have seen him as dull, routine, and stupid. It
is true that he is often inaccurate and that there are many things
he does not know—what I.N.R.I., I.H.S., and AE stand for; what
parallax is; the first name of Carey the Invincible; what the Italian
teco means—but it has seldom been suggested that a man who has a
touch of the poet in him must also have the true pedantic stink. Like
most of us, Bloom is not gifted with total recall. And unlike most
readers of *Ulysses*, his education is minimal and his reading severely
limited. He knows a little school Latin but pretends to no modern
languages. The few foreign phrases he recalls are from songs he has
heard, often songs in Molly's repertory. He is no scholar, nor does he
pretend to be.[15]

But he enjoys words and takes an almost Elizabethan delight in
seeing what they can be made to do. He finds significance in the
similarity of *Carmel* and *caramel* (*U* 155), makes a rather obvious
pun on *Methodist* ("method in his madness") (*U* 161), refers to
Mrs. Purefoy's children as "hardy annuals" (*U* 161), to Queen
Victoria as a "good layer" (*U* 161), and to Farrell's going outside
lampposts as "one way of getting on in the world" (*U* 160). He
describes the well-fed nuns at Mt. Carmel as "buttering themselves in
and out" (*U* 155), Alderman Robert O'Reilly as "Bobbob lapping

[his soup] for the inner alderman" (*U* 155), and persons who are accepted into the Chiltern Hundreds as retiring "*into* public life" (*U* 165). (Italics mine.)

From the start of the episode where he imagines Edward VII seated on his throne "sucking red jujubes white" (*U* 151), Bloom's wit moves frequently and with obvious relish into the grotesque. His notion of visiting the Guinness Brewery leads to:

> Regular world in itself. Vats of porter, wonderful. Rats get in too. Drink themselves bloated as big as a collie floating. Dead drunk on the porter. Drink till they puke again like christians. Imagine drinking that! Rats: vats. Well of course if we knew all the things (*U* 152).

The eating habits of the aristocracy call up "That archduke Leopold was it? No. Yes, or was it Otto one of those Hapsburgs? Or who was it used to eat the scruff off his own head?" This information any one of his acquaintances might have given him. The clincher is all Bloom: "Cheapest lunch in town" (*U* 175). Equally grotesque are the pictures drawn in the following passages:

> Hot fresh blood they prescribe for decline. Blood always needed. Insidious. Lick it up, smoking hot, thick sugary. Famished ghosts (*U* 171).

> All kinds of places are good for ads. That quack doctor for the clap used to be stuck up in all the greenhouses. . . . Strictly confidential. Dr Hy Franks. Didn't cost him a red . . . . Got fellows to stick them up or stick them up himself for that matter on the q.t. running in to loosen a button. Fly by night (*U* 153).

Ready as he is to skewer Dr. Franks with a pun, he is equally ready to make himself the butt of one of his private jokes. Seeing a flock of pigeons whirling about the Parliament House doors, he imagines their conversation: "Who will we do it on? I pick the fellow in black. Here goes. Here's good luck" (*U* 162).

The wit which we have seen Bloom display derives in part from a fascination with language but equally in most instances from a shrewd perception of relationships. Throughout "Lestrygonians" Bloom reveals himself to be a keen observer of what is going on in his vicinity and a knowledgeable, even subtle, commentator on its significance. Here again we find more than a touch of the artist in old Bloom.

He misses very little. When he meets Josie Breen in Westmoreland Street, he notes the contents of her handbag, that she is still wearing the "same blue serge dress she had two years ago," that she has lines around her mouth, "flakes of pastry on the gusset of her dress," and a "daub of sugary flour stuck to her cheek" (*U* 157-158). When he enters the Burton, we are treated, in a passage too long and too well known to be reproduced here, to a stomach-turning account of what he perceives. In the hour or so it takes him to make his way from O'Connell Bridge to the National Museum he observes a thousand details, all of which are carefully recorded for us.

But Bloom does more than merely look about him. Detached as he is from the prejudices and presuppositions which condition the responses of other Dubliners, he can cut deftly through surface appearances to the truth they hide. His judgment on evangelism is a curt "Paying game" (*U* 151). A glimpse of Dilly Dedalus in rags, her health undermined by malnutrition, and he begins to think of the forces responsible for her condition:

> Fifteen children [Dedalus] had. Birth every year almost. That's in their theology or the priest won't give the poor woman the confession, the absolution. Increase and multiply. Did you ever hear such an idea? Eat you out of house and home. [Priests have] no families themselves to feed. Living on the fat of the land . . . . All for number one (*U* 151-152).

As we have seen, the sight of John Howard Parnell brings thoughts of his brother. Bloom had supported the older Parnell and had attended his rallies. A great day in his life was the one on which he returned the great man's hat after it had been knocked off by someone in a mob. But his judgment in 1904 is wholly unsentimental: "His brother used men as pawns. Let them all go to pot" (*U* 165). Nothing separates Bloom from his companions more effectively than this clear-eyed estimate of the Chief. For enthusiasts generally he has little use. Thinking of the Irish patriots and their hopes for "the not far distant day," he muses, "Home Rule sun rising up in the northwest. . . . Useless words. Things go on same; day after day" (*U* 164). "The patriot's banquet," he concludes, is "eating orange-peels in the park" (*U* 165). He knows that youthful radicals rush "into the army helterskelter" when war comes and that half are magistrates or civil servants in a few years (*U* 163); he thinks also that peace and war really depend "on some fellow's digestion" (*U* 172). Equally penetrating are his comments on the essential ingratitude of men (*U* 162), on the methods of informers (*U* 163), on why men go on benders (*U* 167), on the food men eat (*U* 174, 176), and on the power of judges (*U* 183).

Bloom is not, however, merely a commentator. Despite his detachment from many of the concerns of his fellow Dubliners, his musings reflect an intense involvement with the world that streams by him as he walks. Again and again in "Lestrygonians" he expresses his genuine concern for those who are trapped in the cruel mechanisms of society: for Dilly Dedalus, innocent victim of others' beliefs; for Josie Breen, saddled with a lunatic husband; for Minna Purefoy with her unremitting pregnancies and painful deliveries; for the blind piano tuner ("Where is the justice being born that way?" [*U* 182]); for the barefoot arab standing over the gratings at Harrison's restaurant breathing fumes of food he cannot buy (*U* 157); and even for the gulls, whom he feeds, and the "wretched brutes there at the cattlemarket waiting for the poleaxe to split their skulls open" (*U* 171). For all of these Bloom has sympathy—as ultimately he has for himself and for Molly and even for Boylan—because he knows that we cannot help ourselves, cannot help being what we are.

Throughout "Lestrygonians" his concern for individuals and for his country leads him to consider the passing of time and its relation to the human condition. Twice in the early pages of the episode he refers to the stream of life (*U* 153, 155), but his most extensive consideration of the historical process occurs as he passes the gates of Trinity College:

> His smile faded as he walked, a heavy cloud hiding the sun slowly, shadowing Trinity's surly front. Trams passed one another, ingoing, outgoing, clanging. Useless words. Things go on same; day after day: squads of police marching out, back: trams in, out. Those two loonies mooching about. Dignam carted off. Mina Purefoy swollen belly on a bed groaning to have a child tugged out of her. One born every second somewhere. Other dying every second. Since I fed the birds five minutes. Three hundred kicked the bucket. Other three hundred born, washing the blood off, all are washed in the blood of the lamb, bawling maaaaaa.
>
> Cityful passing away, other cityful coming, passing away too: other coming on, passing on. Houses, lines of houses, streets, miles of pavements, piledup bricks, stones. Changing hands. This owner, that. Landlord never dies they say. Other steps into his shoes when he gets his notice to quit. They buy the place up with gold and still they have all the gold. Swindle in it somewhere. Piled up in cities, worn away age after age. Pyramids in sand. Built on bread and onions. Slaves. Chinese wall. Babylon. Big stones left. Round towers. Rest rubble, sprawling suburbs, jerrybuilt, Kerwan's mushroom houses, built of breeze. Shelter for the night.
>
> No one is anything (*U* 164).

Small wonder that his next comment is, "This is the very worst hour on the day. . . . Fell as if I had been eaten and spewed."

Bloom, like Stephen, sees history as inimical to man. But his is not a nightmare full of shattered glass and toppling masonry which must be actively resisted because it stands between him and his future as a creative artist, which must be smashed with an ashplant in Bella Cohen's brothel. Characteristically, Bloom's vision of history is less dramatic than Stephen's, if no less moving and no less real. History is not to be resisted, it is to be accepted. For him the past and the future combine to form an essentially meaningless continuum. Things do not change day after day; they go on the same. Behind them civilizations leave a few artifacts—pyramids, walls, towers, stones—but the rest is rubble. Sustained by no faith, buoyed by no hope, Bloom accepts the ultimate implications of this view of the operations of time: "No one is anything." In the eye of history, the individual is literally nothing. At times in "Lestrygonians" even his own identity in the present seems about to escape him. Thinking of the early years of his marriage, before Rudy was born, when he and Molly were happy if they ever were, he says, "I was happier then." But promptly he wonders, "Or was that I? Or am I now I?" (*U* 168).[16] A few moments later he is saying, "Can't bring back time. Like holding water in your hand," and wondering, "Would you go back to then?" (*U* 168). Since the question is academic, he turns again to the tasks of the present with what Goldberg calls "his humble courage and his unselfconscious aspirations to moral integrity."[17]

Even so brief a survey of one segment of *Ulysses* should demonstrate that Bloom is indeed an extraordinary man. He is "ordinary" only in the eyes of his fellow citizens and in the appurtenances of his life: a routine job, a home like thousands of other middle-class dwellings in Dublin, a very modest bank account, a sketchy and inadequate education, and a wife and child to support. But the real man, whom Dublin never sees but whom we are privileged to observe from a thousand different angles, is quite out of the ordinary, a man with more than a touch of the artist about him, a man whose essentially prosaic mode of thought can even rise to the poetic under the stress of great emotion:

> Hidden under wild ferns on Howth. Below us bay sleeping sky. No sound. The sky. The bay purple by the Lion's Head. Green by Drumleck. Yellow-green towards Sutton. Fields of undersea, the lines faint brown in grass, buried cities. Pillowed on my coat she had her hair, earwigs in the heather scrub my hand under her nape . . . . . O wonder! Coolsoft with ointments her hand touched me, caressed . . . (*U* 176).

From "Lestrygonians" to Ithaca the road is long and hard, and Ulysses-Bloom is sorely tried. He is betrayed, insulted, and abused by inhabitants of the city. As style begins to dominate the book, his image is wrenched and contorted for us as if he were trapped in a house of distorting mirrors at a carnival. But in the end the image of Bloom which Joyce creates in the early sections remains essentially unaffected. As the day wears on, the wit, the perception, the compassion, the "justness and reasonableness"[18] of Bloom prevail.

Lawrence University

NOTES

1. Frank Budgen, *James Joyce and the Making of "Ulysses"* (1934; Bloomington: Indiana University Press, 1960), p. 116.

2. "Bloom on Joyce; or, Jokey for Jacob," *Journal of Modern Literature*, 1(First Issue 1970), 23.

3. *The Joyce Paradox: Form and Freedom in His Fiction* (London: Routledge & Kegan Paul, 1966), p. 83.

4. *The Classical Temper: A Study of James Joyce's "Ulysses"* (London: Chatto and Windus, 1963), p. 107.

5. *The Art of James Joyce: Method and Design in "Ulysses" and "Finnegans Wake"* (New York: Oxford University Press, 1964), pp. 39-40.

6. There is one intrusive element, to be sure: the multitudinous references to food and its consumption, which are designed to satisfy the Odyssean parallel. However, despite their ubiquitousness, they are so closely tied in with Bloom's activities during the episode that for most readers they are not really a distorting mechanism.

7. *Ulysses on the Liffey* (New York: Oxford University Press, 1972), p. 29. Hereafter *UL*.

8. Interestingly, he seems to have had some good friends in the past—his schoolmates Percy Apjohn and Owen Goldberg and neighbors Mastiansky and Citron—but by June of 1904 all are dead or have moved away.

9. In fact, we see very little of Dublin city through Stephen's eyes. We find him in the Martello Tower, in a private school, on Sandymount Strand, in a newspaper office, in the National Library, in the maternity hospital, in Bella Cohen's, and in 7 Eccles Street. In "Aeolus" he and the newspapermen go from the *Freeman* office to Mooney's; but they are in animated conversation during their walk. In "Eumaeus" he does take to the streets; but then he is in the company of Bloom, and are given little evidence of his reactions, and the streets are empty. The characteristic pattern of the Stephen episodes which take place in the city is a prolonged discussion in which Stephen plays a leading role, followed by an eruption into the street and a prompt ending. Although we are led to believe that Stephen spends some time wandering alone in Dublin, we are not permitted to see him do so, except for two brief glimpses in "Wandering Rocks."

10. In the famous letter to Grant Richards, May 5, 1906. *Letters* II, 134.

11. This tiny dot in the vast mosaic of *Ulysses* will reappear slightly altered in "Circe," where Mananaan MacLir (AE) chants: "I am the light of the homestead, I am the dreamery creamery butter" (*U* 510).

12. The fact that Bloom's memory brings together two unrelated phrases from the speech only emphasizes the validity of his condemnation of Dawson's empty rhetoric.

13. In the Burton Bloom considers another aspect of language. Seeing a man "ramming a kniveful of cabbage down," he hits upon a *bon mot*: "Born with a silver knife in his mouth. That's witty I think. Or no. Silver means born rich. Born with a knife. But then the allusion is lost (*U* 170).

14. One might argue that some of the witticisms are not original. The evidence of the text, however, suggests that Joyce wishes us to credit Bloom with all of them. Elsewhere Bloom is scrupulous in acknowledging the source of wit he admires. On p. 165, for example, he refers to what "Simon Dedalus said" about what Parnell would have done if his brother had been elected to Parliament. And in "Hades," on p. 103, we find: "Burst sideways like a sheep in clover Dedalus says

he will. . . . Most amusing expressions that man finds." There is nowhere any suggestion that all of the puns, parodies, and other examples of wit which I have cited are not to be taken as the products of Bloom's own imagination.

15. A few years ago Edward C. McAleer provided us with a comprehensive listing of Bloom's errors and a brief comparison of the "Brilliant," "provocative" Stephen with poor old bumbling Bloom. Not surprisingly, McAleer's bias led him to the conclusion that Bloom's "is essentially the mind of a business man." ("The Ignorance of Mr. Bloom" in Richard Beale Davis and John L. Livesay, eds., *Studies in Honor of Hodges and Thaler, Tennessee Studies in Literature,* Special Number, 1961, pp. 121-29.)

16. In this episode Bloom looks frequently back to the happier days. On p. 155 he thinks of Molly at the Glencree dinner in 1894: "Happy. Happier then." And on pp. 175-76 he relives the afternoon on Howth and thinks: "Me. And me now." His thoughts about his own identity echo Stephen's on pp. 189-90 and in *A Portrait,* p. 240.

17. Goldberg, p. 262.

18. Joyce's terms. Budgen, p. 116.

Morton P. Levitt

A HERO FOR OUR TIME:
LEOPOLD BLOOM AND THE MYTH OF ULYSSES

I

It is an unalterably boring book, the analyst declared, over seven hundred pages of chaotic nonsense which consistently put him to sleep, a work as readable from the end as from the beginning, infuriating in its difficulty and monotony, "a positively brilliant and hellish monster-birth." Surely, he would never accuse the author of being psychotic, yet somehow it seemed "all too familiar" to him, like "those endless writings of the insane who have at their disposal only a disrupted consciousness and who therefore suffer from a complete lack of judgment and from atrophy of all their values." Even the dense accuracy of its detail was infuriating—"If worms were gifted with literary powers they would write with the sympathetic nervous system for lack of a brain. I suspect that something of this kind has happened to Joyce...."

This is Carl Gustav Jung speaking, in 1932, not of a single chapter from *Work in Progress* but of the whole of *Ulysses*, ten years after its publication.[1] Jung eventually finished reading the novel, found it in some ways instructive, perhaps even as affirmation for some of his own psychoanalytic theories.[2] But he persisted in viewing it as essentially negative, a work of art without a soul, its creator "more 'bereft of gods' than Nietzsche himself ever dreamed of being." "What is so staggering about *Ulysses*," he went on, "is the fact that behind a thousand veils nothing lies hidden; that it turns neither towards the mind nor towards the world, but, cold as the moon looking on from cosmic space, allows the drama of growth, being, and decay to pursue its course. I earnestly hope that *Ulysses* is not symbolic, for were it so it would have missed its aim. What kind of carefully guarded secret might it be that is hidden with matchless care under seven hundred and thirty five unendurable pages?"

And yet, paradoxically, in a way that its author could not have anticipated, Jung concluded that the novel was valuable precisely because it was soulless, because its disjunction of character, incident and form reflected perfectly the anarchy of its times: "all that is negative in the Joycean work, all that is coldblooded, bizarre and banal, grotesque and devilish, are positive virtues for which it deserves praise. . . . [For] in this mudhole is reflected with a blasphemous distortion very nearly all that is highest in religious thought, exactly as in dreams."

132

It is easy to judge Jung harshly from the perspective of 1972. We know a great deal today about the symbolic levels of *Ulysses*, about the meticulous care which Joyce brought to its construction, about the many ways it can delight the attentive reader. Most of all, we know something of what has happened in the world during the past forty years—about Dachau and Hiroshima and My Lai. Jung spoke of the novel as a manifestation of "the collective unconscious of the modern psyche," and perhaps it is—although hardly in the negative sense that he intended. For the seeming disjunction that he found in *Ulysses* may appear to us now not simply as a sign of the chaos and anarchy that govern our lives, but as a way out of this modern dilemma, as a partial solution to the existential *angst* that affects us all. Had he been a more patient reader, Jung might have found in *Ulysses* verification of his own most significant literary and social theories—evidence of the continued functioning of mythic archetypes and of their relation to modern society and to the whole of human history. *Ulysses* is more than the compilation of mythic formulas that we may have viewed it as; it is itself a new myth, a new sense of commitment to life, and the drama of being and growth which it develops does not end with decay.

II

Of all the critical clichés inspired by *Ulysses*, none is more persistent than the belief that this is a novel whose characters and events are derived from a unique amalgam of myths and that its central myth is provided by the *Odyssey* of Homer. We know that Joyce was interested in the character of Ulysses from adolescence, that he read widely as an adult in the post-Homeric Odyssean tradition, that he named the chapters of his novel for Homeric episodes, omitting the titles only in his final manuscript and then ensuring their continued use through the chart he provided for Stuart Gilbert. " 'I am now writing a book,' " Joyce told Frank Budgen in the summer of 1918, " 'based on the wanderings of Ulysses. The Odyssey, that is to say, serves me as a ground plan. Only my time is recent time and all my hero's wanderings take no more than eighteen hours.' "[3] The contradictory body of scholarship arising from these few indisputable facts is quite extraordinary.

Larbaud spoke out first: the *Odyssey*, he claimed, was "the very web" of *Ulysses*, the key to understanding the characterization and plot of the novel.[4] To this T. S. Eliot added that the Homeric analogue provided as well a kind of moral order for Joyce, a means of giving shape and definition to "the immense panorama of futility and anarchy which is contemporary history."[5] Thus, the basic argument was framed within a year of the novel's publication: to appreciate *Ulysses* fully, we were told, we must first understand the use which the novelist has made of the Homeric original. But other early critics were less favorably impressed with Joyce's epic endeavors. The parallel with Homer, they argued, was "far-fetched" and "nonsense,"[6] for literal correspondences alone could not recreate the true spirit of the epic;[7] and besides, they said irritably, Joyce was not even a very good classicist.[8]

Even to some of its admirers, the Homeric plan of *Ulysses* has seemed rigid and unnatural,[9] or merely superficial in the way that it actually functions,[10] its symbolic components only remotely analogous to the realistic events which dominate the novel.[11] At best, it seemed that Homer might have provided what Harry Levin called the "scaffolding" upon which Joyce constructed his narrative, to be removed when the edifice was completed. "The immediate effect of this [symbolic] method," Levin pointed out, "is to reduce his characters to mock-heroic absurdity."[12] *Ulysses* in this view is not basically mythic at all; it makes use of Homer only as an aspect of its parody and social satire, in order to demonstrate the inversion of mythic values in modern times.[13] The comparison between Bloom and Odysseus thus becomes one more way of reminding us ironically of the diminution of the epic spirit in our own meager lives. Yet even Levin agreed that the irony implicit in Joyce's handling of myth in some way magnified the characters as it diminished them, for it gave them the dignity at least of universality.

This ambiguity about Bloom as hero has degenerated more recently into an argument about plot—and a conjectural plot at that: the probable events of June 17, 1904, and their implications for the Blooms and indeed for all of mankind. Ordering breakfast in bed somehow makes Bloom heroic, we are told, or fails to do so; somehow it represents new life for him and for Molly—and thus for us all—or else is no more than a tired man's natural request.[14] This hardly seems the stuff of heroism whatever its implications, but perhaps it is the best that we can attain to in our century.

Finally, there is that body of scholarship which suggests that the Homeric analogy is simply one part of a complex matrix of specific bodies of myth—including among others Shakespeare, Aristotle, Blake, Dante and the gods and heroes of ancient Ireland[15]— which together enable us to judge the actions of Bloom and Stephen and Molly and the rest. It is in this spirit that we are now confronted with explanations of why Bloom masturbates, of why Molly menstruates, of why Stephen picks his nose: metaphysical problems as well as mythical ones.[16]

In retrospect, this entire argument about Homer is as irrelevant today as it once seemed inevitable. We have been reminded in this anniversary year that the Homeric parallels which Joyce had in mind were many and detailed—whether he provided them for Gilbert and Gorman or for Carlo Linati; and we have been told once again that they function thematically along with the bodily organs associated with each chapter, as well presumably as with the colors and art forms that Joyce listed alongside them. But today we may be harder to convince of their significance than we once were.

We may well wonder today precisely how the Homeric parallels are supposed to help us to understand the action and themes of the novel. Does it help, for example, to link the narrator of "Cyclops" with the scurrilous Thersites? to find Joyce listing Alcinous and Arete among the implicit characters of "Nausicaa"? to look for the old nurse Eurycleia in "Ithaca"? even to view Stephen as Telemachus? For what does it really tell us about Stephen Dedalus to identify him with the Ithacan prince? That as a child he was almost sacrificed by his father as a means of escaping the draft? that he is desperately striving to salvage his patrimony from a mother who seems unable to control her own affairs? that he competes with his father to bend the great bow and annihilate the suitors? that in a later myth he will kill off his father by means of a surrogate and then marry his mother, again through a surrogate? Only the general parallel is truly helpful: like Telemachus, Stephen is a young man anxiously working to find himself, to develop functional values in a world given over to chaos, perhaps even, as the cliché has it, to find a surrogate father. But we need not label him "Telemachus" in order to learn any of this.

The Homeric myth in *Ulysses* serves three main functions, none of them quite as vital or as pervasive as we have sometimes believed. (1) It does provide character and incident, and even structure and theme, for Joyce's narrative but only to a limited extent, for the parallels are not particularly close: on the simplest level, as when the moly of Odysseus becomes Bloom's potato, they are little more than a kind of ironic joke; at their best, they may function as metaphor, enabling us at times to see new possibilities in the naturalistic events of the novel—the near-blindness of the bar dwellers in "Cyclops" acts in this way. (2) It offers as well a certain ironic counterpoint between Homeric ideals and those of our time, reinforcing our awareness of the decline in our values. Here too, however, this aspect of Homer relates not so much to the pro-tagonists as to such minor characters as Gerty MacDowell and Mr.

Deasy. For them, briefly as they appear, we are content with the note that reminds us, "this is our Princess Nausicaa; this is what has become of the wisdom of Nestor." But we know too much about Stephen and Bloom to be content with such facile formulations about them; for them we need more precise images, a more telling myth. (3) Finally, and most significantly, the frequent analogues from Homer—we might almost call them post-Homeric similes—create a sense of continuity between Mycenaean civilization and our own, an awareness that the problems confronting Bloom are strangely like those which Odysseus must deal with, indeed which all men must face. But even here the *Odyssey* is one aspect only of the larger pattern of myth that operates in the novel—not as a collection of individual myths but as a collective archetype—the pattern that Jung should have seen but could not.

III

"The universal hero myth . . . always refers to a powerful man or god-man who vanquishes evil in the form of dragons, serpents, monsters, demons, and so on, and who liberates his people from destruction and death."[17] This is Jung speaking again, and he hardly appears to be speaking of Bloom. We have only to compare Joyce's hero with a contemporary figure, the Odysseus of Nikos Kazantazakis' *The Odyssey: A Modern Sequel*, to see how little the Jew seems to fit Jung's mythic archetype. Kazantzakis' character is larger than life-size, more powerful by far than the heroes around him, more demanding even than his prototype. He too contends with the forces of society and nature, contends with himself and with God, as he seeks what Jung labels "the soul of man"—the union of civilized consciousness and basic instinct—the goal of all human mythmaking. He is the product of a long series of fertility archetypes, not only of Homer's Odysseus, but of Mithra and Buddha and Christ, and we sense that such a hero could surely free us all by his example.

Poor Bloom, in contrast, seems even more of a schlemiel. And yet Bloom too attains a certain mythic dignity—and not merely as the first of our anti-heroes; he too has his dragons to kill, and in strange, paradoxical ways, he too may be able to liberate us. In the microcosmic world of Homer's epic, the original Odysseus could serve as representative of all Mycenae and of all Bronze Age values; yet there has long been ambiguity about the worth of his character, a controversy going back at least to Hesiod and Pindar and perhaps even to Homer and his sources.[18] Kazantzakis as well, writing at the same time as Joyce, could draw upon the unique history and culture of his native Crete and posit a hero able to surmount the despair that surrounds him; yet there is a certain atavism in his personality that almost inevitably offends Western sensibilities. In a world suddenly bereft of Homeric virtues, in a world in which ambiguity is everywhere, Leopold Bloom—neither a powerful man nor god-man—is more of a hero than he could ever imagine. With overpowering irony, Bloom, who can father no son, becomes in a sterile universe a sort of archetype of fertility.

Once freed of Homer, Bloom appears as both less and more than a modern Odysseus. He is a schlemiel, to be sure, but he almost alone perseveres: we need only to look at his fictional successors to appreciate this—at Malamud's Fixer and Bellow's Mr. Sammler, at the dying Artemio Cruz in the novel by Carlos Fuentes, at the nearly despairing protagonists of Claude Simon, at the whole town of Macondo in *One Hundred Years of Solitude*, by Gabriel García Márquez, even at Updike's Rabbit. In the midst of defeat, they too somehow affirm traditional humanistic values in a seemingly valueless world, and it is the lesson of Bloom that leads them to this somewhat victory. The fertility archetype develops throughout the novel, but it grows most notably in "Ithaca," as Bloom returns home from the wasteland.

IV

From Agendath Netaim, the "planter's company" (*U* 60) of the pork butcher's handout, Bloom has drawn in his mind a verdant picture of the Zionist homeland. But the passing grey cloud, as well perhaps as untouched memories of Rudy, turns it into a seering image of the wasteland of life: "A barren land, bare waste. Volcanic lake, the dead sea: no fish, weedless, sunk deep in the earth. No wind would lift those waves, grey metal, poisonous foggy waters. . . . A dead sea in a dead land, grey and old. . . . Now it could bear no more" (*U* 61). Yet almost immediately, Bloom makes an unconscious affirmation of life, as he echoes unawares the words of Abraham offering up Isaac for sacrifice: "Henani, Lord, I am here." "Well, I am here now," thinks Bloom, who has no son to give to his God (*U* 61). Bloom of course is no Abraham; he himself demonstrates this when he confuses the patriarch with his son (*U* 76). (The story that he soon starts to tell of the near drowning of Reuben J. Dodd's son may even be a parody of the Biblical scene.) But he does represent a certain ethnic and spiritual continuity of his own.[19]

Bloom refuses as well to be Lazarus, to be Christ, to be Parnell or Moses, but the fertility symbolism inherent in each of these figures carries over in part to him. The raising of Lazarus, he decides, is absurd: "The resurrection and the life. Once you are dead you are dead. That last day idea. Knocking them all up out of their graves. Come forth, Lazarus! And he came fifth and lost the job" (*U* 105). When THE END OF THE WORLD does come up in Nighttown, it is to the tune of a Scottish dance and the revivalist dicta of "A.J. Christ Dowie and the harmonial philosophy" (*U* 508), that same "Alexander J. Christ Dowie that's yanked to glory most half this planet from 'Frisco Beach to Vladivostok" (*U* 428). Yet Bloom is sympathetic to the picture of Mary and Martha, the sisters of Lazarus, and implicitly to the Savior that they are the first to acknowledge (*U* 79, 117). To the extent that Martha of Bethany is identified in his mind with that other Martha from Dolphin's Barn, we might almost contend that Bloom himself becomes Jesus, and at the same time his predecessor, Lazarus—except, of course, that he is obviously unaware that they are all related. And although he claims a certain kinship with Jesus (*U* 342, 643), his knowledge of the Savior is limited and his reactions to him ambiguous. Presumably he has read both *The Hidden Life of Christ* (*U* 709) and *Was Jesus a Sun Myth?* (*U* 485); he recalls with mixed admiration and scorn an advertisement for a luminous crucifix: "Wake up in the dead of night and see him on the wall, hanging. . . . Iron nails ran in" (*U* 151); he reacts with impatience to Father Vaughan's sermon on the need to make moral choices: "Christ or Pilate? Christ, but don't keep us up all night over it" (*U* 82). Yet it is to Bloom that the Daughters of Erin pray for salvation (*U* 498), and Bloom who wears amidst the phoenix flames the robe marked I.H.S. "I have sinned," it proclaims, "or no: I have suffered, it is" (*U* 81).

A martyr like Parnell, with something of the great man's own "fascination" (*U* 163)—note the various women attracted to him— Bloom too has a dream of a Promised Land in which all men can prosper. "The new Bloomusalem in the Nova Hibernia of the future" he calls it (*U* 484), and in his hands it turns into a comic mélange of fantasy and reality, of individual citizens and their universal dreams. It is not political independence that they demand from Parnell-Bloom, or even mere moral probity, but legal and medical advice that they desire, scientific and astrological data, suburban gardens and mixed bathing. He is, we must remember, "the funniest man on earth" (*U* 491) and not a parliamentarian.

A false Messiah he may be, a scapegoat without doubt (*U* 497),[20] but he is also a good deal more. "In Bloom," declares one critic, a bit hyperbolically no doubt, "Stephen finds his Moses."[21] A Joking

Moses perhaps, for this character too he distorts: what catches his eye
in the bogus Mosaic text that he finds on the Bedford row bookstall
is hardly the revelation of the Law: "How to soften chapped hands.
Recipe for white wine vinegar. How to win a woman's love" (*U* 242).
Yet Moses of Egypt is one of his guises (*U* 495), as well as progenitor
of that long line of saviors whose culmination is Bloom. Like Moses,
he will view the Promised Land only from afar; his Pisgah Sight
of Palestine is in imagination alone.

Bloom, we must reluctantly agree, is no resurrection deity to in-
spire us, no more convincing as Parnell or Moses than he is as Abraham, Lazarus or Christ. Yet the fertility echoes persist, accompanying him throughout the day, in "Lestrygonians" and "Nausicaa,"
in "Circe" and especially in "Ithaca." We perceive them in his attraction to the sensuality of the East and in his attraction to women;
in the seedcake that Molly passes to him on Howth Hill (*U* 176—
leave it to Bloom to reverse the usual process); in the globe that he
Paris-like passes to Gerty-Aphrodite and in the "warm flush" that he
draws to her cheeks (*U* 356); even in his Onanism on the beach (another fertility image that he manages to distort, becoming with Onan
the very name for reluctance). There are the naked goddesses from
the Kildare street museum: Venus Callipyge of the well-shaped
buttocks, Venus Pandemos, patron of marriage and family life,
Venus metempsychosis (*U* 490); there is his marriage to Selene,
goddess of the phases of the moon (*U* 483), still another role
for Molly; there is even his well-borne potato, his "heirloom"
and "talisman" (*U* 476), a symbol of the continuity of life (and thus
traditionally eaten with hard-boiled eggs after Jewish funerals). To
the dying Veiled Sibyl, he is "my hero god," and, like a god of the
corn, he is finally done in by "midsummer madness" (*U* 492). But
Bloom will live to return home once again.

V

For Odysseus—in both Kazantzakis and Homer—the quest is more
real than the goal. (Thus virtually his first words to Penelope in the
Odyssey are to tell her of the prophecy that he must soon be travel-
ling again, while the modern sequel deals almost exclusively with
those final voyages.) For Bloom, however, not the journey but
Ithaca is all. It is in this seemingly anticlimactic chapter, especially
after Stephen's departure, that we see the culmination of fertility
images in Eccles Street, the full development of Bloom as archetype.

Even the form of the chapter is appropriate to the myth: the
questions and answers of Bloom's silent monologue suggest a kind of

popular catechism of the rationalism of the age, that ethic of faith in reason to which Bloom is devoted but which has so patently failed him. "Modern man," wrote Jung, "does not understand how much his 'rationalism' (which has destroyed his capacity to respond to numinous symbols and ideas) has put him at the mercy of the psychic 'underworld.' He has freed himself from 'superstition' (or so he believes), but in the process he has lost his spiritual values to a positively dangerous degree. His moral and spiritual tradition has disintegrated, and he is now paying the price for this break-up in worldwide disorientation and dissociation. . . . There are no longer any gods whom we can invoke to help us."[22] Bloom has long since discovered this fact, for there have never been gods upon whom he could call. Nevertheless, no matter how alien he may be to his neighbors, he has never been alienated from life.

"Ithaca" is filled with minor echoes of fertility myths: the solar year (U 668), the end of the drought (U 671), the healing hand of the god as surgeon (U 674); Bloom's symbolic name with its various anagrams (U 678) as well as his multiple baptisms (U 682); the "heaventree of stars" looking down upon him and Stephen (U 698), the affinities between the moon and the woman (U 702), their paean of praise to the moon goddess above them (U 702); even the church bells that ring out Stephen's guilt (U 704) sound the future resurrection of man. Neither separately nor together do these echo that Bloom will redeem us, but a related pattern may suggest just that: these are the images of the Passover, the feast that celebrates the symbolic death and rebirth of the Jewish people.

They begin with Stephen and Bloom in the kitchen, again in a minor key—in the songs sung by Stephen, in the scene that he narrates for his host, in the verse recited by Bloom. They also tell us something of the character of the celebrants. The anti-Semitism of "Little Harry Hughes" (U 690-91) is a Christian perversion of the Passover ritual and its implications for moral renewal; that renewal is at least partly thwarted during the Exodus from Egypt (U 698), as Moses must view the Promised Land from afar (A Pisgah Sight of Palestine, U 685): these signs of failure are delivered by Stephen. Bloom sings of hope for the future in the Zionist anthem (U 689)— although of course he remembers it only in part.

After Stephen has left, Bloom the Wandering Jew—"suncompelled," "a sleeper awakened," he would "obey the summons of recall . . . [and] reappear reborn . . ." (U 728)—makes up the sum of his day's activities, recollects the key events of his life. Nearly all are connected in some way with Passover and Palestine. Thus, Agendath Netaim, once a wasteland in Bloom's consciousness, becomes again the land of promise and honey, of olive groves and orange fields and melon plantations. Early in the day it recalled the sterility of both Bloom and his people; now it is merely a practical affair foreseen by a man of science (*U* 718). Through the objective format of "Ithaca" Bloom can disguise even to himself the emotional depths of his responses. But we cannot forget its reminder of Rudolph and Rudy, of the dead heir and the seemingly dying tradition; not coincidentally, the ancient hagadah and the suicide note of his father now reappear together (*U* 723). In the prayer book for Passover— a fertility festival founded on a kind of symbolic sterility (the death of the first-born of Egypt) and itself the source of its own replacement in myth (the Last Supper)—we find a sign of continuing tradition; in the suicide note and its inevitable recollection of Rudy, we see the apparent death of tradition. Bloom, the "last [of] my race" (*U* 285), will reach Palestine only in imagination ([*U* 726]—and even here his journey ends at the Dead Sea); he has found no surrogate son on this night and will likely make no new one of his own in the morning. No resurrection deity indeed, yet there are overtones of rebirth even as he falls into sleep: the womb, the roc's auk's egg, Sinbad the Sailor and Darkinbad the Brightdayler (*U* 737) are all images of awakening from sleep.

Bloom fails as businessman, fails as husband and father, fails even as Jew to understand his sole heritage. The first of the modern schlemiel heroes, he seems on the surface to justify fully Jung's complaints about disorder and disorientation. Yet somehow we sense that the fertility echoes—inconsistent as they may be—are perhaps a warning that Bloom cannot be dismissed so easily, that the disjunction surrounding us is not in his life but in ours, that Bloom may represent one of the few remaining paths to the Promised Land in our time. Again, we turn to Jung: "When we attempt to understand symbols, we are not only confronted with the symbol itself, but we are brought up against the wholeness of the symbol-producing individual. This includes a study of his cultural background. . . . If we try to see such a situation with the eyes of the believer, we can perhaps understand how the ordinary man can be liberated from his personal impotence and misery and endowed (at least temporarily) with an almost super-human quality. Often enough such a conviction will sustain him for a long time and give a certain style to his life. It may even set the tone of a whole society."[23] Bloom is sustained by the remnants of a cultural heritage that insists that individual lives do have merit, that there is meaning to life in general, that there can be dignity and order even in the midst of disorder. The Passover images—never fully unified and at times even comic in their misapplication ("that brought us out of the land of Egypt and into the house of bondage," as he remembers a prayer, [U 122])—are an ever-present sign of that heritage.

Bloom is hardly a true believer, but he does believe in his heart of hearts that he could well be the Savior ("and his name shall be called Emmanuel," [U 496]). In an earlier day, we would undoubtedly have chosen a hero less ambiguous and more compelling, but in the urban world in which we all live, no man could be more representative.[24] It is thus no longer sufficient to agree that Bloom in his way is affirmative,[25] that he is ennobled in part by the parallel with Odysseus,[26] or that *Ulysses* is a modern translation of Homer, akin in both situation and spirit.[27] It is, in effect, a new myth of its own, borrowing from the old yet perfectly appropriate to its own time, and Bloom is its indispensable, albeit not unambiguous hero.

VI

Leopold Bloom is no fertility godhead, not even a distant descendant of the godlike heroes whose names are associated with his, and the images of Passover and Palestine—of the remnants of his Jewishness—are no substitute for Homeric mythology. However, they do make explicit the essential creativity of this unexpected hero and his value for a world searching anxiously for value. The only affirmation that we at one time could see in *Ulysses* was that of James Joyce himself, the artist who had completed his act of creation—the Modernist view;[28] only now can we begin to perceive that Bloom is not merely a Modernist hero announcing the breakdown of traditional values, but perhaps even the first of our positive post-Modernist heroes, holding out by his example the possibility of re-integration in life: the symbol of one generation and herald of the next. The myth of *Ulysses*, according to such a schema, is thus not merely a means of ordering art but a way of giving meaning to life, not simply a borrowing from earlier myth but itself the source of new borrowings. Half a century of chaos has made this view increasingly convincing and ever more necessary.

If each age invents its own Homer, as T.S. Eliot and Hugh Kenner suggest,[29] then why not a new Joyce for each new generation? Surely *Ulysses* is as seminal a work for us as the *Iliad* and *Odyssey* were for Vergil, Dante, Milton, Pope, Keats and for Joyce as well. And we surely have need in 1972 of some confirmation of the continuity of tradition and culture. Fifty years ago, Joyce could tell us with a shock of recognition that the orderly world of the Victorians had disintegrated forever, that the new reality supplanting that of Thackeray and Dickens was nonomniscient, nondirective, ambiguous. But even his ambiguity did not unsettle us totally. He rattled the poles of reality, but he did not uproot them; there was as yet no need for reassurance fifty years ago that life still had value, that life would go on. Looking back on 1922 from the perspective of the most self-destructive half-century in history, we may find the Joycean discontinuity perversely affirmative, for it seems now to assure us that at least there still is a reality, even if it is no longer objective, that our sense of the meaning of life may have changed, but that the surface of life at least can go on as before.

Saul Bellow speaks of the urban world of 1972, the world mirrored by Joyce, the world that Joyce helped to create: "It is the deep conviction of vast numbers of individuals that they have no proper story. Their personal experience of storylessness, and hence of value-lessness, is very great. . . . Joyce meant to say, I think, that there is a remaining significance in myth which sustains the individual. . . . What is truly human for Joyce turns out to be protean comical unfitness, a defeatedness which may secretly be victorious, an acceptance of huge and hopeless disorder and impotency which, alone, can liberate great energies and give the human being transcendent powers denied the ambitious and purposive." "Joyce's purpose," Bellow concludes, "is to bring us through the hell of modern consciousness, to master the schizophrenia it induces, to purge us, to redeem us."[30]

This, it seems, may be the ultimate function—for 1972 at least—of the myth of *Ulysses*. Even in apparent mediocrity, Bloom is consoling today precisely because nothing is foreign to him, because nothing in him is foreign to us. In him we discover almost willing alienation, the acceptance of outsiderness as an act of potential creation. Bloom is an ironic hero for our time, but unlike Lermontov's uneasy and disjointed hero, who is one of his ancestors, he will survive, and perhaps he will help us as well—outsiders all—to survive. This may well be the most fertile myth that we today can create. "With the light of inspiration shining in his countenance and bearing in his arms the secret of the race" (*U* 676), Bloom points the way to a renewal—of sorts—for us all, to the possibility of new life in an impoverished world.

Temple University

NOTES

1. "Ulysses," *Europäische Revue*, 9 (1932), 547-68, as rpt. under the title "Ulysses—A Monologue" in *Nimbus*, 2 (1953), 7-20. "There is no way of assessing the influence of 'Ulysses,' the essay published by Carl Jung in 1932, although almost every book about *Ulysses* or Joyce's work which was published after that date mentions it explicitly; but whatever its influence, Jung appropriately created the archetype" (Stanley Sultan, *The Argument of "Ulysses"* [Columbus: Ohio State University Press, 1964], p. 9).

2. "What, if anything, Jung got out of 'Circe' to suggest or support his theory of Anima-Animus is entirely uncertain; but what he published more than ten years later in the chapter entitled 'Anima and Animus' in *The Relations Between the Ego and the Unconscious* certainly helps the reader to understand better the transformations that take place in Nighttown" (Elliott Coleman, "A Note on Joyce and Jung", *JJQ*, 1 [Fall 1963], 11).

3. Frank Budgen, *James Joyce and the Making of "Ulysses"* (1934; Bloomington: Indiana University Press, 1960), p. 15.

4. Valery Larbaud, "James Joyce," *Nouvelle Revue Francaise*, 18 (1922), 385-405, rpt. in *James Joyce: The Critical Heritage*, ed. Robert H. Deming (New York: Barnes and Noble, 1970), I, 261. Hereafter *CH*. The most detailed explications of the Homeric analogues may be found, of course, in Stuart Gilbert's *James Joyce's "Ulysses,"* 2nd ed. (1930; New York: Knopf, 1952), as well as in Joseph Prescott's *Exploring James Joyce* (Carbondale: Southern Illinois University Press, 1964). Howard Jacobson in "Joyce and the *Iliad*: A Suggestion," *JJQ*, 7 (Winter 1970), 141-42, adds that parallels from the *Iliad* supplant those from the *Odyssey* in the climactic confrontation between Stephen and Bloom in "Eumaeus." Cf. W. B. Stanford, *The Ulysses Theme: A Study in the Adaptability of a Traditional Hero* (Oxford: Basil Blackwell, 1954): "Some Iliadic qualities are also noticed. Bloom . . . is not without secret ambitions to excel as a *politique* . . . (p. 216).

5. "Ulysses, Order, and Myth," *The Dial*, Nov. 1923, rpt. in *James Joyce: Two Decades of Criticism*, ed. Seon Givens (New York: Vanguard Press, 1963), pp. 198-202.

6. Sisley Huddleston, *Back to Montparnasse* (1931), rpt. in *CH* II, 549.

7. Rebecca West, "James Joyce and his Followers," *New York Herald Tribune* (Jan. 12, 1930), rpt. in *CH* II, 534-37.

8. The conservative English and Irish positions may be found, respectively, in Herbert Read, "The High Priest of Modern Literature," *Listener* (Aug. 20, 1930), rpt. in *CH* II, 520-22, and the anonymous A Fellow Dubliner, "The Veritable James Joyce according to Stuart Gilbert and Oliver St. John Gogarty," *International Forum* (July 1931), rpt. in *CH* II, 556-69.

9. Edmund Wilson, "Ulysses," *New Republic*, 31 (July 5, 1922), 164-66.

10. Elliot Paul, "Farthest North: A Study of James Joyce," *Bookman*, 75 (1932), rpt. in *CH* II, 372-74.

11. Desmond MacCarthy, "Le roman anglais d'après-guerre," *Revue de Paris* (May 1932), rpt. in *CH* II, 574-76.

12. *James Joyce: A Critical Introduction* (Norfolk, Conn.: New Directions, 1941), pp. 71-6.

13. Rudolph Von Abele, "*Ulysses*: The Myth of Myth," *PMLA*, 69 (1954), 358-64. The suggestion that myth functions as parody in *Ulysses*—either serious in intent or simply as comedy—has been advanced by Richard M. Kain in *Fabulous Voyager: James Joyce's "Ulysses"* (1947; New York: Viking Press, 1959) and by

William York Tindall in *A Reader's Guide to James Joyce* (New York: Noonday Press, 1959). It has been rejected, however, by Richard Ellmann in "Ulysses the Divine Nobody," *Yale Review*, 47 (Autumn 1957), 56-71 and Hugh Kenner in "Joyce's *Ulysses*: Homer and Hamlet," *Essays in Criticism*, 2 (Jan. 1952), 85-104. Vivienne Koch, in "An Approach to the Homeric Content of Joyce's *Ulysses*," *Briarcliff* (now *Maryland Quarterly*), 1 (1944), 119-30, avoids the issue of parody but contends that the correspondences are not literal but of tone and quality, as an inevitable demonstration of the change from Homer's time to our own.

14. The issue of Bloom's breakfast and its potential implications was originally raised by Wilson, but its most forceful exposition comes from Sultan: "*Ulysses* asserts that Bloom's only salvation is in becoming a proper husband and father again, and provides not only personal and social but also explicitly religious grounds for the assertion; . . . *Ulysses* presents, as an instrumental factor in the rescue of its protagonists, direct divine intervention in events—that is to say, miracle" (p. 455).

15. Virtually everyone who has written on the novel has dealt to some extent with the influence of Shakespeare and Dante, Kenner most specifically perhaps on the mythic possibilities of *Hamlet* for Stephen; the subject of Blake as myth in *Ulysses* has been put forth by S. Foster Damon, "The Odyssey in Dublin," *Hound and Horn* (1929), rpt. in Givens, 203-42; of Aristotle by Ellmann; of Irish folklore by Howard Emerson Rogers, "Irish Myth and the Plot of *Ulysses*," *ELH*, 15 (1948), 306-27.

16. These questions, along with the Linati schema mentioned in the following paragraph, are found in Ellmann, *Ulysses on the Liffey* (New York: Oxford University Press, 1972).

17. C.G. Jung, "Approaching the Unconscious," in *Man and his Symbols* (New York: Doubleday, 1968), p. 68.

18. W.B. Stanford traces this controversy in detail, but see also Philip Edwards, "*Ulysses* and the Legends," *Essays in Criticism*, 5 (1955), 118-28, who argues that Joyce's use of Homer cuts both ways, diminishing the present surroundings and those of the past as well; and Andrew Rutherford in "Joyce's Use of Correspondences," *Essays in Criticism*, 6 (1956), 123-25, who responds that "this view depends to some extent on a misreading of the *Odyssey*, which is *not* a story of consistently high ideals and satisfactory relationships. . . . Joyce therefore thought that he had a precedent in Homer (or tradition), for many of Bloom's qualities and defects" (p. 124). Kazantzakis in particular makes effective use of this potential ambiguity in the reputation of Odysseus.

19. See my article, "The Family of Bloom" in *New Light on Joyce from the Dublin Symposium*, ed. Fritz Senn (Bloomington: Indiana University Press, 1972).

20. See R.P. Blackmur, "The Jew in Search of a Son," *Virginia Quarterly Review*, 24 (1948), 96-116. Offered in isolation, the view of Bloom as scapegoat appears to be something of an oversimplification.

21. Roderick Davis, "The Fourfold Moses in *Ulysses*," *JJQ*, 7 (Winter 1970),127. Davis's reading of Moses as inevitable forerunner of Christ is the sort of Christian misinterpretation that poor Bloom has always to contend with.

22. Jung, "Approaching the Unconscious," pp. 84, 91.

23. Ibid., pp. 81-2 and 68.

24. The Jew in the West has been a city dweller, and Joyce, says Frank O'Connor, "is probably the most exclusively urban writer who ever lived. . . . Jewish literature is the literature of townsmen, and the greatest Jew of all was James Joyce" (*A Short History of Irish Literature* [New York:.Putnam, 1968]), p. 198. ──

25. Among others, and for different reasons, Tindall, *James Joyce: His Way of Interpreting the Modern World* (New York: Scribners, 1950); S.L. Goldberg, *The Classical Temper: A Study of James Joyce's "Ulysses"* (London: Chatto and Windus, 1961); Ellmann, "Ulysses the Divine Nobody"; and Northrop Frye, "Myth, Fiction, and Displacement," in *Fables of Identity: Studies in Poetic Mythology* (New York: Harcourt, Brace & World, 1963), agree that Bloom is essentially affirmative and that this fact may have mythic implications beyond his own limited lifetime. As Tindall puts it, "At best, whether ironic or solemn, the modern myth is pseudo-myth. But its function for the maker is identical with that of ancient myth. And if, like Joyce's myths, the modern myth has a public level, it can do for us what myths did for our ancestors. *Ulysses* and *Finnegans Wake* have a social function; for modern man needs to be assured of his humanity" (p. 104). Starting from an almost opposite premise, Goldberg reaches a similar conclusion, as he denies the presence of archetypes in the novel yet manages somehow to assert them: "Bloom is no Ulysses or Christ, yet in truth he is; . . . and Bloomsday exhibits as well as the social contours of today the permanent contours of human life" (p. 209). Previously, he wrote, "whatever the role and effect of mythic Archetypes in *Finnegans Wake*, what we actually feel in *Ulysses*, and especially in 'Ithaca,' is its force of affirmation, and affirmation not of any doctrine superhuman or supernatural, but of *the mythopoeic imagination itself*. It is as if we come to apprehend in and through Bloom and Stephen . . . the vital truth of the myths of Ulysses and Christ and the Wandering Jew and Sinbad and so on" (p. 203).

26. The ethical parallel is emphasized by Stanford in "Ulyssean Qualities in Joyce's Leopold Bloom," *Comparative Literature*, 5 (1953), 125-36 and by Frye's "Quest and Cycle in *Finnegans Wake*," in *Fables of Identity*, although the latter contends that it is feminine principle that is ultimately affirmed in the novel.

27. See especially Kenner, "*Ulysses*: Homer and Hamlet." And also Stanford, *The Ulysses Theme*, p. 214: "The basic humanistic elements in conduct, motive, and environment, are identical for the Prince of Ithaca and for this humble citizen of Dublin."

28. The best statement of this Modernist viewpoint is that of Maurice Beebe in "Joyce and the Meanings of Modernism," in *Litters from Aloft: Papers Delivered at the Second Canadian James Joyce Seminar, McMaster University*, ed. Ronald Bates and Harry J. Pollock (University of Tulsa Department of English Monograph Series, No. 13, 1971), pp. 15-25.

29. See Kenner's essay "Homer's Sticks and Stones," *JJQ*, 6 (Summer 1969), 285-98.

30. In a lecture at Franklin and Marshall College, Lancaster, Pa., on April 20, 1972.

Richard M. Kain

THE SIGNIFICANCE OF STEPHEN'S MEETING BLOOM: A SURVEY OF INTERPRETATIONS

With *Ulysses*, as with *Hamlet*, commentary, already an immense mass, threatens to become a morass. In both cases the bulk of interpretation is, to me, evidence of the works' evocative powers. In neither does there seem to be any consensus of opinion. What does happen in *Ulysses?* Is the meeting of Stephen and Bloom significant?

It would be impossible to review all of the comment on this point, but several positions may be identified. Earliest, represented by Stuart Gilbert, Frank Budgen, Harry Levin, and Hugh Kenner, is that the meeting points up a tragic abyss between two temperaments, representative of the modern cultural crisis. Thus Stuart Gilbert concludes his chapter on "Paternity" in his basic study, *James Joyce's "Ulysses,"* with these words:

> The last pages of the *Portrait* . . . are clearly an invocation to fatherhood—but to what father, whether to the artificer Daedalus, or to a heavenly or an earthly father, it is difficult to say, perhaps Stephen himself hardly knows. Even the meeting with Bloom is, for him, no release from his hopeless quest . . . . Stephen's attitude is really one of despair; he has not lost a father, like Telemachus, but he can never find one.[1]

Frank Budgen uses an appropriately nautical metaphor, himself having been a merchant seaman: "They are like two ships bound for different ports that come within hail and disappear into the night."[2] Harry Levin finds the characters "complementary . . . . Yet the attraction of opposites is not enough to produce a synthesis,"[3] an opposition which Hugh Kenner attributes to Bloom as a figure in the Dublin milieu in contrast to Stephen as "anarchic aesthete."[4]

On the literal level of the text, no meaningful outcome of the meeting seems probable. Stephen and Bloom are separated by gulfs of temperament ("The scientific. The artistic" [*U* 683]), of race ("He thought that he thought that he was a jew whereas he knew that he knew that he knew that he was not" [*U* 682]), education (*U* 682), and experience. Their past contacts had been few, and accidental (*U* 680), their points of agreement minimal. Their divergent postures are shown by Bloom's singing the Jewish anthem, which Stephen counters with an anti-semitic ballad (*U* 689-91). To Stephen the "Ha Tikvah" suggested "the accumulation of the past," and Bloom felt in his visitor "the predestination of a future" (*U* 689).

As for the invitation to spend the night, Stephen's refusal re-enacted that of Bloom, who had been invited to dinner by the Dedalus family twelve and a half years before (*U* 680). Why, one wonders, did Joyce overlook the possibility of making this previous encounter sixteen years before, a number which we shall see is emphasized elsewhere in *Ulysses*? Stephen's reply seems un-equivocal: "Promptly, inexplicably, with amicability, gratefully it was declined." Though other proposals were "advanced, accepted, modified, declined, restated in other terms, reaccepted, ratified, re-confirmed" (*U* 696), their fulfillment, we are told, was "rendered problematic" by "The irreparability of the past" and "The im-previdability of the future" (*U* 696).

No, the clown at Hengler's Circus was not Bloom's son, nor was the florin Bloom once notched ever returned. Despite his pathetic eagerness to shelter Stephen, and to see in him his own lost son, the past is irreparable, the future imprevidable. No. 7, Eccles Street is truly a "house of bondage" (*U* 697), no less to Stephen than to Bloom.

Though the Isolation Theory, if I may term it so, has a long and respectable pedigree, the matter seems not to rest there. A counter proposal had been made as early as 1931 by Edmund Wilson in *Axel's Castle*, and perhaps earlier, in one of his perceptive essays on *Ulysses* from which the Joyce chapter was derived. Wilson writes:

> As for Stephen, unresponsive as he has seemed to Bloom's interest and cordiality, he has at last, none the less, found in Dublin someone suffi-ciently sympathetic to himself to give him the clew, to supply him with the subject, which will enable him to enter imaginatively—as an artist—into the common life of his race. It is possible that Molly and Bloom, as a result of Bloom's meeting with Stephen, will resume normal marital relations; but it is certain that Stephen, as a result of this meeting, will go away and write "Ulysses."[5]

Wilson cites the remark of Buck Mulligan that Stephen says he is to write something in ten years.

Why did Joyce not confide some such significance to any one of his inner circle, we may ask, especially Frank Budgen, his first close associate, or perhaps Ezra Pound, to whom he was so indebted, or to Stuart Gilbert, whose work is dependent upon Joyce's guidance? It may be, of course, like a private joke, that the author delighted in hiding his meaning even from his leading expositors and defenders. The Sphinx remained silent. He was ready enough to parcel out some information (the *schema* could be used by Gilbert but not be Budgen), but not this. While all of the Paris circle were continuing to commemorate Bloomsday each year, Joyce may have been chuckling to himself about how little they knew of its meaning for him.

If he were not to put his imprimatur on any reading of this point, he could drop hints within the text which might be picked up by the wary. Thus would his celebrated cunning be demonstrated.

William York Tindall is the most eloquent and persistent advocate of the argument that the meeting is a fulfillment of Stephen's "unconscious quest," as a result of which "Discovering Bloom . . . , Stephen discovers mankind."[6] I quote from *A Reader's Guide to James Joyce*, as his fullest exposition, although he had suggested this reading as early as 1950 in *James Joyce: His Way of Interpreting the Modern World*. His arguments are ingenious and diverse:

1. Bloom's offer of coffee and bun in the cabman's shelter is an "unsubstantial communion," consisting of bread and wine (*coffee*, from Arabic, originally meaning wine) (*U* 634; *RG* 217).

2. Stephen murmurs " *Christus* or Bloom . . . *secundum carnem*" (*U* 643), which "seems a recognition of Bloom's humanity and humanity itself" (*RG* 217).

3. In "Ithaca" the shelter scene is described as a rite of "atonement" (*U* 729; *RG* 222).

4. Stephen drinks the "massproduct, the creature cocoa" (*U* 677), a four word phrase which suggests the Mass, "creative power," while cocoa is botanically *theobroma* or " 'god food' " and even "may imply co-co or with-with" (*RG* 222 and 222n).

5. The light in Molly's window is described by Joyce as "a visible luminous sign" (*U* 702; *RG* 224).

6. Mutual urination (*U* 702) is an "inconsiderable creation celebrating all creation" (*RG* 225).

7. Suggestions of Dante are found in Stephen's intonation of Psalm 113 (*U* 698), cited by Dante in his epistle to Can Grande elucidating the four-fold meaning of the *Commedia*. Other hints are the stars and the "concentric circles" of Molly's lamp (*U* 736; *RG* 225 and 225n).

8. Marion, the name a derivative of Mary, was born on the day of the Nativity of the Blessed Virgin, September 8 (*U* 736; *RG* 226).

9. Moses is intimated by Psalm 113, by the "Pisgah Sight of Palestine," and by Molly's "female hemispheres, redolent of milk and honey" (*U* 734; *RG* 226).

An almost convincing list this is, though it has come in for some severe criticism. Thus S. L. Goldberg, in *The Classical Temper*:

"What rather shakes our confidence is Mr Tindall's trust in abstract and mechanical 'symbolism'—in particular, his surely excessive faith in cocoa."[7] Without committing oneself to Tindall's interpretation, it may be said that Mr. Goldberg displays an excessive faith in his word "surely." We must be wary of any such positiveness in dealing with Joyce. It was Joyce, not Tindall, who first set up systems of "abstract and mechanical 'symbolism,' " and for the present we had better keep an open mind regarding that "faith in cocoa." *Ulysses* is filled with inconsequential objects, the junk of ordinary life, and Joyce often invests these items with surprising vitality and significance—Stephen's ashplant, Mulligan's boots, Bloom's potato, etc. The midden heap of *Finnegans Wake* is the ultimate in a series of unpoetic symbols. Revolt, irony, and cunning may be motivations, the Holy Office of literary and self purgation.

Cunning is possibly illustrated by Stephen's ashplant. John Garvin remarked to me that the rowan or ash is, in the Irish alphabet, attached to the month of February, Joyce's birth month. Hence, perhaps, Richard Rowan and the ashplant.

Mr. Goldberg also takes exception to urination as creative, which to him "seems questionable, both physiologically and poetically," since it is merely "to eliminate waste-matter . . . and Stephen creates neither life nor art."[8] In *The Conscience of James Joyce* Darcy O'Brien agrees:

> Mr. Tindall here demonstrates the lengths to which one must go to try to find some kind of positive value or hope in the meeting of Stephen and Bloom. The two characters acknowledge nothing more here than the fullness of their bladders . . . .[9]

An infantile joke at best, we might think, in questionable taste, but Freud had a good deal to say on the subject, and the scatalogical is one form of anti-climax Joyce delights in using—witness the conclusion of "The Sirens" and elsewhere. In my experience I have found this type of snickering more common in Ireland than in this country, attributable perhaps to comparatively primitive sanitary conditions, as well as to reaction against religious discipline. Regarding full bladders, one is reminded of the legendary Emer, mentioned by Yeats in his "Crazy Jane on the Mountain":

> Great-bladdered Emer sat,
> Her violent man
> Cuchulain sat at her side.

If urination be considered creative, or, as Freud would argue, a matter of pride, then the scene in the garden may constitute another of Joyce's sneers at art as worthless waste, a forgery. Shem, we recall, was "a sham and a low sham."

The ambiguity of *Ulysses*, and Joyce's own personal ambivalence, render neither the negative nor the affirmative conclusions completely satisfactory. It is possible that Joyce, like the author of *Hamlet*, achieved an artistically viable ambiguity, consciously or not, and that both works derive an ever constant imaginative energy from this inherent tension. They continue to be of a tantalizingly almost-solvable nature. As in Kafka's work, where incidents can support religious, sociological, psychological, and existential interpretations, Joyce contrives complex sequences of screens or mirrors which reflect the observer, and indeed give different images at different times. Witness S. Foster Damon's 1947 postscript to his pivotal 1929 essay. In 1929 *Ulysses* seemed to Damon "a study in loneliness," with no hope of friendship. Yet in 1947 Damon feels that "Stephen accepts the Christ in Bloom" and thus finds "something he can accept as Father, something to which he can devote his life." In this way "Bloom's deed" of protectiveness "becomes the long sought inspiration for *Ulysses*."[10] Damon here echoes Edmund Wilson, with theological overtones (one is reminded of Stephen's aside to himself while he expatiates on Shakespeare: "Just mix up a mixture of theolologicophilolological" [*U* 205]).

William Empson, in the course of elaborating his own theory, which will be discussed later, gave a somewhat mocking but clever definition of the Ambiguity Theory. He is discussing *Exiles*, and defines Joyce's aim

to write a Profound Play, like Euripedes and Shakespeare as well as Ibsen, which would have university lectures given on it in later years.[11]

We remember Joyce's own humorous disclaimer regarding the *schema*:

"If I gave it all up immediately, I'd lose my immortality. I've put in so many enigmas and puzzles that it will keep the professors busy for centuries arguing over what I meant, and that's the only way of insuring one's immortality" (*JJ* 535).

There are innumerable unreconciled oppositions in Stephen's character. In contrast to the Homeric son in search for a father, he is depicted as aloof, independent. In the words of "The Holy Office" (1904):

> . . . the self-doomed, unafraid,
> Unfellowed, friendless and alone,
> Indifferent as the herring-bone
> Firm as the mountain-ridges where
> I flash my antlers on the air

The stag image had been used the same year in the "Portrait" essay: "Let the pack of enmities come tumbling and sniffing to the highlands . . . he flung them disdain from flashing antlers."[12] The herring-bone, I learn from J. S. Atherton, derives from judicial oaths on the Isle of Man.[13] Yet Joyce, one sentence later, finds in his Ibsenesque stag "evident self-flattery" and "a danger of complacence."

A variant on the animal at bay passes through Stephen's mind as he expounds his theory of Shakespeare:

> Christfox in leather trews, hiding, a runaway in blighted treeforks from the hue and cry. Knowing no vixen, walking lonely in the chase (*U* 193).

On Sandymount Strand he had imagined himself back in Viking days: "I spoke to no-one: none to me," and, a moment later, "I just simply stood pale, silent, bayed about" (*U* 45). Less Byronic in his conception of the artist's destiny as a return to self, but only after many meetings:

> We walk through ourselves, meeting robbers, ghosts, giants, old men, young men, wives, widows, brothers-in-love. But always meeting ourselves (*U* 213).

This return to self is, like Stephen's theory of Shakespeare, a contradiction of the concept of aesthetic indifference.

Far from being "like the God of the creation . . . refined out of existence" of Stephen's definition of the artist in *A Portrait*, Joyce is always interposing himself between the work and the reader. One of the subjects of *Ulysses* is the writing of *Ulysses*. Joseph Prescott suggested to me years ago that there are many intimations which indicate Stephen's awareness, on June 16, of a time when he will look back upon what is now known as Bloomsday. We all remember Mulligan's sneer:

> —Ten years, he said, chewing and laughing. He is going to write something in ten years (*U* 249).

The passage which prompted my query to Prescott was the intrusion in "Aeolus" of Stephen's sense of an epiphany in the striking of a match, "that small act, trivial in itself . . . that determined the whole aftercourse of both our lives" (*U* 140). Others, one of which Mr. Prescott cited in a letter to me, are in the library episode: "See this. Remember" (*U* 192); "in the future, the sister of the past,

I may see myself as I sit here now but by reflection from that which then I shall be" (*U* 194); "One day in the national library we had a discussion" (*U* 215). In "Aeolus," under the headline "YOU CAN DO IT!'", Crawford had urged Stephen "to write something . . . with a bite in it," going on to say:

> Put us all into it, damn its soul. Father Son and Holy Ghost and Jakes M'Carthy (*U* 135).

Throughout the day Stephen has a sense of impending destiny. His dream of the night before, "That man led me, spoke" is set in a "Street of harlots" and associated with a melon "he held against my face" (*U* 47). We all know the hide-and-seek meetings and near misses of Stephen and Bloom—en route to the funeral (*U* 88), and at the news office (*U* 129, 131)—before their contacts late in the day. "Evening will find itself" (*U* 50) he had thought prophetically, and, as he leaves the library portico he recalls watching the birds "for augury" (an echo from *A Portrait*) and thinks again of his dream (*U* 217). Always meeting ourselves, Stephen had stepped aside to let Bloom go out between himself and Mulligan—possibly a significant trinity—and in a forward glimpse he sees Bloom as his future self. At least that is my interpretation of the passage:

> The moment is now. Where then? If Socrates leave his house today, if Judas go forth tonight. Why? That lies in space which I in time must come to, ineluctably (*U* 217).

Observant readers will recall the Maeterlinck passage on Socrates and Judas quoted by Stephen a few moments earlier (*U* 213). More remote is the association with Bloom's "Step of a pard" as he leaves (*U* 218). The dog on the beach was thought of as "a pard, a panther" (*U* 47), the panther being a recall of Haines's nightmare and also, as we learn in "Circe," of the legend that a Roman by that name was the father of Jesus (*U* 521). Perhaps the trinity is that of Stephen-Socrates, Bloom-Christ, and Mulligan-Judas.

One can play games with dates, and Joyce did. Bloom, 38 years old, is the age of Joyce in 1920. Sixteen years separate him from Stephen, as sixteen years separate 1904 from 1920. In "Circe" there is another coincidence. Bloom speaks of injuring his hand when he was sixteen, whereupon Stephen says:

> See? Moves to one great goal. I am twentytwo too. Sixteen years ago I twentytwo tumbled, twentytwo years ago he sixteen fell off his hobbyhorse. (*He winces.*) Hurt my hand somewhere (*U* 563).

Mathematics is carried to the height of absurdity in "Ithaca," where the ratio between the ages of Stephen and Bloom is extrapolated into impossible longevities of 374, 646, and finally 83,300 years (*U* 679). Robert M. Adams points up errors which might indicate that Joyce thought so little of his joke he didn't care about rechecking.[14]

Joyce could, above all, play with words, and we read of "Stoom" and "Blephen," another symbol perhaps, but the Spoonerism trails into inconsequence.

Another part of the puzzle is Shakespeare. We can see Stephen in his theory, and in "Circe" Shakespeare, Bloom, and Stephen are linked:

> God, the sun, Shakespeare, a commercial traveller, having himself traversed in reality itself, becomes that self. . . .   Self which in itself was ineluctably preconditioned to become. *Ecco!* (*U* 505).

Just as we try to unravel the cat's cradle of Joyce-Stephen-Bloom-Shakespeare-the sun and God, we are brought up short by one of Joyce's puncturing ironies. When Stephen and Bloom look into the mirror Shakespeare's face appears, but it bears the marks of paralysis (*U* 567), and we know what paralysis meant to Joyce. A coy and oblique identification of Joyce and Shakespeare through the Irish predecessor Patrick Weston Joyce is made in "Cyclops," where amid an absurd miscellany of names is "Patrick W. Shakespeare" (*U* 297). The same deflationary technique follows the list of novae near the births of Shakespeare, Bloom, Stephen, and Rudy. The series verges on meaningfulness until we hear of similar phenomena "some years before or after the birth or death of other persons" (*U* 701).

Thus far we have considered four theories—those of Isolation, of Creativity, of Deliberate Ambiguity, and the concept that *Ulysses* is about the writing of *Ulysses*, which might be called Trinitarian, since it involves Stephen, Bloom, and Joyce. From the latter it is but a step to the Classical Temper Theory, which I have the effrontery to name from the title of S. L. Goldberg's profound study. To simplify again, the following digest may be helpful:

1. Five common readings of *Ulysses* are inadequate: those regarding it as a bar-room comedy, or as nihilistic, esoteric, satiric, or an affirmation of life.

2. Critical analysis tends to make Joyce's techniques mechanical, espcially irony, Homeric parallelism, realism, symbolism.

3. Joyce's irony is not best shown in obvious forms, such as parody, but in his insight into Bloom's qualities and shortcomings, the contrast between "the stunted and unrealized possibilities that represent his bondage to the world, and the substantial human integrity that constitutes his freedom from it" (p. 137).

4. It is we, the readers, not Stephen or Bloom, who reach the point of artistic detachment, sympathy, and understanding.

5. Again, only we become freed from the nightmare of history by "*the mythopoeic imagination itself*" (p. 203). It is to this goal that the Homeric and other parallels lead.

6. Though Joyce verges towards extremes of realism (put everything in) and of symbolism (everything means something else), he does project "The gradual realization, by reader and artist, of a sense of the wholeness of life, of its ironical paradoxes, its intermingled decay and vitality, its absurdity and mystery" (p. 313).

Goldberg is both eclectic and original. He accepts the partial truth in most of the interpretations of *Ulysses*, and by subtle examination of the book's tonal and technical aspects reaches a view of *Ulysses* as neither a rejection of life nor its acceptance, but an aesthetic *stasis* of understanding. Joyce leads the perceptive reader to this plane through his varied styles and structures. We reach this *stasis* through our awareness of the author's presence and his artistic control.

Arnold Goldman, in *The Joyce Paradox*, follows a hint earlier suggested by Father William T. Noon, that *Ulysses* may be interpreted in the light of the categories of Soren Kierkegaard. In this reading Stephen and Bloom are "border-figures," the young artist poised between the aesthetical and ethical, the older man between the ethical and the religious. "As such, they are *either* figures moving from one condition to another *or* fixed in one realm." The question remains open, in Goldman's opinion, and instead of trying "to discover which of the alternatives is right, we wish to enjoy the drama of the alternatives."[15] E. M. Forster and Ford Madox Ford are cited as exemplars of this open indeterminate mode.[16] Stephen is presented as facing a crisis of identity, Bloom one of integrity.

A related interpretation is that of Edmund Epstein, whose book, *The Ordeal of Stephen Dedalus*, fascinates through the miscellany of out-of-the-way information and the author's depth of insight. He rejects the idea that the son is searching for a father: "The son is striving to *become* a father, to fulfill his Aristotelian drive toward completeness" and creativity.[17]

The temptation to identify Stephen with Joyce remains almost irresistible, ·despite critical admonitions, and we turn now to biographical theories. These may be distinguished as regards the presumed conscious or unconscious intention of Joyce. On the one hand we have the theory of biographical fact, that *Ulysses* tells of an experience Joyce actually had on June 16, 1904. On the other hand are speculations about the novel as a projection, a fiction which embodies the conflicts and obsessions of the author.

According to the dogmas of the no-longer-New Criticism, the Intentional and the Affective Fallacies are the Scylla and Charybdis of literary interpretation, with the Biographical Fallacy a Wandering Rock somewhere in the vicinity of Intention (this begins to sound as if the *Odyssey* were written by Bunyan!). Though never strong on dogma, especially in criticism, I think that these "fallacies" have to be reckoned with. An example of the confusions attendant upon biographical speculation is the essay by William Empson on "The Theme of *Ulysses*." Its most recent, expanded and modified version is found in *A James Joyce Miscellany, Third Series*. The original text of 1954 here is revised by addenda of 1956 and 1962. The first version made these points:

1. *Ulysses* celebrates an actual sexual experience which liberated Joyce from Dublin (p. 131).

2. Joyce's reference to "Ithaca" as the ugly duckling of the book suggests that it will become a swan (p. 133).

3. Like Ibsen, Joyce aims "to thrust on the reader a general problem, so one mustn't make it easy for the reader by 'ending with a particular solution" (p. 134). This seems to modify the positiveness of the first item.

4. Stephen will return, for his anti-semitism is merely an instance of his tendency to be "automatically nasty." This point rests on the reply to "Condense Stephen's commentary" (*U* 692), which describes "the victim predestined" who is led "to a secret infidel apartment" where he is immolated, "consenting." One may question Empson's assertion that this comment "has rather little to do with the song." It, in fact, paraphrases the song. Moreover, in following questions it is Bloom who is identified with both victim and infidel (p. 135).

5. Empson emphasizes the word "counterproposals" (*U* 696). He suggests that it was Stephen who made another proposal (Empson forgets that there were several), and that "this was ratified." The one Empson singles out was Italian lessons, the others being voice lessons and "intellectual dialogues." Had Empson considered all three, he might have attributed them to Bloom, counterproposal not necessarily demanding a suggestion made by a different person.

6. Hiding the meaning (see #3 above) involved making Bloom Jewish, and was appropriately Joycean: "The whole game of keeping his secret while telling the truth on such a big scale was obviously a great spur to his invention, and also gave him a great deal of innocent glee" (p. 139).

When Empson begins to speculate on what did actually happen to Joyce on June 16, he is not only entangled in the Biographical Fallacy but involves himself in what might be termed seven types of contradiction. In 1954 it seemed to be Joyce's "first real sexual experience" (p. 133); by 1956, commenting on the notes for *Exiles*, Empson finds them academic: "They smack of no direct experience" (p. 146). Yet a page later, though judging the notes disgusting, he thinks Joyce's mind "is obviously working on something that really happened." He tends to distrust Byrne's account in *Silent Years* of the shattering experience Joyce encountered in 1909, when he feared that he had been betrayed by Vincent Cosgrave (Lynch), since neither Byrne nor Ellmann in "The Backgrounds of *Ulysses*," (*Kenyon Review*, Summer 1954) give sources. Though dubious about Byrne's (Cranly's) story, Empson writes, "I cannot get away from feeling that at least an approach to the situation really happened" (p. 152). By 1962 Ellmann's biography brings Empson back to not thinking that *Ulysses* "describes a real event." He bases his retraction on Ellmann's assertion that Joyce met Nora on June 10, not June 16 (p. 153). Ellmann, however, is merely following Gorman, whose identical dates Empson had cited just two pages before.

Whom can one believe? Byrne, Joyce's notes for *Exiles*, Gorman, Ellmann? Empson had expressed his wariness about the penchant of Dubliners for gossip:

> by the way it is a nuisance, when you consider how ready some Dubliners are to give you a good story for another pint and then jeer at you for believing it (p. 150).

Despite this canny observation, he seems to swing with the wind, now accepting, then rejecting hearsay.

Literary critics are rightly skeptical of psychoanalytic interpretation. In addition to its tendency toward reducing art to neurotic causation, one may question the validity of analysis itself, not only on grounds of insufficient evidence, but also on those of the competence of the analyst. He, whatever his own school of thought, be it Freudian, neo-Freudian, or some other variant, has to thread his way carefully through mazes of hints and shreds of evidence, with the cooperation of his patient. Joyce took his secrets to the grave, although he did leave a trail of evidence—the *Exiles* notes, the letters to Nora, the works themselves. Though Stephen's aesthetic theory in *A Portrait* is a model of indifference, it is contradicted by the Stephen in *Ulysses*. Flaubert is often invoked as progenitor of the pure artist, yet we note his own identification with Emma Bovary.

On Sandymount Strand Stephen meditates on his role as observer and interpreter: "Signatures of all things I am here to read, seaspawn and seawrack, the nearing tide, that rusty boot." But this sentence is preceded by the phrase, "thought through my eyes" (*U* 37). The subjectivity of the artist's vision seems to be indicated. Stephen's Shakespeare does abide his question, and is not free, to paraphrase in reverse Matthew Arnold's sonnet. Shakespeare is wounded, like Richard Rowan in *Exiles*, suffering the anguish of sexual jealousy, troubled by self-doubt, feeling guilt at his father's death. These anxieties were Joyce's. Note the cry in "Ecce Puer":

> O, father forsaken
> Forgive your son!

As Stephen says of Shakespeare, Joyce "has hidden his own name" in his work (*U* 209). Impersonality seems unattainable, for, as Stephen comments on the Maeterlinck passage, " We walk through ourselves . . . . always meeting ourselves" (*U* 213).

Such considerations lead us "behind or beyond or above" the work itself, where we see Joyce, not, to continue the well-known definition of *A Portrait*, not "invisible, refined out of existence, indifferent, paring his fingernails," but more like "The fox burying his grandmother under a hollybush" (*U* 27), whose scraping is as much to call attention as to hide the scene of his activities. Hence the frequent over-elaboration of details not fully realized imaginatively, the occasional shrillness of bad humor and ill-naturedness which we can detect in *Ulysses*. One of the most recent studies, *James Joyce* by John Gross, emphasizes the role of the man behind the works. The book is a marvel of compactness, less than a hundred pages in length, but it touches upon most of the central issues. If the author were "to identify Stephen too positively with the Joyce of 1904," Gross argues, "he would be in danger of appearing to boast openly about how far he had come," and, as for Bloom, he is in part "the surrogate on whom Joyce had no qualms about heaping the psycho-sexual aberrations and indignities which he couldn't quite bring himself to attribute directly to Stephen."[18] The theme of paternity, Gross believes, "can easily be made too much of, or at any rate, taken too literally," with Bloom at once too young to be a convincing father and Stephen too old to be searching for one. Bloom can, however, help Stephen "to release, not only the frustrated artist locked up inside him, but the potential husband and father too . . . ."[19]

My survey of theories is designed to present alternatives, leaving decision to the reader. No one could be more aware than the author of its limitations. A thesis or book-length treatment would be necessary to cover the subject adequately. Questions may be raised regarding my grouping of tendencies, or my assignment of interpretations to their respective critics. At least an attempt has been made to touch upon what seem to be the major types of readings. In conclusion, I list these theories in order to facilitate discussion.

1. Isolation: the meeting is fortuitous and unimportant, a demonstration of modern keylessness or of the existential position of man.

2. Creativity: Stephen becomes a discoverer of mankind, through communion with Bloom.

3. Ambiguity: Joyce's mode of contrasting symbols and his penchant toward anti-climax render any single theory suspect.

4. Trinitarian: Joyce seems to indicate a subtle relationship of himself, Stephen, and Bloom.

5. Classical Temper: the book reveals the wholeness and complexity of life.

6. Existential: Bloom and Stephen reach a point of crisis, the outcome of which is problematic.

7. Biographical Fact: *Ulysses* dramatizes a crucial personal experience of the author.

8. Psychological Projection: Stephen and Bloom are fictional surrogates for Joyce's own conscious and subconscious drives.

In summarizing this paper for the Colloquium, the author was able to add two recent contrasting views unavailable to him at the time of writing. They show that the question remains open. Richard Ellmann, in *Ulysses on the Liffey* presents a "resurrection," with the three major characters forming "a human improvement upon the holy family."[20] At the opposite pole is the position of Hélenè Cixous, *The Exile of James Joyce*, that *Ulysses* presents "the tenuous, difficult, and even morbid relationships" of three people "who can never satisfactorily achieve their communion."[21]

A few remarks made in the discussion period and in seminar are worth recording. One listener expressed concern that after a fifty year "crash program" of interpretation and exegesis no consensus had been reached. I cited *Hamlet*, which T. S. Eliot had considered a failure for a similar reason. A psychological explanation was proffered: that Bloom was unable to project himself into the role of fatherhood. Several questions were raised as to how many of the interpretations could be compatible, and as to the speaker's preference. I opted for the area of ambiguity, which, it seems, could include Joyce's own role within the book as well as the classical and existential theories. Ambiguity, several agreed, best reflects the richness and mystery of life.

University of Louisville

NOTES

1. *James Joyce's "Ulysses"* (1930; New York: Vintage Books, 1959), p. 64.

2. *James Joyce and the Making of "Ulysses"* (1934; Bloomington: Indiana University Press, 1960), p. 259.

3. *James Joyce: A Critical Introduction*, rev. ed. (1941; Norfolk, Conn.: New Directions, 1960), p. 83.

4. *Dublin's Joyce* (Bloomington: Indiana University Press, 1956), p. 171.

5. *Axel's Castle: A Study in the Imaginative Literature of 1870-1930* (1931; New York: Scribner's, 1939), p. 202.

6. *A Reader's Guide to James Joyce* (New York: Noonday Press, 1959), p. 221. Hereafter *RG*.

7. *The Classical Temper: A Study of James Joyce's "Ulysses"* (London: Chatto and Windus, 1961), p. 28.

8. Ibid., p. 329n.

9. *The Conscience of James Joyce* (Princeton: Princeton University Press, 1968), p. 195n.

10. "The Odyssey in Dublin: *With a Postscript, 1947*," in *James Joyce: Two Decades of Criticism*, ed. Seon Givens (1948; New York: Vanguard Press, 1963), pp. 221, 242.

11. "The Theme of *Ulysses*," in *A James Joyce Miscellany, Third Series*, ed. Marvin Magalaner (Carbondale: Southern Illinois University Press, 1962), p. 145.

12. *The Workshop of Daedalus: James Joyce and the Materials for "A Portrait of the Artist as a Young Man,"* ed. Robert Scholes and Richard M. Kain (Evanston: Northwestern University Press, 1965), p. 61.

13. "Hall Caine and the Isle of Man," *A Wake Newslitter*, N.S. 2 (Aug. 1965), 6.

14. See *Surface and Symbol: The Consistency of James Joyce's "Ulysses"* (New York: Oxford University Press, 1962), p. 183.

15. *The Joyce Paradox: Form and Freedom in his Fiction* (London: Routledge & Kegan Paul, 1966), pp. 77, 78.

16. Ibid, pp. 78, 111.

17. *The Ordeal of Stephen Dedalus: The Conflict of Generations in James Joyce's "A Portrait of the Artist as a Young Man"* (Carbondale: Southern Illinois University Press, 1971), p. 173.

18. *James Joyce* (New York: Viking Press, 1970), pp. 45, 47.

19. Ibid., p. 48.

20. *Ulysses on the Liffey* (New York: Oxford University Press, 1972), pp. 149, 150.

21. *The Exile of James Joyce*, trans. Sally A.J. Purcell (1968; New York: David Lewis, 1972), p. 703.

Robert Scholes

ULYSSES: A STRUCTURALIST PERSPECTIVE

"We are still learning to be Joyce's contemporaries." So run the opening words of that extraordinary achievement in biography, Richard Ellmann's *James Joyce.* I take it that a conference on *"Ulysses:* From the Perspective of Fifty Years" is asking for a progress report on our attempt to become contemporaneous with Joyce. What have we learned in fifty years that enables us to see *Ulysses* more clearly than it could have been seen by those who were contemporary with it in mere chronology? And by this question is implied some progress not only in that narrow domain called "Joyce studies," to which some of us present here may claim a partial title, but in the larger world of humane learning as a whole.

My response to this question is a fairly simple thesis. I believe that the most important thing we have learned in the past fifty years is a way of thinking called "structuralism," which is based on linguistics and cybernetics, and has profoundly altered our ontology and our epistemology. Or rather it *should have* altered our fundamental concepts of being and mind, but it has met with a very understandable resistance—especially in literary studies. We men of letters have been reluctant to give up a view of the human situation that has seemed correct since Copernicus, and which we hold responsible for all individual achievement since the Renaissance. As a part of my thesis, I will maintain that the reluctance of many critics to accept the later Joyce (and by this I mean the last chapters of *Ulysses* as well as *Finnegans Wake*) is an aspect of this larger reluctance to accept the structuralist revolution. In a very real sense, some of us do not *want* to become Joyce's contemporaries, and we find the collapse of individuated characterization in the later Joyce as threatening as the loss of our own identities in some dystopian nightmare of the future. In this perspective the closing words of the first mini-version of *A Portrait*, which once seemed merely the posturings of a confused young idealist, appear much more concrete and consequential:

Perhaps his state would pension off old tyranny—a mercy no longer hopelessly remote—in virtue of that mature civilization to which (let it allow) it had in some way contributed. Already the messages of citizens were flashed along the wires of the world, already the generous idea had emerged from a thirty years' war in Germany and was directing the councils of the Latins. To those multitudes, not as yet in the wombs of humanity but surely engenderable there, he would give the word: Man and woman, out of you comes the nation that is to come, the lightning of your masses in travail; the competitive

161

order is employed against itself, the aristocracies are supplanted; and amid the general paralysis of an insane society, the confederate will issues in action.[1]

This passage could be dissected at length, for it is a strange and wonderful combination of Marx, Nietzsche, and D'Annunzio. Certainly that brand of National Socialism which came to be called Nazism might seem to have been rooted in this kind of thought. But it should be clearly noted that the worst crimes of Nazism had to do with its nationalistic character (nationalism leading naturally to racism, genocide, and even ecocide) rather than with its socialism. Joyce's "nation that is to come" is not a nation state but a kind of global village: individuals cybernetically related through "the wires of the world." As I say, it is tempting to dwell on this passage and explore its implications, but more pertinent matters lie ahead. Let it serve notice here that what I am going to call the revolutionary aspects of the later Joyce are not revolutionary merely from my own perspective, as a critic writing in 1972. Over seventy years ago, Joyce saw himself as one who "would give the word" to those not as yet in the wombs of humanity. Though we have been learning to read him, he may speak more clearly and more powerfully to our children. And the word he brings, in his final work, is the good news of a structuralist revolution.

Of course, both of these terms are so abused currently that it takes some temerity to introduce them in a serious discussion such as this one. If it is possible to have a "bell bottom revolution," or a "hot pants revolution," and so on, what mild shift in the breezes of fashion can not be proclaimed revolutionary? "Structuralism," too, has suffered from linguistic inflation, acquiring meanings not only in the sciences but, as Jean Piaget has ruefully noted, "at cocktail parties." Both of these terms are disturbingly modish, and I can only partially take the curse off them by trying to give the phrase "structuralist revolution" a clearly delimited meaning for the rest of this discussion. Once that is accomplished, we may turn more directly to *Ulysses*.

First of all, let it be clear that by revolution I mean a turning-over of our ways of thinking. Of course, such turnings-over have political implications. The medieval world view and the feudal political system stood and fell together. But revolution in the sense of a single action confined to the political sphere is not what I am thinking about here. I mean revolution in the larger sense—as we might say that the American revolution and the French revolution were instances of some larger meta-revolution called "liberalism" or "democracy" or some such thing. The revolution I am calling structuralist begins, then, with a turning-over of our ways of thinking. This turning-over is summed up neatly and vigorously in a recent collection of essays by Gregory Bateson called *Steps to an Ecology of Mind:*

> In the period of the Industrial Revolution, perhaps the most important disaster was the enormous increase of scientific arrogance. We had discovered how to make trains and other machines. . . . Occidental man saw himself as an autocrat with complete power over a universe which was made of physics and chemistry. And the biological phenomena were in the end to be controlled like processes in a test tube. Evolution was the history of how organisms learned more tricks for controlling the environment; and man had better tricks than any other creature.
>
> But that arrogant scientific philosophy is now obsolete, and in its place there is the discovery that man is only a part of larger systems and that the part can never control the whole.[1]

In short, this revolution has put something like God back in the universe—but not a God made in man's image, bursting with individualism and subject to temper tantrums when His will is thwarted. But a God who truly "is not mocked" because It *is* the plan of the universe, the master system which sets the pattern for all others. This God cannot intercede for His chosen favorites and suspend the natural law. Nor can He promise comforts in some afterworld for pain endured here. Here is where It is. God is immanent. It offers us only the opportunity to learn Its ways and take pleasure in conforming to them. For certainly there is only frustration in trying to thwart them. If in some ways this resembles the theology of Dante, then so be it. It would be a strange comment on the ecology of ideas if Catholicism could persist for two millennia without a grain of truth in its theology. It is not Catholic theology which has made the Church obsolescent, but Catholic fundamentalism. Freed from the letter, the spirit of Catholic theology is quite capable of accommodating all the truths of science. But lest I sound too much like an Apologist for the Church I left some twenty years ago, let me hasten back to Joyce.

The point of this particularly "commodius vicus of recirculation" is that Dublin's Dante could work himself into a structuralist position more easily by taking medieval theology as a point of departure than could someone handicapped by conversion to a more "reasonable" world view. Thus, I submit that Joyce, taking a few ideas well learned from Catholic theology, and adding notions from Vico and others, worked himself into an intellectual position which has much in common with that of Lévi-Strauss, or Piaget, or Bateson. Let us listen to Bateson again, with Joyce's later work specifically in mind:

Ecology currently has two faces to it: the face which is called bio-energetics—the economics of energy and materials within a coral reef, a red-wood forest, or a city—and, second, an economics of information, of entropy, negentropy, etc. These two do not fit together very well precisely because the units are differently bounded in the two sorts of ecology. In bioenergetics it is natural and appropriate to think of units bounded at the cell membrane, or at the skin; or of units composed of conspecific in-dividuals. These boundaries are then the frontiers at which measurements can be made to determine the additive-subtractive budget of energy for a given unit. In contrast, informational or entropic ecology deals with the budgeting of pathways and probability. The resulting budgets are fractionating (not subtractive). The boundaries must enclose, not cut, the relevant pathways.

Moreover, the very meaning of "survival" becomes different when we stop talking of something bounded by the skin and start to think of the survival of the system of ideas in the circuit. The contents of the skin are randomized at death and the pathways within the skin are randomized. But the ideas, under further transformation, may go on out in the world in books or works of art. Socrates as a bioenergetic individual is dead. But much of him still lives as a component in the ecology of ideas.[3]

It is clear to me that Joyce is one of the few writers of his time, perhaps the only one, who arrived at a concept of fiction which is cybernetic rather than bioenergetic. As his career developed, he accepted less and less willingly the notion of characters bounded by their own skins, and of actions which take place at one location in space-time, and then are lost forever. Unlike Lawrence, for in-stance, who reacted against "the old stable ego of the character" simply by giving us characters with unstable egos, Joyce attacked the ego itself, beginning with his own. But not initially. The cybernetic serenity of his later work was long coming and hard won. For he had a good deal of ego to disperse. Nothing could be sharper than the division between self and others as we find it in his early Epiphanies, with their focus upon the verbal or gestural "vulgarity" of others and the "memorable" phases of his own mental life. This same bioenergetic separation persists through *Stephen Hero*, *Dubliners*, and *A Portrait*. Though there are hints of it in this latter work, it is only in *Ulysses* that we really find the ego breaking down. I think it is reasonable to say that Stephen Dedalus is Joyce's bioenergetic self-portrait, while Leopold Bloom is his cybernetic self-portrait.

Since Ellmann's biography of Joyce, we have complacently referred to Bloom as well as Stephen as "autobiographical"—but surely we need to distinguish between these two kinds of autobiography. And it is not enough to say that Stephen is a young Joyce and Bloom is a mature Joyce. For Stephen "is" Joyce in a different way from the way Bloom "is" Joyce. Stephen is Joyce in his skin, with all the significant features that would make him recognizable. And with no features that Joyce himself did not possess. Insofar as Joyce could create a "true" self-portrait, Stephen is that portrait (somewhat retouched from book to book). But Bloom contains large elements of Joyce's neural circuitry without being recognizable as Joyce; and at some important levels of experience he is a "truer" representation of Joyce than Stephen. But that cellular integrity which marks Stephen as Joyce himself and not any other person is lacking in Bloom. He is a Joyce interpenetrated with others: with the far-wandering Odysseus and with a pathetic Dubliner that the Joyce family actually knew. (And with other figures from life and art as well.) This characterization of the peripathetic Bloom is remarkable not because it shows Joyce creating a great character who is un-autobiographical, but because it shows us an autobiographical characterization without egocentricity.

If Flaubert truly thought of Emma Bovary on occasions as himself ("*C'est moi!*"), he must have donned her skin with a naturalistic *frisson*, prompted by his sense of how different it was from his own. But for Joyce in *Ulysses* there is no hint of such *nostalgie de la boue*. He lived *là-bas*, and thus his works lack the delight in slumming which is often one aspect of naturalism. And by *Finnegans Wake* he had come to accept the Homais in himself as Flaubert never could. It might also be well to recall at this point how in the *Wake* Joyce's ego is not only diffused among the whole range of major figures and minor; it has also spread out to include the "inanimate" rivers, rocks, and trees of Dublin and the world. Which ought to remind us that if Beckett is Joyce's heir, he is a model of filial rebellion. For the nausea and alienation which he has chronicled so articulately are the very antitheses of the acceptance of the ecosystem that animates *Finnegans Wake*.

It should be clear by now that from my perspective on *Ulysses* "fifty years after," it is a transitional work *par excellence*. It is transitional in Joyce's treatment of his own ego and in many other respects as well. This very transitional nature of the book has led one school of critics (call it the Goldberg variation) to see the book as a failed novel, which goes off the novelistic track in the later chapters due to Joyce's self-indulgence in various linguistic capers. It would be just as reasonable to invert this critique and see the early chapters as a false start of somewhat too traditional flavor, corrected by the brilliant new devices of the last part. These views I reject as equally wrong. *Ulysses* is a transitional work for us as well as for Joyce. In reading it we learn how to read it; our comprehension is exercised and stretched. We are led gradually to a method of narration and to a view of man (the two inseparable) different from those found in previous fiction. This method and this view I am calling structuralist, asserting that Joyce's later work can not only be seen more clearly from a structuralist perspective but that it is structuralist in its outlook and methodology.

In testing this thesis against the mass of *Ulysses* in such short space, much will have to be taken for granted. But I will try to look at certain representative aspects of *Ulysses* in the light of a few structuralist notions derived from Saussurian linguistics and the genetic epistemology of Jean Piaget, beginning with Piaget's definition of structure:

> In short, the notion of structure is comprised of three key ideas: the idea of wholeness, the idea of transformation, and the idea of self-regulation.'

This triad leads to a more satisfying esthetic than the one Joyce called "applied Aquinas," and in fact it is more applicable to Joyce's later work. But before applying it we must elaborate on it a little bit. By *wholeness* Piaget indicates elements arranged according to laws of combination rather than merely lumped together as an aggregate. Such wholeness is a quality of all recognizable literary works. It is, in fact, one way we recognize them. They have the wholeness of all linguistic utterances and the more intense wholeness of discourse specifically literary. Since this is a characteristic of all fiction, it need not be especially remarked in *Ulysses*. By *transformation* Piaget means the ability of parts of a structure to be interchanged or modified according to certain rules, and he specifically cites transformational linguistics as an illustration of such processes. In *Ulysses* the metempsychotic way in which Bloom and Odysseus are related is one notable principle of transformation, and there are other transformational aspects of the book to which we will return. By *self-regulation* Piaget refers to the "interplay of anticipation and correction (feedback)" in cybernetic systems and to "the rhythmic mechanisms such as pervade biology and human life at every level." Self-regulating structures are both "self-maintaining" and "closed." I would like to suggest that in *Ulysses* the Homeric parallels function as a kind of feed-back loop, operating to correct imbalance and brake any tendency of the work to run away in the direction of merely random recitations from Bloom's day. And there are many other such loops. Each chapter, in fact, is designed to run down when certain schematic systems are complete and when a certain temporal segment of the Dublin day has been covered. Whereupon the next

Homeric parallel is activitated to provide a diachronic scheme for the following chapter.

This system can be illustrated by a brief consideration of the much maligned "Oxen of the Sun" chapter. It exhibits all of the structural properties I have been discussing, and can thus serve to illustrate their working in some detail. This chapter is basically a simple narrative segment of the day: Stephen and Bloom happen to come to the same place, a lying-in hospital where Mrs. Purefoy is engaged in a long and difficult accouchement. After young Mortimer Edward is born, Stephen and some medical students, accompanied or followed by Bloom, go off to a pub for some superfluous drinking. This base narrative is transformed according to a complex set of rules. Rule 1: the events must be narrated by a sequence of voices that illustrate the chronological movement of English prose from the Middle Ages to contemporary times. Rule 2: each voice must narrate an appropriate segment of the events taking place. That is, a Pepysian voice must deal with Pepysian details and a Carlylean voice with a Carlylean celebration. Which assumes Rule 3: the voices must be pastiches or parodies of clearly recognizable stylists or stylistic schools.

The purpose of these rules is not merely to show off Joyce's skill as a parodist and pasticher, which is considerable, but to enrich our experience of the characters presented and events narrated. And it is their interaction which gives shape to events that in themselves are only minimally shapely. In this chapter Joyce operates with roughly six sets of narrative materials, to be arranged according to these rules. He has Bloom's present words and deeds, plus his thoughts of the past, and the same two sets of present and past for Stephen. He also has the simultaneous actions of the medical students, Haines, and so on, along with a sixth item, the birth itself. The selection of what comes when, in the necessarily linear sequence of prose narrative, is thus the result of a complex interaction among these rules and sets of possibilities. (The Homeric parallel, in this chapter, offered the initial idea, but had less influence on structure than in some other chapters.) In this chapter, the selection of the moment of birth, for instance, is saved from arbitrariness by the appropriateness of the voices of Dickens and Carlyle to celebrate the new arrival. And if *they* are to celebrate him, young Mortimer must appear in the middle of the nineteenth century, the era of phyloprogenitiveness. Similarly, the drunken conversation that closes the chapter functions in a structural way because it is a linguistic transformation of the anti-structural randomization of an afterbirth: a melange of entropic noise. It is what structure prevents

Ulysses from becoming, though for those who cannot perceive the structure it is precisely what the book seems to be.

This kind of structure, of course, is a function of Joyce's massive unwillingness to get on with it and tell a simple linear tale. And thereby hangs a good deal of critical hostility. In discussing this aspect of *Ulysses* some terminology from linguistics will be helpful. Saussurien structuralism is founded on a distinction between synchronic and diachronic views of language. From this initial position a further distinction between the syntagmatic and paradigmatic aspects of any particular utterance has been derived. In a given sentence, for example, the meaning of a single word is determined partly by its position in the sentence and its relation to the other words and grammatical units of that sentence. This is the word's syntagmatic aspect, often conceptualized as a horizontal axis along which the sentence is spread out in its necessary order. The meaning of a single word in a sentence is also determined by its relation to some groups of words *not* in the actual sentence but present in a paradigmatic (or "vertical") relationship to the actual word. A word is thus defined partly by all the words which might have filled its place but have been displaced by it. These displaced words may be conceived as belonging to several paradigmatic sets: other words with the same grammatical function, other words with related meanings (synonyms and antonyms), other words with similar sound patterns—these are three obvious paradigmatic sets. Our actual selection of a word in a sentence involves something like a rapid scanning of paradigmatic possibilities until we find one that will play the appropriate role in the syntax we are constructing. In structuralist literary theory, it is customary to see narrative literature as a transformation by enlargement of our basic sentence structure. Characters are nouns; their situations or attributes are adjectives; and their actions are verbs. And fiction is defined by its emphasis of the syntagmatic or linear (horizontal) dimension of linguistic possibilities, whereas poetry is less concerned with syntagmatic progression and more inclined to play with paradigmatic possibilities.

Joyce, in *Ulysses*, is often very reluctant to speed along the syntagmatic trail like an Agatha Christie. Often, it is as if he cannot bear to part with many of the paradigmatic possibilities that have occurred to him. He will stop and climb up the paradigmatic chain on all sorts of occasions, such as the various lists in "Cyclops" (I shall resist the temptation to pause and make a meta-list at this point), in which displaced possibilities are allowed to sport themselves and form syntagmatic chains of their own. These list *do be-come* syntagmatic in themselves, and they further relate to other lists and other parts of the whole narrative in a syntagmatic way. A book as long as *Ulysses* which was really paradigmatic in its emphasis would be virtually impossible to read—as *Ulysses* is for those who do not see its structure. But even the lists in *Ulysses* if examined closely will prove to have both an internal syntagmatic dimension and an external one.

The lists in "Cyclops," for instance, tend to follow some basic comic laws which depend on syntagmatic expectation. For instance, they may establish an innocent pattern, apparently a simple process of repetition, and then violate it while appearing to continue in the same manner—as in this sequence from the opening of the list of ladies attending the "wedding of the grand high chief ranger of the Irish National Foresters with Miss Fir Conifer of Pine Valley. Lady Sylvester Elmshade, Mrs Barbara Lovebirch . . . ." and so on (*U* 327). We quickly pick up the basic principle of these names—or we think we do. There is to be an appropriateness between the first and last names of these arboreal damsels which makes it amusing to consider them. Such names further down the list as "Miss Timidity Aspenall" or "Miss Grace Poplar" are constructed by animating an attribute of the tree names in the last name and deriving a first name from this attribute. Poplars are graceful and aspens may easily be thought of as timid. (And by extension, Miss rather than Mrs. is appropriate for them too.) In this list, the opening "Fir Conifer" and "Sylvester Elmshade" establish this pattern without being as clever as some of the later combinations—thus allowing for some syntagmatic pro-gression. But this pattern is enriched by some others, which add a different kind of comedy to the list and complicate its syntagmatic relationships. That third name, "Barbara Lovebirch" introduces into this green world the whole motif of sado-masochistic perversion which will culminate in the "Circe" chapter. The name "Lovebirch" not only includes the masochistic idea but refers to the author of the pornographic novel *Fair Tyrants* (James Lovebirch), which Bloom has inspected in "Wandering Rocks" and rejected ("Had it? Yes.") as not so much in Molly's line as *Sweets of Sin*. And of course in "Circe" Mrs. Yelverton Barry accuses Bloom of making "improper overtures" to her under the *nom de plume* of James Lovebirch. Among the list of innocent trees the barbaric lovebirch is comically sinister. And once directed this way the reader may well see sexual connotations lurking beneath every bush. Is "Mrs Kitty Dewey-Mosse" innocent? Thus even what appears to be a purely paradigmatic excursion in *Ulysses* proves to have a system of its own and beyond that to exhibit connections of the syntagmatic sort with other events and episodes.

The process illustrated here in little is related to the larger processes of the book. The "Oxen of the Sun" is written as it is not merely to vary our perspective on Stephen and Bloom, showing aspects of them that could only be shown through the styles employed. The chapter also represents an acknowledgment of all the narrative voices that have been displaced by Joyce in uttering *Ulysses*. The whole chapter is a climb up a particular paradigmatic ladder on the level of style. And it serves not only to throw new light on Bloom and Stephen. It also takes Bloom and Stephen and the whole world of *Ulysses* back through the system of English literature and allows this work of 1922 to intermingle with the past. If Carlyle's voice can celebrate Theodore Purefoy in 1922, then Carlyle's cybernetic self still lives through Joyce's agency. And if the "Oxen of the Sun" chapter serves partly to install Bloom and Stephen among the literature of the past, the "Ithaca" chapter serves a similar purpose with respect to science.

The technological and scientific perspectives of "Ithaca" extend Bloom and Stephen to new dimensions without aggrandizing them. (And without dwarfing them as is sometimes contended.) Space-time does not permit me to trace this process in detail, but I want to close by focussing on what I take to be the final lesson of "Ithaca" and one of the most deeply embedded meanings in the entire book. At the end of this chapter, after a day of anxiety, Bloom rearrives at an equilibrium which is not merely that of a body at rest but that of a self-regulated system operating in harmony with other systems larger than itself. He views his wife's adulterous episode "with more abnegation than jealousy, less envy than equanimity" for a very important reason. Because it is

> not more abnormal than all other altered processes of adaptation to altered conditions of existence, resulting in a reciprocal equilibrium between the bodily organism and its attendant circumstances . . . (*U* 733).

Blazes Boylan is Molly's adjustment to Bloom's sexual retreat. As she might say herself, "It's only natural." Bloom is homeostatic man, centripetal, his equilibrium achieved. And Stephen is young, therefore centrifugal, and therefore to be forgiven. In time he too will return, like Shakespeare reading the book of himself, and writing it too. Stephen and Bloom and Molly have other roles to play in

Finnegans Wake, permutations and combinations hardly dreamed of in 1922. And for this total achievement, we may say of Joyce what Bateson said of Socrates. As a bioenergetic individual he is indeed dead. "But much of him still lives in the ecology of ideas."

Brown University

NOTES

1. "A Portrait of the Artist," in *The Workshop of Daedalus: James Joyce and the Materials for "A Portrait of the Artist as a Young Man,"* ed. Robert Scholes and Richard M. Kain (Evanston: University of Illinois Press, 1965), pp. 67-8.

2. *Steps to an Ecology of Mind* (New York: Ballantine Books, 1972), p. 437.

3. Ibid., p. 461.

4. *Structuralism,* trans. Chaninah Maschler (New York: Basic Books, 1970), p. 5.

Maurice Beebe

ULYSSES AND THE AGE OF MODERNISM[1]

Almost everyone seems to agree with Leslie Fiedler's contention that "the literary movement which we have agreed to call 'Modernism,' and at the center of which Joyce stands, is a literary movement which is now dead."[2] But we disagree about the value of that movement. We are still trying to establish the dates of its birth and its death. We are in fact still waiting for someone to answer with authority the question which Harry Levin asked as far back as 1960: "What Was Modernism?"[3]

That question, interestingly raised but only partly answered by Professor Levin, lay dormant for almost a decade. Aside from the valuable collection of primary materials collected by Richard Ellmann and Charles Feidelson, Jr. in *The Modern Tradition: Backgrounds of Modern Literature* (1965) and Irving Howe's useful anthology of essays on *The Idea of the Modern in Literature and the Arts* (1967), very little was published on the subject until the 1970s. Now Modernism is the literary topic of the day. Numerous books and articles are in print or in progress; there are several recent doctoral dissertations on the subject; the Autumn 1971 issue of *New Literary History* is devoted entirely to Modernism; and the first issue of *Boundary 2: A Journal of Postmodern Literature* (Fall 1972) was devoted largely to a symposium on how the new literature differs from that of the Modernist age. Both the University of Toledo and Temple University held conferences on the Age of Modernism during the past year, and we have been told that the main theme of the Fourth International James Joyce Symposium in Dublin next June will be not Joyce alone, but his ties and affinities with the other major writers of the modern period.

In view of all this activity, it may well be important to decide "What *Was* Modernism?" One way to answer the question—or, rather, to evade an answer—is to say that Modernism may be assimilated within that broader movement called Romanticism which has been with us for almost two hundred years. Morse Peckham in the title essay of his recent collection sees modern literature as *The Triumph of Romanticism* (1970), and for some time Harold Bloom has been arguing almost persuasively that not only Yeats but other modern writers may be easily accommodated within the Romantic tradition. In *Dionysus and the City: Modernism in Twentieth Century Poetry*, Monroe K. Spears begins by surveying previous definitions of Modernism, cites three versions of the argument that Modernism is a continuation of Romanticism—his three authorities are no less than Edmund Wilson, Northrop Frye, and Frank Kermode—and though conceding that "modernism is, of course, an impossible subject,"[4] seems to go along with these eminent critics by stressing in his own worthy study the "Dionysiac" elements of modern literature.

Formidable opposition indeed. But working with literary terms is, of course, tricky business. Jacques Barzun has shown that there are more than one hundred separate meanings for the word "romantic."[5] It is therefore easy enough to understand how virtually everything may be called "romantic" in one way or another. I do not have the time nor the ability to work my way through this semantic jungle. I would rather assume that most students of literature have a generally valid even if vague idea of what Romanticism means, and I should then like to argue that Modernism means something quite different. If we see modern poetry as a current which moves from Whitman to Frost to Graves to Ginsberg (to Bob Dylan?) and if we see Lawrence, Hesse, Hemingway, and Mailer as the major novelists of the twentieth century, then I suppose it may be possible to see Modernism as only another wave in the incoming tide of Romanticism. But what then do we do with Flaubert, James, Conrad, Ford, Woolf, Forster, Shaw, Pound, Stein, Cummings, Eliot, Auden, Mann, Kafka, Proust, Gide, Stevens, Williams, Faulkner, Beckett, Nabokov, Warren, Durrell—and James Joyce? To label these writers Romantic seems to me a clear case of mistaken or insufficient identification, and to reduce them to the status of minor writers would violate all sense of critical justice. Monroe Spears says that "if any god personifies modernism, it is Dionysus,"[6] but try to imagine Henry James on a Dionysiac frolic with Virginia Woolf and Thomas Mann. Surely a stronger case could be made for the major Modernists as Apollonian. The period which Hugh Kenner calls *The Pound Era* (1971) seems to me distinctively different from the Age of Wordsworth.

We may grant that the cycle has turned again, the pendulum swung back in such a way that much contemporary literature of the Post-Modernist period does indeed seem to represent a return to Romantic attitudes and values. Spears writes: "Graham Hough and Robert Graves among the British and Karl Shapiro in America . . . proclaim exultantly that modernism died and was succeeded by neo-Romanticism in 1957, if not before; and they have many followers"[7] I can go along with this view, for it at least has the merit of distinguishing Modernism from Romanticism. But I cannot share the opinion that Modernism was only "a detour or dead end

away from the main highway of tradition."⁸ I would prefer to see
it as an island, separate from the mainland and made up largely of
rich estates. The Age of Modernism was an incredibly vital period
in the history of literature, perhaps the greatest since the
Renaissance, and it should require no apologists. Modernism may be
dead, but it is still far from buried.

Unlike Spears, who dates the Age of Modernism from 1909 to
1957 perhaps because he is more interested in poetry than in fiction
or the other arts, I see Modernism as an international current of
sensibility which dominated art and literature from the last quarter
of the nineteenth century until about 1945—from the
exhibitions of the 1870s and the first writings of Henry James to
about the time of the Second World War. This period of about
seventy years, the Age of Modernism proper, was the time of the
great masters, the myth-builders and world-creators like Yeats and
Joyce, Proust and Mann, James and the early Faulkner—writers
who gave us such an abundance of riches that it is perhaps well that
the great surge of creative Modernism began to lose its charge
during the 1940s and was succeeded by a quarter century of assimilation and assessment that deservedly has been called the Age of
Criticism. Modernist literature did not end in the 1940s. Modernist
artists are still alive and active in the Post-Modernist, Neo-Romantic
age in which we are now groping our way—Beckett, Nabokov,
Durrell, Warren, Bellow, not to mention Picasso and Dali—but
the great monuments of literary Modernism had appeared by 1950.
In fact, it makes sense to say that the movement reached its crest in
the 1920s, then slowly diminished in strength as the necessity for
critical analysis and assessment became increasingly urgent in proportion to the abundance of riches already accumulated. As in an
Impressionist painting, the edges may be blurred between these
overlapping periods, but the over-all design seems clear enough.

I have not yet answered the question, "What *Was* Modernism?"
The best way to define the literature of any historical period is
to determine the main characteristics of the literature produced
by the most significant and representative writers of the age. When
I first attempted to do this several years ago, I found an abundance
of general affinities and similar themes among the major Modernists,
but I soon realized that many of these were common not only to
modern literature but to all literature—the quest theme, for example,
or the search for a father; the techniques of literary symbolism;
and a philosophy neatly summarized by Henry James as "the free
brave personal way" that has been the dominant philosophy of

artists as artists for centuries, though we did not give it the label "existentialism" until the twentieth century. My task became somewhat easier when I began to look for traits of Modernist literature which clearly distinguish it from the literature of the early nineteenth century and that of today.

I finally settled on four such characteristics. First, Modernist literature is distinguished by its formalism. It insists on the importance of structure and design—the esthetic autonomy and independent whatness of the work of art—almost to that degree summarized by the famous dictum that "a poem should not mean but be." Secondly, Modernism is characterized by an attitude of detachment and non-commitment which I would put under the general heading of "irony" in the sense of that term as used by the New Critics. Third, Modernist literature makes use of myth not in the way myth was used earlier, as a discipline for belief or a subject for interpretation, but as an arbitrary means of ordering art. And, finally, I would date the Age of Modernism from the time of the Impressionists because I think there is a clear line of development from Impressionism to reflexivism. Modernist art turns back upon itself and is largely concerned with its own creation and composition. The Impressionists' insistence that the viewer is more important than the subject viewed leads ultimately to the solipsistic worlds-within-worlds· of Modernist art and literature.

I have found that these four characteristics work quite well if Modernism is seen as a new and basically independent and autonomous phase in the literary history of the past two centuries—and that indeed the exceptions may prove the rule. Most Modernist writers can be fitted quite comfortably within at least three of my four points, but if Modernism is seen as a continuation of Romanticism, we would have to say that the writer who stands at the center of the movement is not Joyce, but D. H. Lawrence. Measured against my four terms, Lawrence fails on all four counts. His indifference to form and esthetic structure, his almost complete lack of irony, his attempt to restore religious value to myth, and his earnest, if not always successful attempts to acknowledge an otherness beyond his own ego—in all these ways he can be identified as the leading Anti-Modernist of twentieth century literature. It is no wonder that Lawrence and Joyce detested each other's writings, but that they did so justifies our seeing literature of the modern period as a substantial body of writings which may be placed in varying locations between the two poles represented by these two masters. We shall be hearing much this year about the fifty-year anniversaries of *The Waste Land* and *Ulysses*. It may be well to remind ourselves that 1922 saw also the publication of *Women in Love*.

Leslie Fiedler is surely correct in saying that Joyce stands at the center of the Modernist movement. *Ulysses* in particular can be seen as a demonstration and summation of the major features of the entire movement. There are several ways in which this could be shown. That the novel is a profound statement about the condition of modern man has long been recognized, and previous critics have traced in *Ulysses* most of the prevailing themes of modern literature—the quest for a father, the Waste Land, alienation, appearance versus reality, the City, modern man's failure to communicate, and so on. I had hoped to show here that *Ulysses* incorporates the various stylistic isms of modern art and literature, but I find that I have been anticipated. In a just-published Tulsa monograph, *Avant-gardism and Modernity*, Peter Egri, an Hungarian Marxist and disciple of Georg Lukács, shows how *Ulysses* makes use of virtually every important ism of our time—with the exception, ironically, of Marxism.[9] Egri cites passages of *Ulysses* which may be classified under such headings as naturalism, impressionism, expressionism, "constructivism cum cubism," surrealism, and something which is only "one degree short of Dadaism." Neither the thematic nor the stylistic approach to the modernity of *Ulysses* would seem to require much further development, and I shall try to restrict myself to showing how Joyce's novel illustrates my four cardinal points of Modernism.

First, formalism. Good literature of any period may have effective form and structure, but it was not until the beginnings of the Modernist period that writers began to see form as the *primary* requirement of successful art—to insist that form is more important than content. This was especially true of fiction writers. Most novelists of the eighteenth and nineteenth centuries, even those like Fielding and Dickens who were good craftsmen, seem to have taken a modest view of the craft they practiced, and it was not until the time of Henry James, whose essay on "The Art of Fiction" (1883) is one of the first important manifestoes of Modernism, that we find writers of fiction insisting that theirs is an art as exalted as any other and subject to as demanding standards of formal structure as music or poetry. Even in those fields, the very nature of which requires a concern for pattern and rhythm, we find around the turn of the century, in Satie and Pound for example, a new and more sophisticated concern for technique than was apparent during the Romantic decades.

Today a concern with form at the expense of content is likely to seem esoteric and irresponsible. I am told that most undergraduates today have little sympathy for Stephen Dedalus, that proud and independent young man who refused to sign petitions, let alone participate in campus demonstrations, and spent his time instead developing a systematic theory of esthetics that expresses the formalist credo in as definitive a way as can be found anywhere. The theory that Stephen expounds in *A Portrait of the Artist as a Young Man* is couched in pseudo-Thomistic terms which may look like an attempt to adapt classical theories of art to the time of Pater and the French Symbolists. But if one looks closely at Stephen's theory of art as stasis, especially his exposition of the three main qualities of art—*integritas, consonantia,* and *claritas;* wholeness, harmony, and radiance—and compares the theory with Joyce's Thomistic sources and the softer version found in *Stephen Hero,* it becomes apparent that what chiefly distinguishes Joyce-Stephen's final theory is the determination to remove from art everything but art itself. Terms that have a religious significance for Aquinas are entirely secularized by Stephen as he argues that art must be a wholeness independent of what surrounds it, that it must have internal harmony, and that the radiance it finally reveals is not that spiritualized "epiphany" which Joyce left behind in *Stephen Hero,* but the simple, objective *quidditas* or "whatness" of the thing itself. Thus in *Ulysses*—

—History, Stephen said, is a nightmare from which I am trying to awake.
From the playfield the boys raised a shout. A whirring whistle: goal. What if that nightmare gave you a back kick?
—The ways of the Creator are not our ways, Mr Deasy said. All history moves towards one great goal, the manifestation of God.
Stephen jerked his thumb towards the window, saying:
—That is God.
Hooray! Ay! Whrrwhee!
—What? Mr Deasy asked.
—A shout in the street, Stephen answered, shrugging his shoulders (*U* 34).

At the time he wrote *Stephen Hero,* Joyce might have agreed with Mr. Deasy that God manifests Himself in the shout of the street as in everything else, but the Stephen of *Ulysses* feels no thrill of epiphany as he hears the cheering from the playground: a shout in the street, he implies with that shrug of his shoulders, is all the God there is.

That *Ulysses* is an elaborately structured work of fiction is a point which hardly needs laboring. No other novel seems more self-consciously devoted to showing the formal relation "of part to part in any esthetic whole or of an esthetic whole to its part or parts or of any part to the esthetic whole of which it is a part" than this curiously experimental novel. Eighteen chapters, each utilizing a separate and distinct fictional technique, are divided into three unequal but symmetrical parts. Occasionally we may find ourselves lapsing into immersion within the consciousness of Stephen and Leopold, but each new chapter startles us into an awareness that we are "reading an intricate, highly artificial construct."[10] The more often we have read *Ulysses*, the more likely we are to think of the book as a series of separate blocks, almost like the stories of *Dubliners*, rather than as a single sustained narrative. But even as the work threatens to split asunder, Joyce manages to maintain a remarkable wholeness. The simple plot-line is much more easily summarized than in most novels that are easier to read than *Ulysses*, and the work more than adequately meets Aristotelian standards of dramatic unity because in his three parts or "acts" Joyce restricts himself to describing less than twenty-four hours of activity within a single geographical location while concentrating on three main characters (the number is itself a symbol of unity) plus an abundance of minor characters or "counters" carefully interlocked with the three main protagonists. As in a Poe story, nothing in *Ulysses* is extraneous or irrelevant—or everything is.

Still, the *quidditas* of *Ulysses* is worth remarking. In *The Pound Era*, Hugh Kenner singles out "space-craft" as a distinguishing feature of Modernism and reminds us that though we think of *The Ambassadors* as a narrative occupying a period of time, the story of Lambert Strether's visit to Paris, the book itself "is a hundred cubic inches of wood pulp."[11] *Ulysses*, with its eighteen separate parts, is like a cord of cut logs neatly stacked for the fireplace, but there is a single whatness about the book itself which makes it rest solidly and comfortably in our hands no matter what edition, cloth-bound or paperback, we may be using at the moment. Has anyone before suggested that the single word of the title may have been carefully chosen because it is unusually compact? It consists of three syllables in only seven letters, and a typesetter would find it as unsatisfactory to divide the word at the end of a line as the reader of *Ulysses* would find it difficult to consider any one of the three parts of the work in isolation from the others. And those three capital letters at the beginning of the three main parts—whether their enlargement may be credited to Joyce or to

Random House, they are appropriate to Joyce's conception of his book as an object. No matter what those letters may represent symbolically, they call attention to the whatness, the thingness of the book before us. In *Finnegans Wake* Joyce referred to *Ulysses* as that "Blue Book of Eccles," thus punning on Sylvia Beach's first edition, the street where the Blooms lived, and one of Dublin's principal tourist attractions, the Book of Kells, a masterpiece among constructed works of the bookmaking craft which Joyce as a youth must often have seen carefully isolated in a glass case of the Trinity College library, undoubtedly open at a page showing an illuminated letter. One can imagine him visualizing a copy of the first edition of *Ulysses* similarly displayed a thousand years hence.

"I may have oversystematized *Ulysses*," Joyce once confided to Samuel Beckett.[12] Certainly, the *consonantia* of the work is as deliberate as its *integritas* and its *quidditas*. In his new book, *Ulysses on the Liffey*, Richard Ellmann applies the several schemata for the novel which Joyce sent to friends and critics to a close study of the text of the novel and discovers among many other things that in addition to the eighteen-chapter and three-part structures which we have already recognized, there is a carefully worked out pattern of six triads in which the first chapters always offer large gestures and reductions of them, the second chapters present instances of cruelty and good will, and the third chapters accomplish their syntheses. Overlapping that pattern is the division of the novel into two halves of nine chapters each: "The first nine episodes of the book ended with a vision of the act of love as the basic act of art. The last nine episodes end with a vision of love as the basic act of nature" (*UL* 174). To give an example of patterning even more specific, "the first word in the book is *Stately* and the last *Yes*, the first and last letters of each being reversed so that the serpent has his tail in his mouth at last" (*UL* 162). Is Ellmann being over-ingenious, a New Critic at last? Perhaps so, but I would rather think not, for though we cannot be sure that one hundred per cent of everything we find in *Ulysses* was planted there by its author, we can be reasonably sure that about ninety per cent of it was. This is one of the most completely *intended* and *executed* books in the history of literature.

Archibald MacLeish said that "a poem should not mean but be." T. S. Eliot praised Henry James for having "a mind so fine no idea could violate it." And Joseph Conrad attributed his own late discovery of the artistry within him to the fact that he had always viewed life "spectacularly" rather than "ethically." These three examples may serve to illustrate the second of my four cardinal points of Modernism—that attitude of detached non-commitment which the New Critics defined as "irony." Modernist writers refuse to take sides; they would rather straddle a fence than mount a soap-box. Today, in this Post-Modernist Age of Relevance, when we hear much about the necessity for getting involved in the urgent social concerns of our time and when for most people group action seems a better way to get things done than "the free brave personal way," it is no wonder that Modernism has gone out of fashion.

Commentators on *Ulysses* have had no difficulty finding an abundance of meanings in the work. Joyce was well educated in philosophy and no doubt interested in ideas of all kinds. But it seems impossible to pin him down to a belief in any of them. They are merely subjects and themes worked into the complex fabric of Joyce's encyclopedic novel. It is no wonder that critics have been able to find in *Ulysses* almost anything they may have been looking for, including opposites and contradictions, because Joyce seems to have tried to accommodate everything. He is at once the most democratic of writers and the most superior, treating all subjects with equal detachment. Asked if he believes in his own theory of *Hamlet*, haughty Stephen promptly admits that he does not. Through a number of satiric and ironic touches, Joyce manages to detach himself from his own surrogate. Joyce is not on Leopold's side as opposed to Molly's, and in the few instances when he seems to move close to judging a character, as in the depiction of Gerty McDowell, he manages to neutralize his scorn with just the right amount of sympathy. Hundreds of books and articles have been written about Joyce, but no one has tried to write a book on Joyce's philosophy of life in the way that such books have been written about Thomas Hardy, for example, or John Updike. We can trace politics as a subject in Joyce's writings from the lost pamphlet on Parnell through *Finnegans Wake*, but it is impossible to discern a political belief in Joyce that would enable us to label him either a conservative or a liberal, and there is very little to suggest that for the mature Joyce politics was a matter of much concern. Once when his brother Stanislaus wanted to discuss Fascism, Joyce snapped back, "Don't talk to me about politics. I'm only interested in style."[13] And this most presumptuous of literary artists once said to Padraic Colum, "It would be a great impertinence for me to think that I could tell the world what to believe."[14]

In many respects Joyce seems curiously out of place among the subjects treated in the Modern Masters series edited by Frank Kermode and published by Viking Press. These little books are intended to offer concise summaries of the careers and impact of "the men who have changed and are changing the life and thought of our age." So far Kermode's pantheon is composed largely of men of action like Che Guevara, of philosophers like Wittgenstein, Lukács, and Marcuse, and the only other writer of literary distinction besides Joyce to appear thus far—Albert Camus—is at least as important for his thought and his social commitment as for his art. There are indications that John Gross, who wrote the book on Joyce for the series, would have liked to recruit Joyce to the camp of the liberals—"*Ulysses* is among the most democratic of novels" and "firmly rooted in the modern secular world"—but Gross concedes that "the element of ice-cold detachment in the book as a whole"[15] makes it difficult to pin Joyce down to any particular creed. I would go even further and say that Joyce's refusal to "get involved" is precisely what makes him as a literary artist a Modern Master.

Surely it is Joyce's pervasive irony which explains why he could not give *Ulysses* a closed ending. Because the respective quests of Stephen and Leopold are left unresolved as the novel ends, critics have been forced to speculate on what will happen in the future. Edmund Wilson found in Bloom's request that Molly prepare breakfast the next day a suggestion that Bloom would resume manly authority in his home and again have full sexual relations with his wife. William Empson noted that Stephen, though refusing to spend the night, does agree to exchange with Mrs. Bloom Italian for singing lessons—the results of such an arrangement being easily predictable. Ellmann objects to these proleptic interpretations, saying that "if Joyce had wanted to, he could certainly have given the book either Empson's or Wilson's conclusion: to please Empson he might have let Stephen stay the night, to please Wilson he could have had husband and wife resume complete sexual relations for the first time in eleven years. He does neither of these, though in Homer Telemachus presumably sleeps in the palace and Odysseus and Penelope share a bed. Instead of sexual intercourse in the present, Joyce has Molly think of a sexual scene in the past" (*UL* 162). Conceding that Joyce "leaves possibilities at the end like dangling threads" (*UL* 164), Ellmann, like earlier critics, cannot resist the temptation to give the novel an affirmative ending after all: "None of the principal figures is complete in himself, but together they sum up what is affirmable. At the end we are brought back to the earth, to spring, to vegetation, and to sexual love"

(*UL* 167). But the fact that intelligent interpreters of the novel continue to offer us differing responses to Molly, including very negative ones, makes it as difficult to accept Ellmann's view of the conclusion as it was to accept Wilson's or Empson's.[16] In fact, if Ellmann's view is accepted, we would have to turn *Ulysses* over to the camp of those who see Modernism as the triumph of Romanticism, for what could be more Romantic than a book which finally seems to prefer nature (earth . . . vegetation . . . sex) over the intellect? I would insist to the contrary that if there is an affirmation at the end of *Ulysses*, it is an affirmation of art—the triumphant assertion of the artist that he has *made* life without becoming trapped by his own creation. Note the neutralizing adjectives which Joyce used in describing the last episode of *Ulysses* to his friend Frank Budgen: it was, he wrote, a "perfectly sane full amoral fertilisable untrustworthy engaging shrewd limited prudent indifferent *Weib*."[17]

When a writer refuses to shape his materials to illustrate ideas or values, he is left with the problem of how art may be ordered at all. From classic literature to the present writers have used mythic and historical narratives as a ready-made substitution for imaginative invention, telling again old stories in new ways. In *"Ulysses, Order and Myth"* (1923), one of the seminal essays of Modernist theory, T. S. Eliot credits Joyce with something that is distinctively new and original:

> The question, then, about Mr Joyce, is: how much living material does he deal with, and how does he deal with it: deal with, not as legislator or exhorter, but as an artist?
> It is here that Mr Joyce's parallel use of the *Odyssey* has a great importance. It has the importance of a scientific discovery. No one else has built a novel upon such a foundation before: it has never been necessary. . . .
> In using the myth, in manipulating a continuous parallel between contemporaneity and antiquity, Mr Joyce is pursuing a method which others must pursue after him. . . . It is simply a way of controlling, of ordering, of giving a shape and a significance to the immense panorama of futility and anarchy which is contemporary history. . . . It is, I seriously believe, a step toward making the modern world possible for art.[18]

Eliot seems to be saying that though earlier writers may have interpreted the myths of the past or used them as guidelines for belief, it was Joyce's distinction that he used the story of the *Odyssey* simply as a structural device. It provided him with the skeletal framework for a story he wanted to tell about modern life in Ireland, saving him from the necessity to invent a mythology of his own to replace the traditional Christian myth in which he had been raised and educated, as Yeats, for instance, had had to do. The story of Odysseus and Telemachus provides Joyce with a frame of reference against which his contemporary characters may be measured and found wanting.

Although many of us have assumed that Stuart Gilbert's book on *Ulysses* more than exhausted the possibilities of approaching Joyce's novel by way of Homer, Ellmann in his new book finds the approach still useful as he offers his own chapter-by-chapter reading of the novel in terms of Joyce's schema for the novel. He comes up with several new insights and discoveries through the Odyssean parallels and reversals, but does little to change our assumption that the main function of the Homeric framework is seen easily enough. It serves to remind us continually that the modern age is not heroic: Bloom is an inadequate Odysseus, Molly an unfaithful Penelope, and so on. In a recent essay, Weldon Thornton comments:

> The key to the mythical method is not in the use of something mythological, but in "manipulating a continuous parallel between contemporaneity and antiquity," and we could with justification and accuracy rechristen it the "allusive method." For while the *Odyssey* parallel is one of the most pervasive in the novel, its function is not essentially different from that of many others, including *Hamlet*, the Daedalus myth, Shakespeare's life and passion, Mozart's *Don Giovanni*, or Goethe's "Walpurgisnacht." In evoking an earlier context for comparison and contrast, this method imports some of that earlier milieu, some of its values and norms, into the present work. It gives us a means of rising above the exigencies of our present, particular situation by suggesting what it shares with the past. This is especially true of those allusions which occur repeatedly in *Ulysses*, so that we sense a pattern of history of art being continually held up against the present.[19]

Thornton and others have traced in detail how Joyce wove these and other historical and mythical narratives through the fabric of *Ulysses*. This is not the time for further exploration into an area already mined extensively.

But if Eliot is correct in crediting Joyce with a new literary method which has "the importance of a scientific discovery," thus providing us with a clear starting point for one of the major aspects of Modernism, we may wonder if the approach has exhausted its possibilities in this age of Post-Modernism. At least one perceptive critic, Richard Wasson, says that it has. In "Notes on a New Sensibility," Wasson argues that contemporary writers have grown sceptical of the Modernist conception of myth as a valid means of ordering art and of disciplining the self through role-playing. The

Post-Modernists discussed by Wasson—Iris Murdoch, Alain Robbe-
Grillet, John Barth, and Thomas Pynchon—have in common a
"desire to get back to particulars, to restore literary language to its
proper role which for them means revealing 'the raggedness, the
incompleteness of it all.' They want a literature finally which
accurately presents man's place in a world of contingency, a world in
which man is free to cope spontaneously with experience."[20] I am not
sure that Wasson is entirely correct here. The writers he mentions
may want to create a new literature that is free, spontaneous,
and loose, but, like most Post-Modernist writers, they have gone
to school to the Modernists who preceded them and they find it
difficult to break away. Iris Murdoch's novels, for example, are as
liberally studded with allusions as Joyce's, and John Barth, whose
Sot-Weed Factor and *Giles Goat-Boy* are mythic in something like
Joyce's sense, has even given us his own highly intricate and
ingenious version of the story of Telemachus.

Literature comments on literature, and we can expect that
eventually Joyce's *Ulysses* will be used by a writer of the future
in much the way that Joyce used the *Odyssey*. Already Joyce's
book has taken on the stature of *the* modern myth, and it is easy
to see Stephen, Leopold, and Molly no longer as mere characters,
but as archetypes. Not long ago I heard someone say of a certain
robust man that he has played Blazes to many Mollys.

To a considerable degree the history of Modernist literature
could be traced in terms of a progression in three stages from the
early Impressionist focus on the external world *as seen* to the
tendency of turn-of-the-century literary impressionists like James,
Conrad, and Crane to put more emphasis on the observer than on
what he observes to a final stage of complete immersion within
the internal consciousness of the "I" who tells the story or one of
his characters. Among the many techniques of *Ulysses* are all
three phases of this progression, but it is surely significant
that Joyce reserved for the last episode an extended use of stream-
of-consciousness as distinguished from the internal monologues
indulged in sporadically if pervasively throughout the earlier
sections of the work. William Schutte and Erwin Steinberg point
out in a recent essay that long before the eighteenth episode the
reader of *Ulysses* has been conditioned to expect at any point in
the narrative a "movement from rather traditional fictional presenta-
tions to almost total immersion in a stream of consciousness," and
they see the constant shifting about as one way in which Joyce
reminds us that "the author, who seemed to have all but refined

himself out of existence, is back there behind his characters after all."[21]

Post-Modernist writers find especially objectionable the way in which external reality in Modernist writings is appropriated to the subjectivity of the hero, who is himself often a surrogate for the author. Wasson points out that it is largely through the Modernist conception of metaphor that "the outer world becomes the hero's inner world" and "the work becomes a projection of the artist's subjectivity."[22] Thus my fourth cardinal point of Modernism — its tendency to be reflexive and solipsistic. Much Modernist literature is about itself. Proust's *A la Recherche du temps perdu* and Gide's *Les Faux-Monnayeurs* are only two of the more obvious examples of a tendency which pervades Modernist literature. When Shem the Penman "wrote over every square inch of the only foolscap available, his own body, till by its corrosive sublimation one continuous present tense integument slowly unfolded all marry-voising moodmoulded cyclewheeling history" (*FW* 185-86), this is Joyce's way of telling us that he is not only writing *Finnegans Wake* but also fulfilling the mission of that earlier surrogate for Joyce, Stephen Dedalus of *A Portrait*, when he went forth to "forge in the smithy of my soul the uncreated conscience of my race."

As Stephen expounds his theory of *Hamlet* in the library chapter of *Ulysses*, he insists that all of Shakespeare's characters are projections of Shakespeare himself, but none more vitally so than the ghost of Hamlet's father, who "goes back, weary of the creation he has piled up to hide him from himself, an old dog licking an old sore. But, because loss is his gain, he passes on towards eternity in undiminished personality, untaught by the wisdom he has written or by the laws he has revealed. His beaver is up. He is a ghost, a shadow now, the wind by Elsinore's rocks or what you will, the sea's voice, a voice heard only in the heart of him who is the substance of his shadow, the son consubstantial with the father" (*U* 197). It is an old *dog* that licks an old sore, and everyone knows that whenever the word "dog" appears in *Ulysses* we are being invited to reverse the letters and to read instead the word "god." Shakespeare as an artistic creator is analogous to Stephen's detached, indifferent God paring his fingernails—and God is referred to in *Ulysses* as "the playwright who wrote the folio of this world" (*U* 213). Elsewhere I have attempted to show that the reflexive quality of modern literature owes much to the tradition of the artist as God, a tradition which goes back at least to Poe's pre-Modernist but prophetic story "The Fall of the House of Usher."[23] Here it must suffice to say that in the cult of Art as Religion which marks the Modernist period, the artist builds not just an Ivory Tower, but a whole cosmos around himself. That protective bubble is an extension of the artist, and the people who populate his little world are always reflections of their creator. If for Stephen Dedalus every character in Shakespeare's plays is Shakespeare, we can assume that Joyce would acknowledge that Stephen, Leopold, Molly, even Buck Mulligan and Gerty McDowell are somehow all James Joyce. Stephen says to Bloom, "You suspect . . . that I may be important because I belong to . . . Ireland . . . . But I suspect . . . that Ireland must be important because it belongs to me" (*U* 645).

It is to a large extent because of this fourth distinguishing aspect of Modernism, its reflexive solipsism, its just plain arrogance, that the whole movement for many people has begun to seem suspect and vulnerable—"elitist" if you like. Recent novels by Joyce Carol Oates, John Fowles, and John Berger, among others, show that the convention of reflexive art, like the use of myth, is still very much with us, but that it may finally have started to run its course is suggested by the way in which reflexive narcissism is being parodied in elaborately ingenious stories by such contemporary writers as John Barth, Donald Barthelme, Robert Coover, and Ronald Sukenick. There are other signs that Post-Modernist writers may be willing once again to look outside themselves for artistic subjects in order to create what John Bayley has called "characters of love," those which do not reflect only the self of the artist, but convey instead "the joy . . . of one fixed being apprehending another."[24]

I can imagine the reader saying at this point, "All right, you have found it easy enough to show that *Ulysses* illustrates your four cardinal points of Modernism. But you admitted during the course of your argument that critics have always been able to find whatever they may be looking for in Joyce's complex and encyclopedic novel. What, after all, does Ulysses, *not* illustrate?"

If I am right in seeing *Ulysses* as perhaps the single most inclusive and important text of literary Modernism as an independent and autonomous movement, then I should be able to show that it excludes the opposing view of Modernism as an extension of Romanticism. I can do this, but only in part. The only times Joyce ever comes close to passing negative judgments on his characters are when those characters are Romantic in one way or another—sentimental Gerty McDowell, the mystics of the "shadow school" in the library scene, that fiercely committed chauvinist known as the

Citizen, and perhaps that most natural man, Byronic Blazes Boylan. Joyce's training under the Jesuits and his long intellectual apprenticeship to Aquinas and "soldier Aristotle" made it difficult for him to go along with the "dreamy dreams" of his Celtic Twilight contemporaries. Tough-minded and coolly objective, Stephen knows that he must "hold to the now, the here, through which all future plunges to the past" (*U* 186).

Joyce's irony is too pervasive to allow him to take sides, but it is a mark of the greatest literature that it achieve a synthesis of thesis and antithesis. I think that Joyce does this—and meant to do so largely through Molly Bloom's soliloquy. We cannot escape the fact that it is given the honor of the last word. Molly is certainly a Romantic in many ways, though too sensual and earthy to enlist in the shadow school of AE and Lizzie Twigg, and if one sees the final chapter as an exaltation of all that Molly represents, as Ellmann most recently does, it would follow that the novel ends romantically. But Joyce was too cunning to be trapped that easily, and I have already tried to show that Joyce maintains his attitude of "amoral . . . untrustworthy . . . indifferent" detachment as he balances the plus and minus qualities of Molly.

Nonetheless, in one important way at least, the ending of *Ulysses* seems to anticipate Post-Modernism. Molly Bloom is what John Bayley calls a "character of love," and by not only creating her, but by accepting her as well, Joyce achieves a recognition of "otherness" as startling as anything we can find in Lawrence. We know that Joyce's relationship to Nora Barnacle lies somehow at the core of the book—its date, June 16, 1904, presumably chosen because it was the day just before Joyce and Nora reached an intimate understanding. In actual life Joyce was tortured by egoistic jealousy of Nora, yet Joyce could not have written Molly Bloom's soliloquy, that joyous testament of woman's "lapsibility," if he had not somehow found a way in art, if not in life, to recognize the distinct otherness of the loved one. Few male writers have succeeded so well in entering the consciousness of the opposite sex and in presenting Woman with such sympathetic acceptance. By doing so, Joyce invaded Lawrence's camp, doing almost casually what Lawrence keeps struggling to accomplish throughout *Women in Love*. It is no wonder that whenever Frieda wanted to make her husband angry, all she had to do was praise the Molly Bloom chapter of *Ulysses*. Lawrence thought that it was obscene.

Temple University

NOTES

1. The present essay incorporates in a revised and expanded form some portions of my "Joyce and the Meanings of Modernism" in *Litters from Aloft: Papers Delivered at the Second Canadian James Joyce Seminar, McMaster University,* ed. Ronald Bates and Harry J. Pollock (University of Tulsa Department of English Monograph Series, No. 13, 1971).

2. "Bloom on Joyce; or Jokey for Jacob," *Journal of Modern Literature,* 1 (First Issue 1970), 21.

3. Levin's essay, first published in *The Massachusetts Review* in 1960, is now conveniently found in his *Refractions: Essays in Comparative Literature* (New York: Oxford University Press, 1966), pp. 271-95.

4. *Dionysus and the City: Modernism in Twentieth-Century Poetry* (New York: Oxford University Press, 1970), p. 3.

5. As an Appendix to his *Romanticism and the Modern Ego* (Boston: Little, Brown, 1943), pp. 213-30.

6. Spears, p. 35.

7. Ibid., p. 15.

8. Ibid. Where Spears stands may be suggested by the way in which he always capitalizes the first letter of "Romantic" while using only lower case letters for "modernism."

9. *Avantgardism and Modernity: A Comparison of James Joyce's "Ulysses" with Thomas Mann's "Der Zauberberg" and "Lotte in Weimar,"* trans. Paul Aston, ed. with Intro. by H. Frew Waidner III (University of Tulsa Monograph Series, No. 14, 1972), pp. 43-54.

10. William M. Schutte and Erwin R. Steinberg, "The Fictional Technique of *Ulysses,"* in *Approaches to "Ulysses": Ten Essays,* ed. Thomas F. Staley and Bernard Benstock (Pittsburgh: University of Pittsburgh Press, 1970), p. 172.

11. *The Pound Era* (Berkeley: University of California Press, 1971), p. 28.

12. Quoted by Richard Ellmann in *Ulysses on the Liffey* (New York: Oxford University Press, 1972), p. 57. Hereafter *UL.*

13. Quoted by Richard Ellmann in his Introduction to Stanislaus Joyce's *My Brother's Keeper: James Joyce's Early Years* (New York: Viking Press, 1958), p. xix.

14. Quoted by Egri, p. 20.

15. *James Joyce* (New York: Viking Press, 1970), pp. 68, 51, and 50 respectively.

16. See, for example, the contrasting views of Molly offered by David Hayman and Darcy O'Brien in *Approaches to "Ulysses,"* pp. 103-53.

17. Quoted by Ellmann in *UL,* p. 164.

18. Eliot's essay was published in *The Dial,* Nov. 1923. It is quoted here from Weldon Thornton, "The Allusive Method in *Ulysses,"* in *Approaches to "Ulysses,"* p. 242.

19. Ibid., p. 243.

20. "Notes on a New Sensibility," *Partisan Review,* 36 (1969), 476.

21. Schutte and Steinberg, p. 167.

22. Wasson, p. 464.

23. *Ivory Towers and Sacred Founts: The Artist as Hero in Fiction from Goethe to Joyce* (New York: New York University Press, 1964), pp. 114-71.

24. *The Characters of Love: A Study in the Literature of Personality* (New York: Basic Books, 1961), pp. 286-87.

Tom Wood

A PORTRAIT OF THE ARTIST
ACCORDING TO HIS DWELLINGS*

> "Houses of decay, mine, his and all."
> —Stephen Dedalus (*U* 39)

In December 1971, my wife and I traveled to Dublin, London, and Paris to pursue my research on the Lost Generation authors. Armed with our Rolleiflex, assorted other cameras, and addresses from Richard Ellmann's list in vol. II of Joyce's *Letters*, we also photographed some of James Joyce's dwellings—a project into which we were lured by Thomas F. Staley.

As we visited many of Joyce's habitations, we noted that he seemed to have an affinity for good accommodations situated near parks. As he grew older, he kept close to the centers of activity that interested him, which were usually near parks of more than ordinary beauty. Despite tales of penury, it would appear that Joyce never lived in hovels.

Most of Joyce's dwellings are still standing and in use. However, we found that the past fifty years have wrought many changes. At the Fitzgibbon and Hardwicke Street residences in Dublin, for example, we found nothing but scarred vacant lots. In London, the Hotel Belgravia has become the Grosvenor Gardens House; we could find no trace of the Euston Hotel. In Paris, the eye clinic at 39 Rue du Cherche-Midi has been replaced by another building, and at 71 Rue Cardinal LeMoine there was a sign advising motorists that an auto body shop was within.

*Photographs by Tom Wood; captions by John W. Van Voorhis

189

Many of the people where Joyce lived are aware that a great man had once lived on their premises. As might be expected, this knowledge struck each of them differently. At the Hotel Lennox in Paris, I interviewed the owner, Mme. Pelloille, whose enthusiasm for Joyce exceeded her grasp of his works. "The Lennox," she told me through an interpreter, "is where Joyce wrote his last book—*A Portrait of the Artist as a Young Man.*" In Dublin, outside 17 Richmond Place, North, a friendly young man named Emonon (cq) Stringer told us that the owners hoped to have the place declared a national shrine and that it was being renovated to that end; he gladly took us on a tour of the premises. Much more typical of Joyce's Dublin, however, were the guarded comments of our cab driver, who viewed our activities with suspicion, and the observation of a small, worried woman, probably in her seventies, who came to the door of 44 Fontenoy Street while we were photographing the place. "Yes. I know James Joyce lived here years and years ago," she told us, "but that didn't improve our lives any."

University of Tulsa

"Fabulous artificer, the hawklike man. You flew. Where to? Newhaven-Dieppe, steerage passenger. Paris and back."

—Stephen Dedalus (*U* 210)

60 Shelbourne Road, Dublin

"Having borrowed more money . . . , [Joyce] found a very large room that spanned the first floor of a house at 60 Shelbourne Road, where a family named McKernan lived" (*JJ* 157).

"60 Shellburn" (*FW* 421.03).

21 North Richmond Place, Dublin

"The other houses of the street, conscious of decent lives within them, gazed at one another with brown imperturbable faces" ("Araby").

"12 Norse Richmound" (FW 420.23).

Eccles Street (with Saint George's Church in background)

"He crossed to the bright side, avoiding the loose cellarflap of number seventyfive. The sun was nearing the steeple of George's church. Be a warm day I fancy."
—Leopold Bloom (*U* 57)

"But real adventures, I reflected, do not happen to people who remain at home: they must be sought abroad" ("An Encounter").

Hotel Belgravia (now Grosvenor Gardens)
  "27 April 1931   Hotel Belgravia, Grosvenor Gardens, Victoria, London S.W. 1"
(*Letters* III, 217)

"Elizabethan London lay as far from Stratford as corrupt Paris lies from Virgin
Dublin."
—Stephen Dedalus (U 188)

Valéry Larbaud's Flat in Rue Cardinal

"Paris rawly waking, crude sunlight on her lemon streets. Moist pith of farls of bread, the froggreen wormwood, her matin incense, court the air" (*U* 42).

"6 November 1939   *Hotel Lutétia, 43 Boulevard Raspail, Paris*
"Nous sommes à l'hotel parce que l'appartement n'est pas chauffé"
(Letters III, 457-58).

Saint George's church, Dublin
  "A creak and a dark whirr in the air high up. The bells of George's church.
They tolled the hour: loud dark iron" (*U* 70).

CONTRIBUTORS

MAURICE BEEBE is Professor of English at Temple University where he edits *The Journal of Modern Literature*. He is author of *Ivory Towers and Sacred Founts* (1964) and edited *Modern Fiction Studies* from 1955 to 1968. He has published widely on various aspects of Modern Literature.

BERNARD BENSTOCK is Professor of English and chairman of graduate studies at Kent State University. He is President of the James Joyce Foundation and author of *Joyce-Again's Wake* (1965). His articles on Joyce have appeared in *PMLA*, *Modern Fiction Studies*, *JJQ*, and other journals.

ROBERT BOYLE, S.J. holds a Ph.D. from Yale and is Professor of English at Marquette University. He is author of *Metaphor in Hopkins* (1961) and has contributed articles to *JJQ*, *Modern Language Quarterly*, *America*, *Victorian Poetry*, and other journals.

RICHARD M. KAIN is Professor of English at the University of Louisville. His books include *Fabulous Voyager* (1947) and *Dublin in the Age of William Butler Yeats and James Joyce* (1962). He is co-editor with Robert Scholes of *The Workshop of Daedalus* (1965) and has published numerous articles, reviews, and notes.

HUGH KENNER holds a Ph.D. from Yale and is Professor of English at the University of California at Santa Barbara. His books include *The Poetry of Ezra Pound* (1951), *Wyndham Lewis* (1954), *Dublin's Joyce* (1955), and *The Pound Era* (1971).

LEO KNUTH teaches in the department of Old Germanic Studies at the University of Utrecht, Holland. He has published many articles on Joyce, has led Joyce seminars in Europe and the U.S.A., and has been visiting professor of English at SUNY, Buffalo and the University of Tulsa.

MORTON P. LEVITT is Associate Professor of English at Temple University. He is author of the recently published *Bloomsday*, with engravings by Saul Field. Prof. Levitt is completing a critical study of the fiction of Nikos Kazantzakis.

A. WALTON LITZ holds a D. Phil. from Oxford and is author of several books on modern literature, including *The Art of James Joyce* (1961) and *James Joyce* (1965). He is co-editor with Robert Scholes of *Dubliners* for the Viking Critical Library. Currently, he is Professor of English and Chairman of the Council of the Humanities at Princeton University.

ROBERT SCHOLES holds a Ph.D. from Cornell and is Professor of English at Brown University. His books include *The Cornell Joyce Collection: A Catalogue* (1961), *Approaches to the Novel* (1961), and *The Nature of Narrative* (1966) co-authored with Robert Kellogg. His articles have appeared in numerous literary journals.

WILLIAM M. SCHUTTE holds a Ph.D. from Yale and is Lucia R. Briggs Professor of English at Lawrence University. He is the author of *Joyce and Shakespeare* (1957) and editor of the Twentieth Century Interpretations volume on *A Portrait* (1968).

FRITZ SENN has recently received the degree of *Doctor philosophiae honoris causa* from the University of Cologne, Germany. With Clive Hart, he is co-founder and co-editor of *A Wake Newslitter*. He has written numerous articles and notes on Joyce and has recently published *New Light on Joyce from the Dublin Symposium*.

MARK SHECHNER is Assistant Professor of English at the State University of New York at Buffalo. His essay "The Song of the Wandering Aengus" is a shortened version of the last chapter of his forthcoming psychoanalytic study of Joyce and *Ulysses*, to be published in Fall 1973 by the University of California Press.

TOM WOOD holds a Ph.D. in European history from the University of Oklahoma and specializes in Lost Generation writers. He is Professor of Journalism at the University of Tulsa and has been a reporter for the *Tulsa Daily World* for nearly 19 years.